Mometrix

TEST PREPARATION

I0891995

SAT

rt (002)

ecrets Study Guide

DEAR FUTURE EXAM SUCCESS STORY

First of all, **THANK YOU** for purchasing Mometrix study materials!

Second, congratulations! You are one of the few determined test-takers who are committed to doing whatever it takes to excel on your exam. **You have come to the right place.** We developed these study materials with one goal in mind: to deliver you the information you need in a format that's concise and easy to use.

In addition to optimizing your guide for the content of the test, we've outlined our recommended steps for breaking down the preparation process into small, attainable goals so you can make sure you stay on track.

We've also analyzed the entire test-taking process, identifying the most common pitfalls and showing how you can overcome them and be ready for any curveball the test throws you.

Standardized testing is one of the biggest obstacles on your road to success, which only increases the importance of doing well in the high-pressure, high-stakes environment of test day. Your results on this test could have a significant impact on your future, and this guide provides the information and practical advice to help you achieve your full potential on test day.

Your success is our success

We would love to hear from you! If you would like to share the story of your exam success or if you have any questions or comments in regard to our products, please contact us at **800-673-8175** or **support@mometrix.com**.

Thanks again for your business and we wish you continued success!

Sincerely,
The Mometrix Test Preparation Team

Need more help? Check out our flashcards at:
http://MometrixFlashcards.com/CEOE

Written and edited by the Mometrix Exam Secrets Test Prep Team
Printed in the United States of America

TABLE OF CONTENTS

Introduction

Thank you for purchasing this resource! You have made the choice to prepare yourself for a test that could have a huge impact on your future, and this guide is designed to help you be fully ready for test day. Obviously, it's important to have a solid understanding of the test material, but you also need to be prepared for the unique environment and stressors of the test, so that you can perform to the best of your abilities.

For this purpose, the first section that appears in this guide is the **Secret Keys**. We've devoted countless hours to meticulously researching what works and what doesn't, and we've boiled down our findings to the five most impactful steps you can take to improve your performance on the test. We start at the beginning with study planning and move through the preparation process, all the way to the testing strategies that will help you get the most out of what you know when you're finally sitting in front of the test.

We recommend that you start preparing for your test as far in advance as possible. However, if you've bought this guide as a last-minute study resource and only have a few days before your test, we recommend that you skip over the first two Secret Keys since they address a long-term study plan.

If you struggle with **test anxiety**, we strongly encourage you to check out our recommendations for how you can overcome it. Test anxiety is a formidable foe, but it can be beaten, and we want to make sure you have the tools you need to defeat it.

Secret Key #1 – Plan Big, Study Small

There's a lot riding on your performance. If you want to ace this test, you're going to need to keep your skills sharp and the material fresh in your mind. You need a plan that lets you review everything you need to know while still fitting in your schedule. We'll break this strategy down into three categories.

Information Organization

Start with the information you already have: the official test outline. From this, you can make a complete list of all the concepts you need to cover before the test. Organize these concepts into groups that can be studied together, and create a list of any related vocabulary you need to learn so you can brush up on any difficult terms. You'll want to keep this vocabulary list handy once you actually start studying since you may need to add to it along the way.

Time Management

Once you have your set of study concepts, decide how to spread them out over the time you have left before the test. Break your study plan into small, clear goals so you have a manageable task for each day and know exactly what you're doing. Then just focus on one small step at a time. When you manage your time this way, you don't need to spend hours at a time studying. Studying a small block of content for a short period each day helps you retain information better and avoid stressing over how much you have left to do. You can relax knowing that you have a plan to cover everything in time. In order for this strategy to be effective though, you have to start studying early and stick to your schedule. Avoid the exhaustion and futility that comes from last-minute cramming!

Study Environment

The environment you study in has a big impact on your learning. Studying in a coffee shop, while probably more enjoyable, is not likely to be as fruitful as studying in a quiet room. It's important to keep distractions to a minimum. You're only planning to study for a short block of time, so make the most of it. Don't pause to check your phone or get up to find a snack. It's also important to **avoid multitasking**. Research has consistently shown that multitasking will make your studying dramatically less effective. Your study area should also be comfortable and well-lit so you don't have the distraction of straining your eyes or sitting on an uncomfortable chair.

The time of day you study is also important. You want to be rested and alert. Don't wait until just before bedtime. Study when you'll be most likely to comprehend and remember. Even better, if you know what time of day your test will be, set that time aside for study. That way your brain will be used to working on that subject at that specific time and you'll have a better chance of recalling information.

Finally, it can be helpful to team up with others who are studying for the same test. Your actual studying should be done in as isolated an environment as possible, but the work of organizing the information and setting up the study plan can be divided up. In between study sessions, you can discuss with your teammates the concepts that you're all studying and quiz each other on the details. Just be sure that your teammates are as serious about the test as you are. If you find that your study time is being replaced with social time, you might need to find a new team.

Secret Key #2 – Make Your Studying Count

You're devoting a lot of time and effort to preparing for this test, so you want to be absolutely certain it will pay off. This means doing more than just reading the content and hoping you can remember it on test day. It's important to make every minute of study count. There are two main areas you can focus on to make your studying count.

Retention

It doesn't matter how much time you study if you can't remember the material. You need to make sure you are retaining the concepts. To check your retention of the information you're learning, try recalling it at later times with minimal prompting. Try carrying around flashcards and glance at one or two from time to time or ask a friend who's also studying for the test to quiz you.

To enhance your retention, look for ways to put the information into practice so that you can apply it rather than simply recalling it. If you're using the information in practical ways, it will be much easier to remember. Similarly, it helps to solidify a concept in your mind if you're not only reading it to yourself but also explaining it to someone else. Ask a friend to let you teach them about a concept you're a little shaky on (or speak aloud to an imaginary audience if necessary). As you try to summarize, define, give examples, and answer your friend's questions, you'll understand the concepts better and they will stay with you longer. Finally, step back for a big picture view and ask yourself how each piece of information fits with the whole subject. When you link the different concepts together and see them working together as a whole, it's easier to remember the individual components.

Finally, practice showing your work on any multi-step problems, even if you're just studying. Writing out each step you take to solve a problem will help solidify the process in your mind, and you'll be more likely to remember it during the test.

Modality

Modality simply refers to the means or method by which you study. Choosing a study modality that fits your own individual learning style is crucial. No two people learn best in exactly the same way, so it's important to know your strengths and use them to your advantage.

For example, if you learn best by visualization, focus on visualizing a concept in your mind and draw an image or a diagram. Try color-coding your notes, illustrating them, or creating symbols that will trigger your mind to recall a learned concept. If you learn best by hearing or discussing information, find a study partner who learns the same way or read aloud to yourself. Think about how to put the information in your own words. Imagine that you are giving a lecture on the topic and record yourself so you can listen to it later.

For any learning style, flashcards can be helpful. Organize the information so you can take advantage of spare moments to review. Underline key words or phrases. Use different colors for different categories. Mnemonic devices (such as creating a short list in which every item starts with the same letter) can also help with retention. Find what works best for you and use it to store the information in your mind most effectively and easily.

Secret Key #3 – Practice the Right Way

Your success on test day depends not only on how many hours you put into preparing, but also on whether you prepared the right way. It's good to check along the way to see if your studying is paying off. One of the most effective ways to do this is by taking practice tests to evaluate your progress. Practice tests are useful because they show exactly where you need to improve. Every time you take a practice test, pay special attention to these three groups of questions:

- The questions you got wrong
- The questions you had to guess on, even if you guessed right
- The questions you found difficult or slow to work through

This will show you exactly what your weak areas are, and where you need to devote more study time. Ask yourself why each of these questions gave you trouble. Was it because you didn't understand the material? Was it because you didn't remember the vocabulary? Do you need more repetitions on this type of question to build speed and confidence? Dig into those questions and figure out how you can strengthen your weak areas as you go back to review the material.

Additionally, many practice tests have a section explaining the answer choices. It can be tempting to read the explanation and think that you now have a good understanding of the concept. However, an explanation likely only covers part of the question's broader context. Even if the explanation makes perfect sense, **go back and investigate** every concept related to the question until you're positive you have a thorough understanding.

As you go along, keep in mind that the practice test is just that: practice. Memorizing these questions and answers will not be very helpful on the actual test because it is unlikely to have any of the same exact questions. If you only know the right answers to the sample questions, you won't be prepared for the real thing. **Study the concepts** until you understand them fully, and then you'll be able to answer any question that shows up on the test.

It's important to wait on the practice tests until you're ready. If you take a test on your first day of study, you may be overwhelmed by the amount of material covered and how much you need to learn. Work up to it gradually.

On test day, you'll need to be prepared for answering questions, managing your time, and using the test-taking strategies you've learned. It's a lot to balance, like a mental marathon that will have a big impact on your future. Like training for a marathon, you'll need to start slowly and work your way up. When test day arrives, you'll be ready.

Start with the strategies you've read in the first two Secret Keys—plan your course and study in the way that works best for you. If you have time, consider using multiple study resources to get different approaches to the same concepts. It can be helpful to see difficult concepts from more than one angle. Then find a good source for practice tests. Many times, the test website will suggest potential study resources or provide sample tests.

Practice Test Strategy

If you're able to find at least three practice tests, we recommend this strategy:

Untimed and Open-Book Practice

Take the first test with no time constraints and with your notes and study guide handy. Take your time and focus on applying the strategies you've learned.

Timed and Open-Book Practice

Take the second practice test open-book as well, but set a timer and practice pacing yourself to finish in time.

Timed and Closed-Book Practice

Take any other practice tests as if it were test day. Set a timer and put away your study materials. Sit at a table or desk in a quiet room, imagine yourself at the testing center, and answer questions as quickly and accurately as possible.

Keep repeating timed and closed-book tests on a regular basis until you run out of practice tests or it's time for the actual test. Your mind will be ready for the schedule and stress of test day, and you'll be able to focus on recalling the material you've learned.

Secret Key #4 – Pace Yourself

Once you're fully prepared for the material on the test, your biggest challenge on test day will be managing your time. Just knowing that the clock is ticking can make you panic even if you have plenty of time left. Work on pacing yourself so you can build confidence against the time constraints of the exam. Pacing is a difficult skill to master, especially in a high-pressure environment, so **practice is vital**.

Set time expectations for your pace based on how much time is available. For example, if a section has 60 questions and the time limit is 30 minutes, you know you have to average 30 seconds or less per question in order to answer them all. Although 30 seconds is the hard limit, set 25 seconds per question as your goal, so you reserve extra time to spend on harder questions. When you budget extra time for the harder questions, you no longer have any reason to stress when those questions take longer to answer.

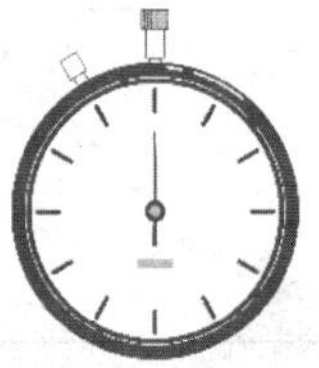

Don't let this time expectation distract you from working through the test at a calm, steady pace, but keep it in mind so you don't spend too much time on any one question. Recognize that taking extra time on one question you don't understand may keep you from answering two that you do understand later in the test. If your time limit for a question is up and you're still not sure of the answer, mark it and move on, and come back to it later if the time and the test format allow. If the testing format doesn't allow you to return to earlier questions, just make an educated guess; then put it out of your mind and move on.

On the easier questions, be careful not to rush. It may seem wise to hurry through them so you have more time for the challenging ones, but it's not worth missing one if you know the concept and just didn't take the time to read the question fully. Work efficiently but make sure you understand the question and have looked at all of the answer choices, since more than one may seem right at first.

Even if you're paying attention to the time, you may find yourself a little behind at some point. You should speed up to get back on track, but do so wisely. Don't panic; just take a few seconds less on each question until you're caught up. Don't guess without thinking, but do look through the answer choices and eliminate any you know are wrong. If you can get down to two choices, it is often worthwhile to guess from those. Once you've chosen an answer, move on and don't dwell on any that you skipped or had to hurry through. If a question was taking too long, chances are it was one of the harder ones, so you weren't as likely to get it right anyway.

On the other hand, if you find yourself getting ahead of schedule, it may be beneficial to slow down a little. The more quickly you work, the more likely you are to make a careless mistake that will affect your score. You've budgeted time for each question, so don't be afraid to spend that time. Practice an efficient but careful pace to get the most out of the time you have.

Secret Key #5 – Have a Plan for Guessing

When you're taking the test, you may find yourself stuck on a question. Some of the answer choices seem better than others, but you don't see the one answer choice that is obviously correct. What do you do?

The scenario described above is very common, yet most test takers have not effectively prepared for it. Developing and practicing a plan for guessing may be one of the single most effective uses of your time as you get ready for the exam.

In developing your plan for guessing, there are three questions to address:

- When should you start the guessing process?
- How should you narrow down the choices?
- Which answer should you choose?

When to Start the Guessing Process

Unless your plan for guessing is to select C every time (which, despite its merits, is not what we recommend), you need to leave yourself enough time to apply your answer elimination strategies. Since you have a limited amount of time for each question, that means that if you're going to give yourself the best shot at guessing correctly, you have to decide quickly whether or not you will guess.

Of course, the best-case scenario is that you don't have to guess at all, so first, see if you can answer the question based on your knowledge of the subject and basic reasoning skills. Focus on the key words in the question and try to jog your memory of related topics. Give yourself a chance to bring the knowledge to mind, but once you realize that you don't have (or you can't access) the knowledge you need to answer the question, it's time to start the guessing process.

It's almost always better to start the guessing process too early than too late. It only takes a few seconds to remember something and answer the question from knowledge. Carefully eliminating wrong answer choices takes longer. Plus, going through the process of eliminating answer choices can actually help jog your memory.

Summary: Start the guessing process as soon as you decide that you can't answer the question based on your knowledge.

How to Narrow Down the Choices

The next chapter in this book (**Test-Taking Strategies**) includes a wide range of strategies for how to approach questions and how to look for answer choices to eliminate. You will definitely want to read those carefully, practice them, and figure out which ones work best for you. Here though, we're going to address a mindset rather than a particular strategy.

Your odds of guessing an answer correctly depend on how many options you are choosing from.

Number of options left	5	4	3	2	1
Odds of guessing correctly	20%	25%	33%	50%	100%

You can see from this chart just how valuable it is to be able to eliminate incorrect answers and make an educated guess, but there are two things that many test takers do that cause them to miss out on the benefits of guessing:

- Accidentally eliminating the correct answer
- Selecting an answer based on an impression

We'll look at the first one here, and the second one in the next section.

To avoid accidentally eliminating the correct answer, we recommend a thought exercise called **the $5 challenge**. In this challenge, you only eliminate an answer choice from contention if you are willing to bet $5 on it being wrong. Why $5? Five dollars is a small but not insignificant amount of money. It's an amount you could afford to lose but wouldn't want to throw away. And while losing $5 once might not hurt too much, doing it twenty times will set you back $100. In the same way, each small decision you make—eliminating a choice here, guessing on a question there—won't by itself impact your score very much, but when you put them all together, they can make a big difference. By holding each answer choice elimination decision to a higher standard, you can reduce the risk of accidentally eliminating the correct answer.

The $5 challenge can also be applied in a positive sense: If you are willing to bet $5 that an answer choice *is* correct, go ahead and mark it as correct.

Summary: Only eliminate an answer choice if you are willing to bet $5 that it is wrong.

Which Answer to Choose

You're taking the test. You've run into a hard question and decided you'll have to guess. You've eliminated all the answer choices you're willing to bet $5 on. Now you have to pick an answer. Why do we even need to talk about this? Why can't you just pick whichever one you feel like when the time comes?

The answer to these questions is that if you don't come into the test with a plan, you'll rely on your impression to select an answer choice, and if you do that, you risk falling into a trap. The test writers know that everyone who takes their test will be guessing on some of the questions, so they intentionally write wrong answer choices to seem plausible. You still have to pick an answer though, and if the wrong answer choices are designed to look right, how can you ever be sure that you're not falling for their trap? The best solution we've found to this dilemma is to take the decision out of your hands entirely. Here is the process we recommend:

Once you've eliminated any choices that you are confident (willing to bet $5) are wrong, select the first remaining choice as your answer.

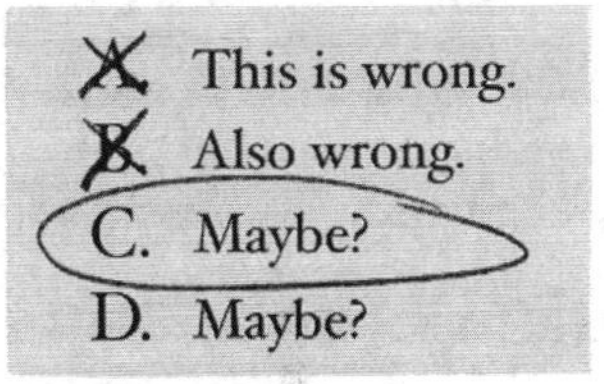

Whether you choose to select the first remaining choice, the second, or the last, the important thing is that you use some preselected standard. Using this approach guarantees that you will not be enticed into selecting an answer choice that looks right, because you are not basing your decision on how the answer choices look.

This is not meant to make you question your knowledge. Instead, it is to help you recognize the difference between your knowledge and your impressions. There's a huge difference between thinking an answer is right because of what you know, and thinking an answer is right because it looks or sounds like it should be right.

Summary: To ensure that your selection is appropriately random, make a predetermined selection from among all answer choices you have not eliminated.

Test-Taking Strategies

This section contains a list of test-taking strategies that you may find helpful as you work through the test. By taking what you know and applying logical thought, you can maximize your chances of answering any question correctly!

It is very important to realize that every question is different and every person is different: no single strategy will work on every question, and no single strategy will work for every person. That's why we've included all of them here, so you can try them out and determine which ones work best for different types of questions and which ones work best for you.

Question Strategies

☑ Read Carefully

Read the question and the answer choices carefully. Don't miss the question because you misread the terms. You have plenty of time to read each question thoroughly and make sure you understand what is being asked. Yet a happy medium must be attained, so don't waste too much time. You must read carefully and efficiently.

☑ Contextual Clues

Look for contextual clues. If the question includes a word you are not familiar with, look at the immediate context for some indication of what the word might mean. Contextual clues can often give you all the information you need to decipher the meaning of an unfamiliar word. Even if you can't determine the meaning, you may be able to narrow down the possibilities enough to make a solid guess at the answer to the question.

☑ Prefixes

If you're having trouble with a word in the question or answer choices, try dissecting it. Take advantage of every clue that the word might include. Prefixes can be a huge help. Usually, they allow you to determine a basic meaning. *Pre-* means before, *post-* means after, *pro-* is positive, *de-* is negative. From prefixes, you can get an idea of the general meaning of the word and try to put it into context.

☑ Hedge Words

Watch out for critical hedge words, such as *likely, may, can, often, almost, mostly, usually, generally, rarely,* and *sometimes*. Question writers insert these hedge phrases to cover every possibility. Often an answer choice will be wrong simply because it leaves no room for exception. Be on guard for answer choices that have definitive words such as *exactly* and *always*.

☑ Switchback Words

Stay alert for *switchbacks*. These are the words and phrases frequently used to alert you to shifts in thought. The most common switchback words are *but, although,* and *however*. Others include *nevertheless, on the other hand, even though, while, in spite of, despite,* and *regardless of*. Switchback words are important to catch because they can change the direction of the question or an answer choice.

☑ Face Value

When in doubt, use common sense. Accept the situation in the problem at face value. Don't read too much into it. These problems will not require you to make wild assumptions. If you have to go beyond creativity and warp time or space in order to have an answer choice fit the question, then you should move on and consider the other answer choices. These are normal problems rooted in reality. The applicable relationship or explanation may not be readily apparent, but it is there for you to figure out. Use your common sense to interpret anything that isn't clear.

Answer Choice Strategies

⊘ Answer Selection

The most thorough way to pick an answer choice is to identify and eliminate wrong answers until only one is left, then confirm it is the correct answer. Sometimes an answer choice may immediately seem right, but be careful. The test writers will usually put more than one reasonable answer choice on each question, so take a second to read all of them and make sure that the other choices are not equally obvious. As long as you have time left, it is better to read every answer choice than to pick the first one that looks right without checking the others.

⊘ Answer Choice Families

An answer choice family consists of two (in rare cases, three) answer choices that are very similar in construction and cannot all be true at the same time. If you see two answer choices that are direct opposites or parallels, one of them is usually the correct answer. For instance, if one answer choice says that quantity x increases and another either says that quantity x decreases (opposite) or says that quantity y increases (parallel), then those answer choices would fall into the same family. An answer choice that doesn't match the construction of the answer choice family is more likely to be incorrect. Most questions will not have answer choice families, but when they do appear, you should be prepared to recognize them.

⊘ Eliminate Answers

Eliminate answer choices as soon as you realize they are wrong, but make sure you consider all possibilities. If you are eliminating answer choices and realize that the last one you are left with is also wrong, don't panic. Start over and consider each choice again. There may be something you missed the first time that you will realize on the second pass.

⊘ Avoid Fact Traps

Don't be distracted by an answer choice that is factually true but doesn't answer the question. You are looking for the choice that answers the question. Stay focused on what the question is asking for so you don't accidentally pick an answer that is true but incorrect. Always go back to the question and make sure the answer choice you've selected actually answers the question and is not merely a true statement.

⊘ Extreme Statements

In general, you should avoid answers that put forth extreme actions as standard practice or proclaim controversial ideas as established fact. An answer choice that states the "process should be used in certain situations, if…" is much more likely to be correct than one that states the "process should be discontinued completely." The first is a calm rational statement and doesn't even make a definitive, uncompromising stance, using a hedge word *if* to provide wiggle room, whereas the second choice is far more extreme.

⊘ Benchmark

As you read through the answer choices and you come across one that seems to answer the question well, mentally select that answer choice. This is not your final answer, but it's the one that will help you evaluate the other answer choices. The one that you selected is your benchmark or standard for judging each of the other answer choices. Every other answer choice must be compared to your benchmark. That choice is correct until proven otherwise by another answer choice beating it. If you find a better answer, then that one becomes your new benchmark. Once you've decided that no other choice answers the question as well as your benchmark, you have your final answer.

⊘ Predict the Answer

Before you even start looking at the answer choices, it is often best to try to predict the answer. When you come up with the answer on your own, it is easier to avoid distractions and traps because you will know exactly what to look for. The right answer choice is unlikely to be word-for-word what you came up with, but it should be a close match. Even if you are confident that you have the right answer, you should still take the time to read each option before moving on.

General Strategies

⊘ Tough Questions

If you are stumped on a problem or it appears too hard or too difficult, don't waste time. Move on! Remember though, if you can quickly check for obviously incorrect answer choices, your chances of guessing correctly are greatly improved. Before you completely give up, at least try to knock out a couple of possible answers. Eliminate what you can and then guess at the remaining answer choices before moving on.

⊘ Check Your Work

Since you will probably not know every term listed and the answer to every question, it is important that you get credit for the ones that you do know. Don't miss any questions through careless mistakes. If at all possible, try to take a second to look back over your answer selection and make sure you've selected the correct answer choice and haven't made a costly careless mistake (such as marking an answer choice that you didn't mean to mark). This quick double check should more than pay for itself in caught mistakes for the time it costs.

⊘ Pace Yourself

It's easy to be overwhelmed when you're looking at a page full of questions; your mind is confused and full of random thoughts, and the clock is ticking down faster than you would like. Calm down and maintain the pace that you have set for yourself. Especially as you get down to the last few minutes of the test, don't let the small numbers on the clock make you panic. As long as you are on track by monitoring your pace, you are guaranteed to have time for each question.

⊘ Don't Rush

It is very easy to make errors when you are in a hurry. Maintaining a fast pace in answering questions is pointless if it makes you miss questions that you would have gotten right otherwise. Test writers like to include distracting information and wrong answers that seem right. Taking a little extra time to avoid careless mistakes can make all the difference in your test score. Find a pace that allows you to be confident in the answers that you select.

⊘ Keep Moving

Panicking will not help you pass the test, so do your best to stay calm and keep moving. Taking deep breaths and going through the answer elimination steps you practiced can help to break through a stress barrier and keep your pace.

Final Notes

The combination of a solid foundation of content knowledge and the confidence that comes from practicing your plan for applying that knowledge is the key to maximizing your performance on test day. As your foundation of content knowledge is built up and strengthened, you'll find that the strategies included in this chapter become more and more effective in helping you quickly sift through the distractions and traps of the test to isolate the correct answer.

Now that you're preparing to move forward into the test content chapters of this book, be sure to keep your goal in mind. As you read, think about how you will be able to apply this information on the test. If you've already seen sample questions for the test and you have an idea of the question format and style, try to come up with questions of your own that you can answer based on what you're reading. This will give you valuable practice applying your knowledge in the same ways you can expect to on test day.

Good luck and good studying!

Materials and Processes

Drawing

ORIGINS, HISTORY, AND USE OF DRAWING

Drawing is a medium that was first used on cave walls as early as 10,000 BC, and it was originally used to express ideas and scenes in these cave paintings. Egyptians used the medium of drawing beginning by 3000 BC. As artists and materials became more refined, drawing was primarily used as a preliminary step before starting a painting. In the Middle Ages, drawings were mainly completed on animal skins, wood, wax, or slate. Artists would keep records of their sketches to use for artwork instead of working from live models. Some artists in the Middle Ages would complete finished drawings as illuminations for manuscripts.

In the Renaissance era, drawing became a more widely used art form of its own. This is partly due to the availability of paper. Drawing was still considered more of a preliminary step before using other media, causing it to be learned on its own as the foundation for these other art forms. Art students during the Renaissance were first taught to draw before painting and sculpting. When large-scale paintings were created, such as in the Sistine Chapel, many preparatory drawings were created to use for the final paintings. In the 1500s in northern Europe, artists began creating drawings as finished works rather than as preparatory materials. Albrecht Dürer and Hans Holbein the Younger created detailed drawings that could stand alone as artworks. Drawing was also used to study and record nature and anatomy. The artists used pen and ink, as well as black and red charcoal.

In the baroque period, drawings were more free-flowing and less exact than those in the Renaissance era. In the 1600s, Rembrandt used pen lines to create expressive drawings, and Dutch artists took their sketchbooks into the fields to capture scenes to paint from later. Artists continued to create sketches prior to finished artworks, but drawing became an accepted medium for a final artwork. Finally, pencils were first manufactured in the 1800s, and they became a widely used drawing tool that helped bring the medium of drawing to an even broader array of artists.

HISTORIC DRAWING MEDIA

- **Charcoal** is an early drawing material made from slowly burned wood. Charcoal was used for cave drawings, when burnt sticks were rubbed on cave walls.
- **Red chalk** is made from iron oxide pigment and refined clay. It was popular in the 16th and 17th centuries, and Leonardo da Vinci used it for many sketches. **Black chalk** is carbonaceous shale, and it is softer than red chalk. It was used in 15th-century Italy for underdrawings for ink or metalpoint artwork. Albrecht Dürer and Anthony van Dyck used black chalk for portraits. **White chalk** is calcium carbonate or soapstone, and it is used for highlights on drawings.
- **Conté crayons** were developed in the early 1800s. They are made in red, black, and white. They are harder than chalk and produce smoother lines.
- **Graphite** is a form of carbon, and it was first discovered in the 1500s. It was later cut into strips and encased in wood for pencils.
- **Ink** is a liquid pigment that can be used with a pen or a brush. It was also commonly used for writing. **Pens** were first made with bird feathers (quills) and reeds, and later they were created with metal tips.

PENCILS AND CHARCOAL

Pencils are made from graphite encased in wood. They are available in a range of hardnesses, from 10H to 10B. A 10H pencil has the hardest lead, and it will stay the sharpest and leave the lightest mark on the paper. A 10B pencil has the softest lead, and it will wear down quickly, leaving the darkest mark on the paper. In the middle are F and HB, which are a medium hardness and darkness.

Charcoal is a lightweight carbon that can be found in stick form or pencil form. Compressed charcoal is a hard charcoal stick, whereas vine charcoal is a thin, delicate stick. Charcoal also comes in different hardnesses, although it is usually just in the B (soft) range. A higher number before the B indicates a softer charcoal.

Charcoal and pencil can be used for sketching and drawing, but pencil will generally give the opportunity for greater detail, since there are harder graphites available. Charcoal is often used for large-gesture drawings and putting ideas onto a canvas prior to painting.

Other Tools for Drawing

In addition to materials used to draw with, there are several tools used along with drawing media. A **tortillon** is a piece of paper wrapped up tightly, ending in a point, that can be used to blend pencil and charcoal drawings. A maulstick, or mahlstick, is a stick with a padded head used to rest and support your hand to keep it steady while drawing or painting. Various **erasers** are used for drawing. A kneaded rubber eraser is one that can be manipulated and rolled into smaller sizes to erase small areas, and it will not leave eraser crumbs behind. A gum eraser is yellowish and will crumble quickly; it is best for larger areas. A pink eraser is firmer and more precise, but it will still leave crumbs on the paper. A large brush can be used to gently brush the eraser bits off of the paper. A dry cleaning pad is a fabric bag filled with pieces of eraser that can be used to clean up fingerprints, smudges, and dust from larger areas of paper.

Drawing Surfaces

A commonly used drawing surface used in the Middle Ages was **parchment**, which was created from animal skin. Paper was first created in 105 AD in China, but it wasn't widely used as a drawing material until it was produced more quickly and more inexpensively in the 1600s.

Paper comes in hot-pressed and cold-pressed surfaces. Hot-pressed paper will be smooth, whereas cold-pressed paper will have a texture. Sketch paper is thinner than drawing paper, which is made to be more permanent. Newsprint is the kind of thin paper that newspaper is printed on, and it is useful for sketching. Illustration board is a thicker cardboard with a hot-pressed or cold-pressed white surface. Bristol board is thicker than drawing paper, and it also comes in hot- or cold-pressed. A smooth surface will allow for greater detail and better control of pencil marks, whereas a rough surface is better suited for looser drawing and sketching or for a drawing with a rough texture.

Paper considered archival will be labeled as acid-free, and it should not yellow and deteriorate over time. Acid-free paper should be used for finished drawings, whereas any paper, including sketch paper and newsprint, can be used for preliminary sketches.

Contour and Blind Contour

A **contour drawing** seeks to define the outline of an object, and it can contain as much or as little detail as the artist desires. This technique uses only lines to delineate the outer edges of the subject; it does not include any shading or other values in the drawing. For a contour drawing, the artist will study the subject and show the proportions and volume, rather than focusing on values or fine details. This type of drawing can be used to quickly capture a subject or scene.

A **blind contour** drawing is used by an artist to practice sketching and perception. To create a blind contour drawing, the artist will look directly at the subject and draw a contour without looking back at their paper. They may occasionally glance at the paper to reorient their drawing tool, but generally will keep their focus on the subject. Rather than being used to capture a subject or scene, this is typically reserved as a drawing exercise to help strengthen the artist's hand-eye coordination.

Gesture and Perspective Drawing

Gesture drawing is a technique used to quickly capture the action and form of a model or subject. A gesture drawing can be completed in as little as 30 to 60 seconds. The artist uses loose lines to simplify and capture the essence of the subject. These drawings are generally done to study and capture different poses of the human figure. Gesture drawings can help an artist choose a pose to use for a more detailed study of the figure.

Perspective drawing is a drawing technique that shows spatial relationships and the illusion of space on a flat surface. An artist can portray a three-dimensional scene on a two-dimensional drawing. One-point perspective shows the objects in the scene receding to one point in the horizon, as shown in the image. Two-point perspective has the scene receding into two points on the horizon. These points along the horizon where the objects disappear to in the distance are called vanishing points.

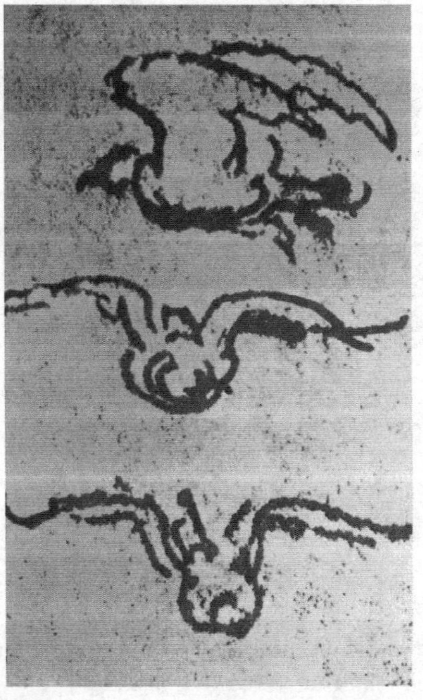

Hatching and Crosshatching

Hatching is a technique that uses closely placed parallel lines to create shading and tones. Crosshatching is when hatching is used perpendicular to itself, creating heavier shades and tones. In this example from Albrecht Dürer, *The Penitent* (1510), he uses hatching heavily throughout the drawing. Notice how the lines are closer together to make darker values and how the lines follow the contours of the objects. On flat walls they are straight, and on the curtains, they follow the curves. Using the lines to emphasize the forms in the artwork helps to create a sense of volume for the viewer.

Dürer uses crosshatching in the heavier shaded areas of the drawing. In the darkest areas, the hatched patterns cross each other to create crosshatching. Again, the lines are closer together where the values are the darkest.

Although this example is a woodcut, these techniques are also used in the printmaking techniques of engraving and etching, as well as drawing.

Shading

Shading adds depth and form to an artwork. An object with accurate shading can appear three-dimensional. To create this illusion with pencils, the artist needs to vary pressure, use pencils of appropriate hardnesses, and understand where the shadows and highlights should be placed. When light hits the object, it creates many different values. The area closest to the light source will have a highlight, which is the whitest part of the drawing. This can be created by leaving that part white or by erasing afterward. As the object gets farther from the light source, it will be gradually shaded darker. A smooth gradation can be accomplished with careful control of the pencil or by using a blending tool, or tortillon, to blend the graphite. If the object is on a light surface, that surface can create a reflection toward the bottom of the object. The object will also cast a shadow on the surface opposite the light source. Careful observation of the object, as well as the values and shadows, will help the artist create a realistic rendering.

Critiquing Drawings

When critiquing a drawing as a finished artwork, you can describe, analyze, interpret, and judge it. Begin by describing the visual facts — what you see in the drawing. Is it representational? What kinds of shapes, lines, or textures do you see? Next, begin analyzing the artwork. Recognize the elements of art and how they are arranged (the principles of design). Do you see shapes arranged in a pattern? Where is the emphasis in the drawing? How are the lines used, and where do they lead your eye? Next, interpret the artwork, or use what you have learned so far to decide what the artist is trying to say. What is the mood of the artwork? What does the subject matter tell you? Why do you think the artist decided to portray it in this way? After completing these steps, you can begin to make your own judgement of the artwork. Did the artist successfully use the principles of design to organize the elements of art? Does the artist successfully convey the feelings, mood, and ideas they were aiming for? Do you see ways that the artwork can be improved?

Following these steps will give you a way to thoroughly and objectively critique a drawing and recognize the successes and failures within it.

CREATIVITY IN DRAWING AND SKETCHING

Drawing and sketching are commonly used to elicit creativity and **refine ideas**. A sketch pad and pencil or pen are easily portable and can be used to quickly jot down ideas or capture a form or scene to be added to a later artwork. Drawings can be completed quickly and started and stopped easily, unlike paintings, which require preparation, more materials, and drying time.

An artist can gather ideas in a sketch book and then look back at them later to think further and get more ideas from them. An artist can also combine their ideas and sketches into a bigger artwork. They can experiment with different pencils, line widths, and techniques to find the ones that work best for them or what will work best for a particular artwork. An artist can observe the world around them and draw what they see and then add those common items into imaginary scenes or draw from the imagination altogether to create new, inventive scenes. Through sketching and experimentation, an artist can prepare their ideas and techniques for a well-planned final artwork that will showcase their creativity.

Painting

OIL PAINTING

Oil painting was developed as a fine art painting medium in the 15th century in northern Europe, and Jan van Eyck is credited with being the first to use oil paint on wood panels. Toward the end of the 15th century, artists began painting on canvas instead of wood panels. The popularity of painting on canvas grew because it was cheaper, easier to transport, and easier to create larger artworks. The canvas was coated with a layer of animal glue and then a layer of lead white paint prior to painting.

Oil paint is made from a pigment suspended in a drying oil. The master painters' apprentices were in charge of mixing and preparing the oil paints. In the late 18th century, prepared oil paints started to be manufactured at scale so they could be purchased.

The pigments and paints used today are more lightfast and durable than the oil paints used in the past. Many times, colors have faded or oxidized due to exposure to light and air, and older paintings do not look as they were intended. One example is Van Gogh's *Sunflowers* (1880s), in which he used a chrome yellow pigment that has turned brown over time.

WATERCOLOR

Watercolor has been used for cave paintings and manuscript illustrations, but it was first widely used as a fine art medium during the Renaissance. Albrecht Dürer was one of the earliest watercolor painters, as seen in *The Hare* (1502). During the baroque period, watercolors were used for sketching and cartoons. In addition to fine art, Renaissance artists used watercolors for botanical illustrations. In the 19th century, John Audubon used watercolors for his well-known bird illustrations.

Watercolor is created by adding pigment to a gum arabic binder. It can be found in a dry cake form, which needs to be wet with water, or in a tube. Watercolor brushes are generally soft and made with natural (sable, squirrel) or synthetic hairs, and they have a shorter handle than oil and acrylic brushes. Watercolors are transparent, meaning they can be layered upon each other and the color underneath and white paper will show through. The most common surface for watercolor painting is watercolor paper, which comes in hot-press (smooth) and cold-press (rough) finishes.

EGG TEMPERA

Egg tempera was a popular painting medium until after 1500, when oil painting became widely used instead. Traditional egg tempera paint is created by adding pigment to egg yolk, which is used as a water-soluble binder. White wine, vinegar, or water can be added in various proportions to keep the dried paint from cracking. When the yolk is exposed to air, it begins to dry, so the artist continually adds water to keep the consistency correct for painting.

Egg tempera paint dries very quickly, so it is applied in thin, transparent layers and usually with short brushstrokes. The technique of crosshatching can be used to layer the colors. Unlike oil paintings, tempera paints have survived over history in much the same condition as they were intended. In the 20th century, some artists began using tempera again, such as Andrew Wyeth, Thomas Hart Benton, and Jacob Lawrence.

Egg tempera is painted onto stiff surfaces such as wood panels or Masonite because a flexible surface would allow it to crack and flake off the support.

GOUACHE

Gouache is an opaque medium with characteristics similar to watercolor. It is traditionally created with gum arabic as the binder, but it also has a filler added to make the paint opaque. Like watercolor, dried gouache can be rewet and reworked. It dries to a matte finish, and it is usually used on watercolor paper or illustration board. With a smooth hot-press surface, an artist can create great detail with gouache. Gouache is commonly used for graphic arts including illustrations, comics, and posters. It has also been used in animation.

The term *gouache* was first used in France in the 18th century to refer to opaque watercolor, but the medium and techniques were used prior to this—as early as the 9th century in Persia.

Gouache is now manufactured as watercolor type and a newer acrylic type. The acrylic gouache is water resistant once it's dry, and it cannot be rewet. It differs from acrylic paint in that it dries to a matte finish and can be worked with for slightly longer.

Common Painting Tools

Paintbrushes used for oils and acrylics generally have a longer handle than do watercolor brushes. Watercolor brushes have soft natural or synthetic hairs, whereas acrylic and oil brushes have stiffer natural or synthetic hairs, including hog bristles. Whereas watercolors and acrylics are water soluble and the brushes can be cleaned with soap and water, oil brushes need to be cleaned with a paint thinner solvent.

Drying oils, such as linseed and poppy oil, can be added to oil paints to decrease drying times and thin the consistency. There are many types of media for acrylic paints that will decrease the drying time or change the texture to thicker or thinner.

Primer is a base for painting, and it is commonly used with oil and acrylic painting. A commonly used primer is called gesso, which is essentially a water-based white paint mixture used to prepare the support.

For watercolors, a **masking fluid** will cover areas of the paper that are needed to stay white for highlights. After the watercolor painting is finished, the masking fluid can be removed, revealing the white paper.

All paints will benefit from the use of a **palette**. A palette can be a basic piece of wood or Masonite, or it can be a more involved structure with divots for each color. A palette is used to organize and mix colors for a painting. The selection of colors and organization is up to the individual artist.

Oil and Water-Based Paints

With advances in **acrylic paints**, an artist can now get similar finished products to that of oil paints, but there are still differences in the media and processes. Oil paint allows for a much longer working time than acrylic. Oil paint will stay workable on the palette for four to eight hours, whereas acrylic paint can dry in less than an hour. A finished oil painting can take six months or more before it is considered dry. The oil paint on the canvas will stay workable to allow for more blending, whereas acrylic dries more quickly and does not lend itself to as much blending. Acrylics turn into a kind of plastic when they dry, so if they dry in the paintbrush, it can be difficult to impossible to clean the brush. Watercolors can be rewet and washed out of the brush at any time, and oil paints can be soaked and removed with paint thinners.

Acrylic can be used as a base for oil paintings, but it cannot be painted on top of oils. When painting with oils, it is important to remember the rule "fat over lean." this means the artist should build increasingly flexible layers on top of each other. The increased flexibility is accomplished by adding an oil medium to the paint and using less solvent.

How the Invention of Invention of Oil Paints Affected Art/Paintings

Prior to the invention of **oil paint,** artists used tempera, fresco, encaustic, and watercolor. Tempera dries quickly, while fresco and encaustic require very specific techniques and conditions for use. Watercolor is limited in textural effects due to its thin nature. The invention of oil paint allowed artists to create more realistic and complex artworks due to the slow drying time. The drying time helped the artist blend the paint on the canvas and add further details. Artists had more control over their work and were able to paint in varied conditions on different surfaces. Oil paint can be applied in a thin glaze or thick impasto, allowing for a range of textures. The paint can be blended or reworked over a long period of time. While oil was used as a binder as far back as the 7th century, Jan van Eyck is credited with perfecting its use in the early 15th century.

How the Invention of Invention of Acrylic Paints Affected Art/Paintings

Acrylic paint was developed around the 1940s. These paints are quick drying, easy to use on various surfaces, and easy to dilute and clean up with water. The flat, bright colors support modern and contemporary artists' methods. The texture and sheen can be altered with a range of acrylic mediums. Acrylics do not yellow over time, and they are more flexible than oil paint once dried. Finished pieces can be created quickly due to the short drying time. Acrylics are used often in school settings due to their low odor and ability to be cleaned up with water. There is a range of acrylics available, from inexpensive student-grade to more expensive artist-grade paints.

How the Invention of the Camera Affected Art/Paintings

The **camera** was invented in the 19th century and had a wide range of effects on art and painting. Artists began to shift their artwork away from realism and toward other styles like Impressionism. They attempted to capture the subjective experience of the scene instead of a photorealistic representation. Artists no longer felt the need to capture minute details since photographs could do that. Photographic portraits led portrait artists to explore stylistic interpretation and depict psychological depth rather than just likeness.

Photography led to new techniques of cropping, angles, and depth of field that artists began to explore in their artwork. For example, depth of field techniques kept the subject in sharp focus while other areas were blurred. Since photography had the ability to capture everyday scenes, the subject matter for other artwork expanded to show domestic scenes and urban life as well. Artwork also began to attempt to show motion, like the works of the Futurists and Marcel Duchamp. Photographs were even included in artworks that blended media, like mixed media and photomontage.

Painting Surfaces

Wood has been used as a support for oil and acrylic painting for centuries. It is rigid and minimizes any flexing or cracking of the paint. Wood should be primed before painting on it to seal the surface and also to make it smoother. For the smoothest surface, layers of gesso can be applied, let dry, and sanded between applications.

Paper is used for watercolor or acrylic, but the oil from oil paints will break paper down, so it is not well suited for oil painting. Canvas has been the most popular surface for oil paints since the 17th century, and it is often used for acrylics, too. **Canvas boards** are now used, which are made from canvas stretched over rigid cardboard and preprimed.

Paper for watercolors, acrylics, and gouache is usually thick to accommodate the amount of paint and water used. Watercolor paper needs to be stretched so that it does not warp after use. Some watercolor pads come with glue around the edges to prevent this warping; otherwise, it will need to be taped to a surface on four sides, then wet and let dry to prepare the paper.

Underpainting and Glazing

Underpainting is a technique used for oil and acrylic painting to create a base for a finished painting. An artist can use the underpainting to lay out the highlights and shadows for their artwork. Underpainting can be used to layer and build up rich color, and it serves as a foundation to establish the tones throughout the artwork. An underpainting for oil can be done with thinned oil paint or in acrylic so it will dry quickly. A tonal underpainting is done with one color of paint, just to establish the layout and tones before beginning the painting.

Glazing is a technique used with oil paints to layer transparent colors over a dried opaque color. Each layer is allowed to dry before another transparent layer is painted on top. The colors interact and visually blend without being physically blended on the palette. Glazing can be used to create skin tones and other complex colors that would be difficult to create otherwise. Some colors are naturally more transparent than others, so the artist needs to know the qualities of the paint and whether to add a medium to increase the transparency.

Dry Brush and Sgraffito

Dry brush is a technique used with water-based and oil-based paints. For acrylic and watercolor painting, the brush is loaded with paint after the water is squeezed or blotted out of it. With oil painting, the brush is loaded with paint after the oil or medium is squeezed or blotted from the brush. Dry brushing creates a scratchy-looking texture on the surface, and the brushstrokes will be evident. This can be used to add texture to a painting, including fur or grass, or it can be used for emphasis and contrast to a smoother area.

Sgraffito is a technique of scratching through a layer of paint to reveal the layer or surface underneath. Sgraffito can be accomplished with a palette knife, the handle end of a paintbrush, or even a stick. This can also be done with only one layer of paint, with the artist scratching through the wet paint and revealing the canvas underneath.

Wet-On-Wet and Wash

Wet-on-wet is a watercolor technique in which the artist paints onto already-wet paper. This will cause the colors to blend and bleed into each other. This technique takes practice because the wetness of the paper, the color already on the paper, the amount of water on the brush, and the color on the brush will all affect the final product. Experience will help the artist know what will happen when they add wet watercolor onto already-wet paper and how the colors will react with each other.

A wash is a technique of adding a large area of color to a watercolor painting. A flat wash is a large area of one color, and a graded wash goes from one color gradually to white or another color. It is easiest to control the wash on dry paper instead of already-wet paper. A large, flat watercolor brush is used to apply the mixture of paint and water. As paint is applied to the paper, it will begin drying; therefore, time is a critical factor to consider in order to achieve an even application of color.

Plein Air and Alla Prima

Plein air is a painting technique that entails painting outdoors. This technique increased in popularity in the 1840s when paint became available in tubes, which is more convenient for travel. The box easel, or field easel, was developed around this time; it is a box that the artist can use to carry their painting materials, and it opens up into an easel. Claude Monet often painted *en plein air* (French for "outdoors"), using the natural light to capture scenes at specific times of the day. This can be done with any painting medium, including watercolors that can be found in small, portable boxes for this purpose.

Alla prima is a painting technique that entails painting wet oil paint onto wet oil layers that have not been allowed to dry. This can also be called direct painting or wet-on-wet. An alla prima painting can be completed in one sitting, unlike an oil painting with multiple layers of glazing, which requires time to dry between layers. Alla prima can create a spontaneous and fresh look in the artwork.

Trompe-L'oeil

Trompe l'oeil is a painting technique that means "to deceive the eye" in French. A trompe l'oeil painting is meant to depict objects in a realistic way to produce the optical illusion that the objects exist in three dimensions. This phrase was first used in the baroque period, but the actual technique was used earlier in Greek and Roman murals.

During the Renaissance, frescoed ceiling paintings were created that used foreshortening and realistic depictions to create the illusion of more space above the viewer. This was called *di sotto in sù*, which means "from below, upward" in Italian.

This painting from 1675 by Cornelis Gysbrechts is an example of trompe l'oeil. The artist depicted objects piled and scattered on a wood surface, and he used realistic colors, proportions, and shadows to achieve a three-dimensional effect. Even the wood surface is carefully and realistically portrayed. This technique requires a great deal of attention to detail as well as a deep understanding of color mixing and oil media by the artist.

Acrylic Paint

Acrylic paint has only been in use since the 1940s, and it has provided an alternative to using oil paints. Acrylic paint has a much quicker drying time than oils, and the finished surface has a greater degree of flexibility, allowing it to be painted on more surfaces with fewer considerations than oils.

Acrylics do not require the use of solvents for thinning or cleaning up the paint. They are water soluble and clean up with water. As a water-based media, more media can be layered on top of acrylics than on oils, making it more versatile for collage art. Acrylics can be used on more surfaces and supports, including cardboard and paper, that are not suitable for oil paints because oil paints will break certain supports down. With a 15- to 20-minute drying time for each layer, acrylic layers can be completed more quickly than can those in an oil painting.

Acrylic paints were first developed for practical applications such as house painting, but when Andy Warhol began using acrylics in his paintings, including *Campbell's Soup Cans*, they gained more recognition as an artistic medium. Other notable artists who used acrylics are Robert Motherwell, Mark Rothko, and Roy Lichtenstein.

Impasto Technique

Impasto is a painting technique in which the paint is laid onto the surface very thickly with a brush or palette knife. With this technique, the brushstrokes are usually very visible, and they can even become purposeful lines that lead the viewer's eye throughout the artwork. When using this technique, the artist can control how light hits and reflects off of the paint surface. It can make the painting appear three-dimensional, and it can also give the painting texture.

In Vincent van Gogh's painting *Wheatfield with Crows* (1890), he uses this technique, laying the paint on thickly with visible brushstrokes. The brushstrokes create lines throughout the painting, and the lines of the brown path lead the viewer's eye to the middle of the artwork. His use of brushstrokes also creates a sense of movement in his works. The dark blues and bold strokes in the sky suggest stormy and turbulent weather. The brushstrokes throughout the wheat field lean to the side and also suggest wind and storms.

Perspective in Paint

Prior to the Renaissance, artists were aware of the varying sizes of elements related to being close or far away, but Renaissance artist Filippo Brunelleschi is credited with discovering geometric perspective in 1413. After this discovery, artists began to use vanishing points and horizon lines to compose their artwork. Decades after Brunelleschi's discovery, Leon Battista Alberti wrote a description of how to properly use perspective.

This image, *The Last Supper* by Leonardo da Vinci, shows the use of one-point perspective. This work was completed between 1495–1496. The lines in this painting converge to one vanishing point in the center of the painting. This serves to draw the focus to the central figure in the painting. Da Vinci's use of perspective masterfully showcases the relatively new technique, gives an architecturally correct feel to the room, and serves as a method of compositional emphasis in the artwork. Due to the discovery of perspective, artists were subsequently able to portray architecture and other scenes with greater accuracy.

Historical Use of Apprenticeship

An **apprentice** was someone who learned to be an artist by working under a master artist. In the medieval era, a painter was thought of as a **tradesman**, and their client would dictate what they would create. The master painter would use helpers, or apprentices, to complete the work. The apprenticeship system began in the medieval era, and it continued through the Renaissance, when a painter was considered an artist.

An apprentice would begin with menial tasks such as cleaning paintbrushes and grinding pigments for the master artist. A student would practice drawing by copying works, and then he or she could move on to painting. The apprentices would paint backgrounds and were trained to work in the style of the master artist.

The master artist might only paint the figures or faces in an artwork, or the apprentices could complete the entire work in the master's style. The master's signature on a work did not indicate that they completed a certain amount of the work, but rather that it was up to their standards. After a certain number of years as an apprentice, an apprentice could reach journeyman status and open their own shop.

Printmaking

Tools for Printmaking

- A **brayer** is a hand tool used for printmaking to smooth out the ink and then roll it onto the printmaking surface for a relief print. It has a handle and a smooth rubber roller.
- A **burnisher** is a smooth metal tool that is used to smooth the surface of a metal intaglio printing plate. Lines are etched into the plate to hold ink, and the burnisher can polish the metal surface to reduce its ability to hold ink. The term burnisher could also refer to a flat disk used to press paper onto a surface to create a print.
- A **plate** is a copper or zinc sheet of metal used for intaglio printmaking. When using a plate, the lines are cut or etched into the surface, and these lines hold the ink, which is the opposite of a relief print in which the raised parts hold the ink.
- A **gouge** is used in relief printmaking to cut away the parts that will not hold ink. Gouges come in different sizes and shapes, including U-shaped and V-shaped, and they are used on surfaces such as linoleum or wood.

Intaglio and Lithography

Intaglio is a printmaking technique in which the image is carved into a surface and the ink is held in those lines for printing. Lines are cut into a metal plate by a burin, which is a handheld metal tool, or by etching, which is a chemical process. For etching, the plate is first covered with an acid-resistant material and then the image is carved into that material to reveal the plate under it. The plate is dipped in acid, which bites only into the lines where the plate is exposed. The acid-resistant material is then removed, and ink is rubbed into the etched or carved lines and wiped off of the rest of the plate. The high pressure of a printing press pushes the paper into the inked grooves to produce the print. The image shown is an example of an etching.

For **lithography**, the artist uses a greasy medium such as a crayon or ink to produce an image on limestone or aluminum. The artist then puts a solution of nitric acid and gum arabic on the surface, and when a roller with oil-based ink is rolled over this, the ink will only stick to the greasy area. This is then run through a press with paper to produce the image.

Relief Printing and Screen Printing

Relief printing is any method in which a raised surface is used to produce the image. Relief printing is commonly done with linoleum and wood, in which the parts that is not wanted to be printed are cut away by the artist with gouges. Letterpress is also an example of relief printing, in which the raised letters are printed onto paper. Ink is applied to the raised surface with a roller, and then paper is pressed onto the surface by hand or with a printing press, to transfer the image onto paper.

For **screen printing**, also called silk screening (as shown in the image), ink is pressed through a fine screen to produce the print. An image is created onto the screen through many different methods, including stencils or photo emulsion, and the parts of the screen that are left open are where the ink will go through to the surface. Ink is pushed through the screen evenly by a squeegee onto paper, cardboard, fabric, or any number of materials. Andy Warhol is famous for using the screen printing technique to produce multiple prints of the same image.

Collagraphy and Frottage

Collagraphy is a printmaking technique in which materials of various textures are attached to a surface. The materials should all be of roughly the same height. Ink is then rolled onto the textured surfaces, and a print is produced on paper by pressing the paper by hand or with a printing press. Different textures and inking methods can produce different results for this technique.

Frottage is a printmaking technique in which the artist gets an impression of the surface of a material. For example, you could place various leaves on a surface, lay paper on top of them, and then carefully rub the side of a crayon onto the paper. The resulting image will show the textures and shapes of the leaves underneath. During the surrealist movement, Max Ernst would take rubbings from various surfaces and use these as a basis for his artworks.

Monotype and Stamping

Whereas most printmaking techniques can produce multiple identical or similar prints, a **monotype** will only produce one print. The artwork is created on a nonabsorbent surface with oil- or water-based ink, and then it is transferred to paper with a printing press. In the process, most of the ink is transferred to the paper, so there is not enough left on the surface to produce another print. The print can then be embellished with ink, by drawing, or by other painting methods.

Stamping is another type of relief printmaking. A stamp can be made from rubber, wax, or other materials, including cardboard or even potatoes. The shape that will produce the image is cut into the material, with the negative space cut away. The shape is pressed into the ink and then pressed onto paper to create the image. A stamped image can be reproduced over and over.

Linocuts and Woodcuts

The process of creating a **linocut**, or linoleum cut, and a **woodcut** are similar. Both of these are relief printing methods, which involve cutting away pieces of the material to produce the image to be printed. For linocut and woodcut, gouges of various shapes and sizes are used to cut away the material. The cut-away areas will not carry ink, whereas the areas left behind will be inked. When the artist is finished cutting away the material, the surface is inked with a roller, and then it is run through a printing press to print the image onto paper. The image can be reproduced repeatedly.

Instead of using the printing press, an artist could use a burnisher to transfer the image to paper. A **burnisher**, or baren, is a disklike hand tool that is flat on the bottom and has a handle. The artist would put the paper on top of the inked surface and then rub the paper evenly with the burnisher to transfer the ink to the paper.

Mezzotint and Aquatint

Mezzotint is a printmaking technique in which the artist works from dark to light. The artist would work on a copper or steel plate and roughen parts of the plate for shading, while smoothing out other parts for the lighter areas. This would increase and reduce the areas' ability to hold ink. The technique was developed in the 17th century, and it could be used to create gradations in the printed work, rather than everything being black and white.

Aquatint is another way to create tonal effects in a print. Fine particles of acid-resistant powdered rosin are melted onto a metal plate, which is then dipped in acid. The acid eats away at the metal around the particles, creating an even, granular pattern that when inked and printed will give an effect similar to a watercolor wash. The darkness of these tones can be controlled by lengthening or shortening the time that the plate is exposed to the acid.

Ethical Standards in Art

Copyright Laws

When creating artwork, it is important to keep in mind copyright issues and not use images or ideas without permission. Copyright is a form of protection for published and unpublished works, and protection begins once the work has been completed. To avoid copyright issues, it is a good idea to work from life or images you have obtained yourself. Copying a famous artwork for your own understanding of the artist's techniques is fine and is commonly done, as long as it is for your own personal use. This artwork cannot be sold or presented as your own work. If using other materials, use materials that are out of copyright, use public domain images, or obtain permission from the originator of the source image. For public domain images, always read the fine print to check for restrictions for using the image. Copyright laws can also vary by state and country, so it is necessary to check specific laws for your area.

> **Review Video: Ethical and Professional Standards**
> Visit mometrix.com/academy and enter code: 391843

Plagiarism

Plagiarism in art refers to when an artist copies the work of someone else and presents it as his or her original work. This is an ethical issue because it fails to acknowledge the origin of the work. Artists who plagiarize might directly copy someone's work or take someone's ideas and present them as their own ideas. They might generate AI art that closely looks like existing artwork.

It can result in serious **consequences** for the artists, and their reputation as an artist can be affected. It also hurts the original artist whose work is used inappropriately. Plagiarism leads to legal consequences, involving lawsuits, fines, and withdrawal of work from an exhibit. Artists can avoid plagiarism by not only giving credit where it is due but also through the creation of their own original artwork. Familiarity with fair use can also help an artist avoid plagiarism. Fair use allows an artist to use copyrighted material in certain ways that may include parody, commentary, and criticism.

Appropriation

Appropriation is the intentional copying, borrowing, or reusing of existing elements from an artwork or culture to make new art. This is a legitimate art technique, but it comes with **ethical** considerations. An artist might appropriate someone's artistic styles or techniques. He or she might appropriate cultural elements, but the artist must approach sourcing elements from a culture with sensitivity to the cultural significance of those elements. Misuse of cultural appropriation can be exploitative or disrespectful. When using appropriated material, the artist should give credit to the original culture or creator. This shows transparency and respect for the origin of the material.

The artist usually creates new meaning when ethically appropriating material. This approach helps the artist to include a thoughtful commentary on his or her process. The artist should transform those elements into something original. The appropriated material should be a jumping-off point for innovation rather than a replication of existing work. The artist must stay within the legal boundaries of copyright laws when appropriating material. Material within the public domain can be appropriated, but the artist should still be respectful of the original work.

Fair Use and Open Source

Fair use is a legal doctrine. It allows for copyrighted material to be used in specific, limited ways without the user asking permission from the copyright holder. Using copyrighted material **ethically** should be done in a transformative way. Fair use in art usually builds on prior works, comments on social, political, or artistic culture, or intertwines with contemporary culture. It should be used for non-commercial purposes. If the artist uses a large portion of the original work in his or her creation, it is unlikely to be considered fair use. The use of a work should not reduce the value of that original work. It should not harm the market for that original work. Fair use does not legally require attribution, but it is considered ethical to provide attribution to the original work.

Open-source materials are works, including artworks, which are freely available for the public to modify, use, or distribute. The user should adhere to the terms of the material's license. This license might require the artist to credit its creator or avoid using the work for commercial purposes. The artist should credit the original creator regardless. If an open-source work is built upon or modified, the artist should be clear about the changes that were made. Users of open-source material should **ethically** give back to the community by sharing their creations. They should respect the integrity of the original work without misrepresenting the intent of the creator.

Sculpture and Ceramics

Ceramics as a Medium

Throughout history, ceramics have been used for fine arts and for functional pieces. Around 24,000 BC, humans began making small figures out of clay. In 9000 or 10,000 BC, the first functional pottery and bricks were made. Glazes were discovered in Egypt around 8000 BC. A potter's wheel was used in Central America around 3000 BC. In ancient Greece, decorative vases depicted daily life and religion and were later decorated with black figures and red figures. Porcelain was developed in China during the Han dynasty (206 BC–220 AD). Pottery now can be mass-manufactured, but many fine artworks and functional pieces are still created by hand.

Ceramics are items produced from clay, including fine artwork, sculptures, figurines, and functional items such as tiles, dishes, urns, and vases. The item is formed, and then it is heated to harden it. A glaze can be applied, and then the item is reheated to harden the glaze. An underglaze can be applied first as a painted decoration. They can be hand built, pressed into molds, or created using a wheel.

Sculpture as a Medium

Sculptures have been created throughout history from many media, and only the most durable have survived. They can be small figures, larger freestanding works, or reliefs attached to walls. The first known prehistoric sculptures are from the Stone Age, approximately 230,000 BC, and they were made from basalt and quartz. Figures called Venuses (shaped as obese women, possibly related to fertility) have been found from the Stone Age and were made from materials such as bone and various stones. Mesolithic sculpture, from 10,000–4000 BC, included freestanding sculptures and bas-relief works. In the Neolithic period (4000–2000 BC), bronze statuettes were created. Classical Greek sculpture is some of the most well known, dating from 500–323 BC, and these superbly crafted figures would only be surpassed by later Renaissance artists. The Renaissance (1400–1600 AD) was a "rebirth" of classical ideals, and the sculptors created figures with great realism. Michelangelo (Michelangelo di Lodovico Buonarroti Simoni) is considered as the greatest Renaissance sculptor. Traditional materials continued to be used throughout history and into the present day, including stone, wood, bone, and metal.

Bas-Relief vs Haut-Relief

In terms of sculpture, a **relief** is a sculpture in which the sculptural elements are attached to a solid background. For the sculpture to appear raised from the background, the background elements are cut away, leaving the subject raised.

A **bas relief** is also called a low relief. The final sculpture has a shallow depth and is not raised far from the background. Coins are a good example of this. In this type of relief sculpture, elements are often distorted by being flattened.

A **haut-relief** is also called a high relief; this is when more than half of the sculptural form is projecting from the background. Heads and limbs might be completely detached from the background in this form of relief. Many ancient Greek relief sculptures used this technique. This image is an example of a high, or haut-relief sculpture. Although the figures are still attached to the background, they are mostly projecting from it, only being attached at their backs.

Materials Used for Sculpture

- **Stone** has been used for sculptures for centuries, and the artist must use the subtractive method—removing pieces of the stone to shape the sculpture. Marble has been a preferred material for traditional sculptors since ancient Greece, but artists also use granite, limestone, sandstone, and alabaster.

- **Wood** has been used historically for carving, and many important sculptures in Africa, China, and Japan were carved from wood. It is lighter and much easier to carve than stone.
- **Glass** can be cast in molds or heated in kilns and then blown or sculpted with hand tools. Larger scale glass sculptures are a modern development. Glass is believed to have been discovered in Egypt around 8000 BC.
- **Clay** has been used for thousands of years to form pottery. The first functional pottery vessels were created in 10,000 BC. People were crafting human and animal figures from clay as early as 24,000 BC. Many cultures have used pottery for fine arts and functional vessels. Clay is a natural material found in the earth, but artists prefer different types. Clay can now be bought commercially, or it can be mixed by the artist.

Glass Sculpture

There are several different processes and materials that can be used to create **glass sculptures**.

- **Molten glass** can be blown and molded into different shapes and designs. Blown glass techniques need a kiln, a blowpipe to blow the glass, a block to shape it, jacks or tongs to control the shape, and shears to cut the shape. Flameworking or lampworking involves using a lamp or torch to melt glass before shaping it into different designs or shapes. The materials for flameworking or lampworking include a kiln, rods or tubes of glass, a torch or lamp, and shapers.
- **Glass casting** involves putting molten glass into a mold to solidify. Glass casting tools include premade molds, a kiln, and glass.
- **Glass fusing** is the process of using a kiln to melt pieces of glass partially or entirely to fuse them together. For glass fusing, the artist needs a kiln, fusible glass strings, and sheets; confetti, frit, and powdered glass to create details; and molds for the glass to slump on.
- **Cold glass** techniques involve etching, engraving, polishing, or cutting glass without heating it. Cold glass techniques require etching cream, engraving burrs, and glass cutters.
- **Stained glass** can be used to create sculptures by coloring molten glass and using shapes of glass to form images or patterns with lead between the glass shapes. For stained glass, the artist needs glass, solder, pliers, and glass cutters.

Wood Sculpture

There are many **materials** to choose from when **sculpting with wood**. Sculptors look for wood with a straight grain, few knots, and soft to moderate hardness. Woods such as basswood, butternut, white pine, or aspen are soft and will not wear down carving tools as quickly, but they are easier to damage. Woods such as walnut, elm, acacia, and alder are moderately hard and are more durable. Sculptors can use hand tools like chisels, gouges, and knives to carve wood. These are available in different sizes, with different shaped tips to carve different effects. A mallet is used to hit the ends of chisels and gouges to help them cut the wood. Tools for power carving include rotary tools with different tips like burs and drill bits, drill presses, band saws, belt sanders, or even chainsaws.

The **process** begins with finding the direction of the wood grain and carving across the grain when possible. Carving along the grain causes the wood to splinter and split. If it is necessary to cut with the grain, the sculptor should make shallow cuts to prevent splintering. The sculptor begins by roughing out the general shape of the sculpture from a piece of wood and then adds the details. Working with wood requires safety glasses and can require a mask if the sculptor is sanding or power carving.

Stone Carving

Several different types of **stone** can be used as material for **sculpting**. Soapstone is soft and can be cut with a knife. Alabaster and sandstone are soft, easy to carve, and suitable for beginners. Marble, granite, and limestone are harder and are more difficult to carve but result in more durable sculptures. The sculptor can carve finer details into harder stone.

To sculpt, the artist will use hand **tools** such as chisels, hammers, and wedges. They can also use powered tools like pneumatic hammers and chisels, as well as rotary diamond burrs and cutters. Manual chisels are used with a mallet or hammer and can provide more control and precision for the sculptor. Powered chisels and tools are useful for large or particularly hard pieces of stone. Sculptors should wear safety goggles when working with stone and should always remember to cut away from themselves rather than toward themselves.

Metal Sculpture

There are several different metal sculpting materials and processes that are used.

- **Lost wax casting** involves creating a wax model and then a mold from the model. Metal is then poured into the mold. Brass, aluminum, stainless steel alloys, or bronze are used for this.
- For **sand casting**, the artist uses sand to create a mold before the molten metal is poured into the mold. Metals with a high melting temperature are used, like steel, nickel, or titanium.
- **Forging** is a process commonly used in blacksmithing to heat metal until it is pliable enough to shape with hammers or presses. Metals used include carbon steel, stainless steel, and copper alloys.
- **Arc, metal inert gas (MIG), and tungsten inert gas (TIG) welding** methods are used to join metals. Some metals are much more ideal for welding, like aluminum, carbon steel, or stainless steel. Aluminum and stainless steel are used for large-scale sculptures that will be exposed to weather. Corten, or weathering steel, is used when a rust-like finish is desired.
- An artist can use acid or chemicals to **etch** the surface of metals to create designs. This works well on titanium, aluminum, copper, and nickel.
- **Chasing** and ***repoussé*** are techniques where the artist hammers metal to make intricate designs. This is done on a smaller scale on metals like gold, silver, bronze, pewter, and copper.
- **Assemblage** is the joining of metals with methods like screws, bolts, and welding. This can be done with a variety of metals.

Clays

Clays can be classified as high fire and low fire. The three most commonly used types of clay are earthenware, stoneware, and porcelain. Earthenware was the earliest clay used, and it is fired to a temperature of less than 1,200 °C. Terra cotta is a type of earthenware that is reddish brown in color. Earthenware is brown, orange, or red in its raw and fired state. Earthenware is more porous than stoneware or porcelain, and it is less durable.

Stoneware is a mid- to high-fire clay that ranges from light gray to brown when fired. Stoneware is nonporous, and it differs from porcelain in that it is more opaque.

Porcelain has a rich history in China, and items made with porcelain are often called china or fine china in some English-speaking countries. Porcelain is a high-fire clay that is made with kaolin, which makes the finished product pure white. Porcelain is fired to 1,800 °C, and when it is fired, it is hard, nonporous, and translucent.

Tools Used for Sculpture

Tools such as chisels, pitching tools, rasps, mallets, and rifflers are used to sculpt stone. A chisel is a piece of steel that is pointed at one end and flat on the other end. A pitching tool is a wedge-shaped chisel. The chisel or pitching tool can be positioned on the stone and hit on the flat end with a mallet to break away unwanted stone. Rasps are flat steel tools with a rough surface, which can be used to wear away excess stone. A riffler is a smaller rasp used for details. Sandpaper or emery (a type of stone) can be used to polish a stone sculpture.

For pottery, an artist uses tools such as cutters and rolling pins for hand building. Ribbon or loop tools are made from a flattened metal ribbon and are attached to a wooden handle. These are used to trim, carve, and hollow out shapes. A wire cutter is used to remove a pot from a potter's wheel. A caliper is an adjustable tool used to measure openings for making lids.

For wood sculpture, similar tools are used as those for stone sculptures: chisels, rasps, mallets, and sandpaper. Gouges are useful for digging into the wood, and knives are also used for carving.

Additive vs Subtractive Sculpture Techniques

Subtractive sculpture is the oldest form of sculpture. This consists of removing material from a larger piece, such as marble, wood, or another material. Michelangelo was a master of this subtractive technique, also known as carving. Michelangelo would begin with a large block of marble, and then he would carve and chip away until he was satisfied with his sculpture. The original piece of material has to be big enough to accommodate the size and shape of the finished work of art.

The additive technique consists of adding material to create an artwork. A soft material, such as clay or plaster strips, is built up over an armature until the final form is achieved. This is also called modeling. With the additive technique, the sculpture can start small and be built larger.

Another additive sculpture technique is assembling. This technique became popular in the 1950s and 1960s. The artist creates a three-dimensional collage by gluing, welding, nailing, and otherwise joining objects—usually found objects. The final product is called an assemblage.

Hand Building and Wheel Throwing

Hand building is working with clay without a pottery wheel. Three methods are slab building, pinch pot, and the coil method. For slab building, clay is rolled into sheets and cut into shapes. The shapes are cut out and then joined together. The artist would score the edges with a sharp clay tool and then add some slip (liquid clay) to join the edges securely.

A pinch pot is created by rolling a ball of clay and then inserting a thumb into the ball. The artist presses the sides out evenly with the thumb on the inside of the pot and the fingers on the outside, until the sides and bottom are of consistent width and are smooth.

For the coil method, the artist first makes a shallow pinch pot as the base. He or she then rolls long coils of clay and builds up the body of the bowl or pot in a spiral, scoring and adding slip as the object is built.

Wheel throwing consists of using a potter's wheel to throw clay objects. The artist will first get any air bubbles out of the clay by wedging (kneading) the item on a surface, and then he or she uses slip to create the object as the clay spins on the wheel.

Modern vs Traditional Sculpture Materials

Traditional sculpture materials include stone, wood, clay, and metal. Stone (including marble) sculptures have survived through the years better than other materials due to their durability. Most works created with wood have been lost to decay, insect damage, and fire. Sculptors in ancient Greece and during the Renaissance focused on depicting the human body, and many ancient sculptures depicted religious or political subjects.

Modern sculptors have moved away from traditional materials and subjects and focus more on assembling and found objects. Picasso changed the direction of sculpture when he began constructing sculptures from different objects, much like a sculptural collage, in the early 20th century. In the 1940s and 1950s, artists began creating abstract and surreal sculptures and experimenting with new materials. This includes Alexander Calder's mobiles and David Smith's stainless steel sculptures. By the 1960s, some artists began creating minimalist works and experimenting with steel and environmental installations. Modern artists have also created sound sculptures, light sculptures, street art sculptures, and kinetic sculptures.

The Stages of Clay

The stages of clay determine how fragile or workable it is and what can or should be done to it next. Clay that has partially dried but is not completely dry is **leather hard.** When a piece is leather hard, the artist can carve the piece or add decorative slip. Handles can be added, and the foot of a pot can be trimmed.

- **Bone dry** refers to when the clay is completely dry. The clay will be a lighter color. The piece will be fragile; attaching and carving cannot be done at this stage.
- **Bisque** is when the piece has been fired once in a kiln. Bisqueware can be glazed and fired again. At this stage, prior to being glazed, the clay is still porous. Prior to being fired, all unfired clay pieces are referred to as **greenware**.
- **Slip** is a liquid clay mixture that can be used to join clay pieces together. Slip is a mix of clay and water, and it has a runny consistency.

The Use and Significance of Ceramics in China

Pottery was first made in China during the Paleolithic era, and it became the most well-known form of art in China. Porcelain, a type of ceramic, is so associated with China that porcelain wares are dubbed "china" or "fine china" in other countries.

Porcelain originated in China, and although proto-porcelain was made as early as 1600 BC, it developed into high-fire porcelain in the Han dynasty (206 BC–220 AD). Later, during the Ming dynasty (1368–1644 AD), China began exporting porcelain wares to Europe. Also during the Ming dynasty, cobalt underglazing was perfected, leading to the production of the iconic blue and white vases from that period. The blue underglaze is painted onto the porcelain, and then a clear glaze is applied, and the piece is fired.

Contemporary artist Ai Weiwei blends modern ideas with historical Chinese materials. One of his performance art pieces involved dropping a Han dynasty urn. Another work involved creating 100 million porcelain sunflower seeds.

Sculptures from Ancient Greece vs Rome

Sculpture in ancient Greece often depicted battles, mythology, and their rulers. Whereas earlier sculptures were made from limestone or bronze, the later larger sculptural works were made from marble or bronze. The classical period of Greek sculpture showed great skill in depicting human anatomy and natural poses. Sculptures were life-sized and realistic. Most bronze Greek sculptures have only survived as Roman copies. The Greeks used the lost-wax technique to create their metal sculptures.

Sculptures in ancient Rome focused more on portrait and less on the idealized human body. The sculptured figures were more rigid and less natural than the Greek sculptures. Their sculptures reflected the current styles and hairdos, and they could even be dated by historians based on these fashions. Romans sought to immortalize and capture a likeness of a person, whereas Greeks sought to idealize them. There are many original Roman sculptures, but there are also many Roman copies of Greek sculptures.

Renaissance Sculpture Subjects and Techniques

The hallmarks of the early Renaissance were classical composition and realism. Artists portrayed their subjects with a naturalism of their clothing, proportions, and perspective. These Italian artists recalled the classical sculptures of ancient Greece, and their subjects and forms. Throughout the Renaissance, sculptors created religious and secular sculptures. Church interiors, palaces, and private homes were elaborately decorated. The Madonna and Child were a popular subject, as well as scenes from the life of Christ. During the High Renaissance, subjects broadened and diverged more away from religious themes to include mythology and other topics.

Lorenzo Ghiberti won a contest to create large bronze doors at the Florence Baptistery, and this is thought of as the beginning of Renaissance sculpture. Donato di Niccolò di Betto Bardi, better known as Donatello, is another well-known sculptor of the 15th century, second only to Michelangelo. Both created many large marble and bronze sculptures. Donatello's most well-known work is his *David*, cast in bronze. Michelangelo is known for many sculptures including the *Pieta* and *David,* both marble. This image is of Michelangelo's *David.*

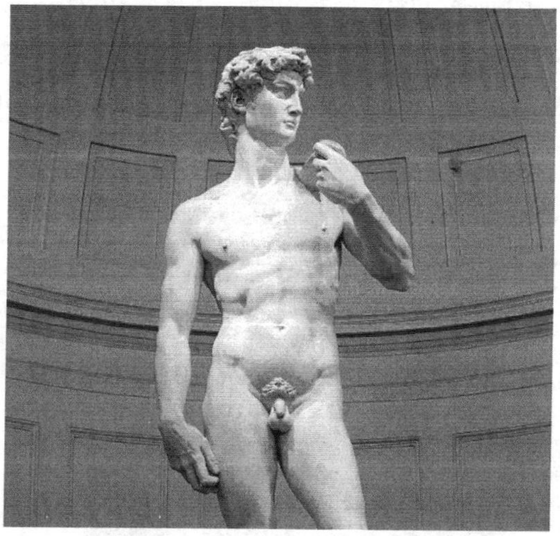

Lost-Wax Casting Technique

Lost-wax casting is a technique in which a metal copy of a sculpture is produced from an original sculpture. This technique was used as early as 3700 BC. To produce a sculpture with this method, a mold is first made of a clay sculpture. The inside of this mold is brushed with wax until the wax is the thickness of the intended metal sculpture. The mold is removed, and the shell of wax is filled with a heat-resistant material. Then a heat-resistant plaster covers the wax, and the assemblage is turned over and placed in an oven. The wax drains away through vents places in the shell; after the plaster mold has been filled with sand, bronze is poured into the void left by the wax. After the whole assemblage has cooled off, the plaster and center are both removed, and the artist can apply any finishing touches to the bronze sculpture.

Fiber Art and Jewelry

Fiber Art as a Medium

The term fiber art was first used by curators after World War II. It described works relating to fabrics, and it includes embroidery, weaving, knitting, crocheting, and sewing. Fiber arts take into consideration the artist's skill and labor to create the work, as well as the materials used, and it focuses more on the aesthetics than on the usefulness of the item.

In the 1950s, fiber artists began weaving more nonfunctional artworks. Then, in the 1960s and 1970s, artists began exploring different techniques including knotting, coiling, and pleating fibers. The feminist movement began using fibers as "high art" and celebrating needlework in the 1970s. From the 1980s to the present, fiber artists have created more conceptual work, influenced by postmodernism. They have focused on cultural issues including feminism, gender, politics, and social sciences. Judy Chicago first used the term feminist art and founded the first feminist art program in the United States. Her work *The Dinner Party* incorporated fiber arts and celebrated the position that needlework and fabric has had in the history of women.

Fibers and Materials

A fiber is a threadlike piece or material created from threadlike pieces. This includes materials such as fabric, yarn, and embroidery thread. Fibers can be made of natural materials, such as cotton, wool from sheep, or silk from a silkworm, but they can also be made from synthetic materials such as acrylic used to make yarn.

Yarn can be bought premade, or it can be spun by the artist. To spin yarn, the artist starts with roving, which is wool that has been run through a mill to brush the fibers in the same direction but hasn't been spun into yarn yet. Yarn can be made with many materials, in many thicknesses and colors. Roving can also be used for felting, which is a process involving hot water and shrinking a wool piece down into a smaller, denser piece.

When using fabrics, the artist can use a sewing machine or sew by hand, but the artist needs to understand the properties of each material and how best to join them.

The Acceptance of Fiber Art

Textile and fiber work, including sewing, embroidery, knitting, and crocheting, have always been considered women's work and have been devalued throughout history. During the suffrage movement of the early 1900s, embroidery was highlighted as a fiber art medium for feminist protests. During the 1950s, artists began creating hanging and freestanding fiber works, but it wasn't until Judy Chicago's work that fiber arts really began to be accepted as an artistic medium. Artists took the perception of fiber as women's work and turned their works into fun and liberating works of art. Her most famous work, *The Dinner Party*, celebrates the accomplishments of 39 important women from history, setting a place at a table for each woman. The work, constructed as a long triangle, incorporates traditional needlepoint and embroidery among other materials. More than 400 people, mostly women, volunteered to assist with aspects of this artwork, and it is still known as the first major feminist artwork.

Knitting, Weaving, and Crocheting

Knitting consists of creating a series of interlocking loops using straight knitting needles that are pointed at one end. The knitter begins by casting on, or creating the first stitches on the needle. A variety of stitches are used; the main stitches are called knit and purl. The basic knitted pattern is called a stocking or stockinette pattern, and the right side looks like a pattern of V shapes.

For weaving, two sets of threads are interlocked in a perpendicular pattern. This can be done by hand or by machine. The lengthwise threads are called the warp and are held stationary on a loom while the other thread (weft) is passed back and forth between them.

Crocheting involves using a stick with a hook at the end, called a crochet hook, and creating stitches to interlock the yarn into a fabric or pattern. With crochet, each stitch is finished before starting the next, whereas in knitting, many stitches are kept open at the same time.

Papermaking

Papermaking is an ancient fiber art involving the use of plant-based fibers to create a pulp that is made into paper. Fibers like hemp, linen, or cotton are broken down into a pulp and diluted with water and then spread onto a mesh screen. The water can then be pressed out, and the pulp can dry into a sheet of paper. It can be used for functional purposes, like manuscripts or documents, or for artistic purposes, like printmaking or drawing.

Other fiber mediums result in a variety of flat or three-dimensional items, while papermaking results in a flat product. Other fiber mediums are generally sewn, woven, felted, knitted, or crocheted and not broken down into a pulp as part of their process. Many other fiber mediums generally still have prominently visible fiber strands, while papermaking results in a more cohesive surface. Both papermaking and other fiber arts can serve both artistic and practical functions.

Sewing Processes

The fiber art of **sewing** involves using a needle and thread for traditional sewing techniques to create contemporary art or for more utilitarian purposes. The end result is an artistic piece that can be narrative, abstract, a textile collage, or part of a mixed media piece. Hand sewing is done with a needle and thread and includes embroidery, which is decorative stitching that makes patterns or images; applique, which is sewing smaller pieces of fabric onto larger fabric; quilting, which is sewing fabric together in a pattern with a layer of batting in between; and beading, which is sewing beads to fabric to create designs and textures.

A sewing machine can be used for many fabric techniques as well, including quilting, patchwork, or free sewing, which is moving the fabric freely through the machine to create designs.

Various types of fabric can be used for sewing, including cotton, silk, synthetics, felt, linen, or wool. Threads can be cotton, silk, metallic, or a variety of specialty types of thread. Embellishments like beads or sequins can also be sewn onto fabric.

Sewing focuses on using a thread and needle to join fabrics together, create patterns, construct garments, or add decoration to fabrics. It can involve a variety of fabrics used in other fabric mediums, but the basic techniques differ from those used for other fabric arts like knitting, felting, weaving, or macramé.

Fashion Design

Fashion design is an applied art that involves using materials as a medium for clothing and accessories. The designer uses creativity and aesthetics to create clothes that are influenced by trends. **Fashion design** is of societal importance because fashion influences identity, culture, and even the economy. It reflects changes in styles throughout the decades, and some clothing is identified as part of a cultural movement. The designed product allows individuals to express their individuality.

Designers must understand classic and historic styles so that they can reinterpret those styles as modern designs. Fashion designers often work for an established fashion house, or they can branch out and create their own fashion label. They combine their creative ability, artistic skills, technical sewing and computer skills, and sense of marketing and branding to succeed in the field.

Materials and Processes for Fashion Design

A **fashion designer** uses many different materials for clothing and accessory design. Some traditional materials include fabric, buttons, and zippers, as well as gold, silver, and precious gemstones for accessories. Newer industry trends include eco-friendly fabrics, smart fabrics that are embedded with digital components, and alternative materials like plastics or faux leather.

The process begins with gathering inspiration and creating a mood board to represent the ideas. The artist then sketches the design by hand or in a computer program. Once he or she has a visually accurate representation of the idea, a pattern can be made. Then, the designer will cut the material, sew the material, and fit it to ensure the product is finished.

Clothing and accessories are created for the consumer, and the designer looks ahead to predict popular fashions. Most clothing is designed for the mass market or for multiple people to purchase. The pieces are created to be both functional and aesthetically pleasing. Clothing created and custom fitted for a specific person is called *haute couture*. Much of the present fashion is ready-to-wear fast fashion that is intended to be inexpensive and worn for a short period of time.

Basketry

Basketry is an art form that involves creating a functional vessel that can also be considered aesthetically pleasing art. It is an old art form used in many cultures, and different cultures use different materials and patterns. Basketry traditionally uses natural materials like reeds, willow, and palm but can use synthetic materials like plastic fibers as well. A basket consists of a base, sides, and a rim and can be created by weaving, coiling, or twining.

While basketry focuses on the creation of three-dimensional functional containers, **other fiber mediums** can be used to make a variety of two- or three-dimensional works with techniques like crochet, weaving, embroidery, or felting. Other fiber arts can also be functional, but many focus on pattern, surface design, and color. Basketry traditionally had a primarily utilitarian cultural role, while other fiber arts like ceremonial textiles, decorative clothing, and artistic home decor are often both utilitarian and aesthetic.

Jewelry as a Medium

Prior to the discovery of precious metals, humans in prehistoric times used bone, shells, antlers, feathers, and pebbles to decorate their bodies. One of the oldest examples of traditional jewelry was discovered in a tomb in Sumer from 2600 BC. The findings included gold pins, amulets, earrings, and a headdress. Evidence was found of Sumerians using techniques such as welding, enameling, stonecutting, and filigree. The tomb of Tutankhamun in Egypt showed mastery of gold and jewelry techniques by the ancient Egyptians. Bracelets, amulets, pendants, earrings, and a large quantity of jewels were found in the tomb, showing a high degree of craftsmanship. Motifs used include the scarab, lotus flower, Horus, eye, serpent, and sphinx, among others. During the Bronze Age, the Minoans in Greece were stamping and cutting gold sheets into beads to form necklaces and decorate clothing. Jewelry making flourished during the Hellenistic period in Greece, and it was used to an even greater extent in ancient Rome. The gold ring became common in ancient Rome, and not just for noblemen. Rings and brooches became widely used in medieval Europe. With a rebirth of classicism, jewelry making reached new heights in the Renaissance era.

Tools and Supplies

Precious metals used for creating jewelry include gold and silver. They are both available in varying purities. 24 karat gold is 24 out of 24 parts gold, and it is also known as pure gold. Fine silver is 99.9% pure silver, whereas sterling silver is at least 92.5% pure silver. Other metals used include brass, which is an alloy of 70%

copper and 30% zinc; copper, a bright reddish-orange element; and pewter, a silver-gray alloy of tin, antimony, and copper.

A soldering iron can be used for joining metal parts together. A jewelry artist will use a variety of pliers, saws, and cutters for working with metal, as well as a polisher to finish the piece. A mandrel is used to size and shape a ring; it is a tapered piece of metal that the ring fits onto. Clamps hold the piece steady for the artist to work on it. A loupe is a magnifier used to see the piece in greater detail. Calipers are used to measure the gauge (thickness) of materials.

Enameling

Enameling involves fusing powdered glass to a surface by heating it to between 750 °C and 850 °C. When fired, the glass powder melts and turns into a smooth, shiny coating. Enameling is often seen on metal jewelry, but it can also be used on glass and ceramics. It can be applied to gold, copper, silver, and aluminum. Commercially, it is often applied to stainless steel. After it is fired, it is durable and resistant to scratching. The finely ground glass used for enameling is called frit, and various minerals are added for coloring. Different colors of enamels can be mixed to create new colors, and enamel can be transparent, translucent, or opaque. Enameling was used in ancient Egypt for the creation of jewelry, as well as in ancient Greece, ancient Rome, and China. In ancient Rome, enamel was also used on glass surfaces.

This image is an example of enamel applied to a copper alloy disk, from between 1290 and 1310 AD. It is a radial pattern with a rose window design.

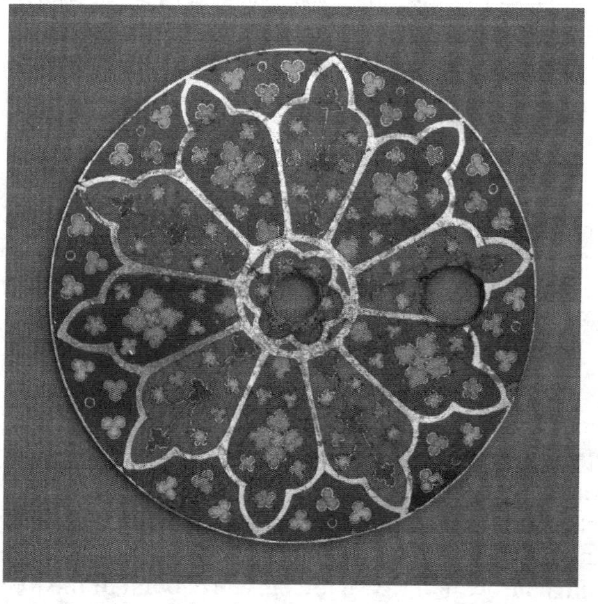

Soldering and Filigree

Soldering can be done on a clean ceramic tile or fire brick. The metal to be soldered should be clean and free of oil or grease. Flux is mixed with water and dabbed on the parts where the metal will be joined. The flux is a chemical used to promote soldering. Tiny pieces of solder are placed onto the fluxed seams of the metal with tweezers. A flame is applied, and the piece is heated evenly until the solder melts and the pieces join.

Filigree is a technique of forming metal threads to resemble a lace pattern. Making a filigree piece involves careful and skillful bending of wire. A filigreed metal piece can be simple or complex, consisting of many pieces carefully formed and combined. Before working with the wire and wrapping it, it should first be annealed. Annealing is a process of heating the metal, then cooling it slowly, so it is easier to work with for a specific technique. This silver ring contains a filigree pattern.

Jewelry Making: Art and Craft

Although art and craft are both thought of as ways to express creativity, the distinction lies in the purpose of the work produced. Crafts are created with an aesthetic and a functional purpose, whereas art is generally decorative but not functional. Based on this, jewelry's functional and decorative nature can be seen as both an art and a craft. Jewelry makers throughout time have used various techniques to create intricate and beautiful works that show superb craftsmanship as well as artistic inspiration. Jewelry making has followed artistic trends throughout major art eras, and the pieces have been used to adorn important leaders, politicians, and the common citizen. Jewelry making requires skill and understanding of the materials, just like when working with oil paints or sculpture materials. The line between art and craft has often been blurred, with artists creating decorative pieces with materials usually used for functional crafts.

Photography and Videography

The Early Camera

The first **photograph** was taken by French inventor Nicéphore Niépce in 1827. In 1837, Louis Daguerre developed the first practical process to create photographs, which was called the daguerreotype. Daguerreotypes create an image on a silvered copper plate, and they require the subject to stay still from 15 to 30 minutes. Henry Fox Talbot next developed the calotype, or talbotype, process. The daguerreotype and the calotype both use two nested boxes as the body of the camera. The calotype used paper coated in silver iodide for the print.

Emulsion plates, or wet plates, using the collodion process followed. They needed much less exposure time than previous methods. Bellows were added to cameras at this time to aid in focusing the image. Ambrotype and tintype were two common emulsion plates. Ambrotype used a glass plate, whereas tintype used tin.

In 1888, George Eastman developed a film camera, and the first one was called the "Kodak." This camera did not require solid plates, and the cost was low enough for the average consumer. The first 35mm camera was available in 1913, but the film was not affordable to average consumers until the 1940s.

The Impact of the Camera

After the invention of the camera in the early 1800s, people began using photographic techniques to attempt to capture reality in a more reliable way than they could by hand. People created millions of daguerreotypes to record images of their families, aware of their own mortality. Photographs were used to capture the atrocities of war, mundane life, and each other. Images of average people could be created as easily as images of important politicians. Action photos as well as posed scenes were created. Images captured in a photograph were more objective than those created by artists, taking out much of the imagination and artistic license, and giving a more reliable representation of the subject. By the mid-19th century, photography was becoming accepted as a powerful tool for communication. When the first mass-produced camera was created, photography became accessible to more people. With advances in equipment, photographers no longer needed to carry plates and chemicals to process their images.

Digital Photography

Prior to the introduction of digital photography, the photographic process was slower and much more expensive. The number of shots was limited to the number available on each roll of film. Film had to be handled carefully and correctly, and then it was taken to a photo developing center, or it could be developed at home in a darkroom using special equipment. Until the pictures were developed, the photographer did not know how their pictures turned out. If the original prints and film were lost, the images could be lost forever.

With digital photography, the number of images is only limited by the storage space on the camera and the size of the digital image. Photographers can immediately review the images, delete unwanted images, and take more photographs until they are satisfied that they have a good shot. Digital photographs can be more easily edited and manipulated on a computer than photos developed in a darkroom. Digital photographs can be stored indefinitely on a digital device and printed inexpensively with online services or on a home printer.

Photography Supplies

Although film cameras are still in limited use, **digital photography** has surpassed them as the medium of choice. Digital cameras range greatly from inexpensive cameras for casual use to high-priced cameras for professionals. Fewer dedicated low-end digital cameras are used now because the ability to take photographs is included in most smartphones.

The **resolution** of a digital camera is determined by its image sensor. A camera with a 1,000 × 1,000 pixel image sensor will take up to 1 megapixel photos. A digital camera may shoot up to 120 megapixels, whereas a smartphone will now commonly shoot up to 12 megapixels. A digital camera can be compact and portable, or it can be larger with removable lenses. A digital single-lens reflex (DSLR) camera contains a mirror at a 45-degree angle to convey the image to the sensor. The DSLR camera will have a higher possible resolution than a compact camera, and it will usually have the option of multiple lenses for different purposes. This image is of a DSLR camera.

Film Photography Supplies

To shoot photographs with a film camera, the correct type of **film** is needed for the photographer's purposes. The most common size is 35mm and speeds range from 100 to 3,200, with consumer film ranging up to 800. The speed of the film is determined by the International Standards Organization (ISO) scale, which dictates how much exposure the film needs to produce an image. Slower film will give better detail and color, but faster film can capture a subject in motion.

To develop the film, the camera back is opened, the film is removed in a completely dark room, and it is coiled into a reel as shown in the image. The reel is placed into the container, and a chemical process consisting of developer bath, stop bath, and fixer bath are introduced into the container. The film can then be exposed to light to be washed and dried.

After the film is developed, the images are printed onto photo paper in a darkroom lit with only a safelight, which will illuminate the room in a red or amber color. An enlarger is used to expose the film to the photo paper.

Parts of a Camera

The main part of a camera is called the **body**. The **viewfinder** is where the photographer looks through the back of the camera to compose the shot. Some digital cameras will have a liquid-crystal display (LCD) screen instead of a viewfinder. The shutter release button activates the shutter, and the amount of time that the shutter is left open is determined by the shutter speed. The lens is on the front of the camera, and it focuses and directs light into the camera. Lenses can either be fixed to the body, or they can be removable. The aperture of the camera controls the amount of light reaching the image sensor. It also determines how much of the image is in focus (depth of field). The aperture is expressed in f-stops. A film advance lever is found on a film camera, and it moves the film to the next frame. A flash can be built in or added to the camera; it adds light to the subject. A flash can be connected to the top of the camera on a socket called a hot shoe.

Similarities between Digital and Film Cameras

Despite the advent of the digital camera, almost all of the components and functions of digital cameras are the same as that of film cameras. Both digital and film cameras use a body to control the shutter speed, a lens to direct the light and control the aperture, but where the two differ is in the way the light is captured. Film cameras use film, which is a chemically reactive, photosensitive paper that captures the negative of the light as it is **exposed** to the light. In a digital camera, the film is exchanged for a photosensitive plate, called a sensor. This sensor captures light and translates the information into a digital format that is stored and interpreted to produce a photo. Where different film has a sensitivity rating (called film speeds) for different environments, such as daylight, inside, or night photography, a digital camera has a variable sensitivity that can be adjusted to match the needs of the moment. In most modern settings, focus is controlled relatively automatically with little input from the user. Digital camera bodies can often track faces and movement and can interpret what is likely to be the focal point of the photo almost instantaneously.

Proper Exposure

As a camera takes a picture, it opens the sensor up to receive light for a short amount of time. The light that is captured becomes an imprint on the sensor. To reach a proper exposure, the sensor needs to capture a certain amount of light. If too little light is let in, the image will be **underexposed** and will appear dark. If too much light is let in, the image will be **overexposed** and will appear too bright, often true white. An image that is under- or over-exposed can often be corrected in editing, but much of the color information is deteriorated or lost. The light that is captured has to be carefully controlled to render a properly exposed and sharp image. The main controls related to a photo's exposure boil down to aperture, shutter speed, and sensitivity (often called ISO).

Aperture

The **aperture** is the size of the hole in the lens that lets light in to reach the sensor or film. Aperture is measured in a ratio called an **f-stop**, which is the ratio of the sensor size to the size of the opening of the lens. Aperture controls the amount of light let in at one time by changing between a bigger and smaller opening to control the **flow of light**. This is similar to the different flow of water possible from a garden hose compared to a fire hose. A bigger hose allows more water through, and the same is true of aperture. If more light is let through at one time, then the shutter speed can be increased, which often results in a crisper picture. Aperture also plays a huge role in controlling the **depth-of-field**, which is used to change the composition of a picture. Shallow depths of fields are often used intentionally in portrait photography to blur out the background of a photo and are often thought to help cover imperfections. Landscape photographers may use smaller apertures to help capture as much detail as possible. Most photographers leave their aperture wide open to capture the most light possible, allowing them to adjust the ISO and shutter speed more freely. The lens in use controls the aperture and plays as a limiting factor for both maximum and minimum aperture. Lenses with large maximum apertures are often very expensive or limited in other ways, such as zoom capabilities.

Shutter Speed

Shutter speed is the **amount of time** that the camera allows light to come in to expose the sensor or film. A fast **shutter speed** is usually desirable, as it helps to keep an image sharp, even when the photographer's hand shakes or when there is a moving object in the picture. Slow shutter speeds often result in blurry photos, but can also be used to artistic effect, such as capturing the motion of an object in an interesting way. Shutter speed is often one of the first controls that a photographer will manually change to adjust to the available light, as it often does not negatively affect the resulting photo. Shutter speed is measured in fractions of a second, such as 1/64th of a second.

Sensitivity or ISO

A camera's **sensitivity**, often referred to as ISO, is related to the way a film photographer would use different films for different ambient lights. A photographer needs to adjust the **ISO** to enable adequate aperture and shutter speed settings. Each of the three main factors of a proper exposure has trade-offs. As aperture increases in size, the depth-of-field decreases. As the shutter speed increases (slows down), the more movement causes a photo to be blurry. As ISO increases, the sensor starts to cause the photos to be **grainy** or have **color degradation**. Out of the three factors, the ISO most directly affects photo output quality. In general, this causes a photographer to seek to leave the ISO as low as possible for the ambient light in the environment and work around other limitations instead.

Lenses

Lenses are arguably the most important component of a camera, as they control both the aperture and the focal length, having the strongest effects on composition of any other factor. The **focal length** is what some might call the *zoom* of the camera, which enables the photographer to capture either wide shots of large landscapes or zoomed in shots of distant subjects, such as at sporting events or wild animals. Some lenses have variable focal lengths, and are called **zoom lenses**. These often come with drawbacks, such as distortion or low maximum apertures. Lenses that have one fixed focal-length are called **prime lenses**. Prime lenses are much less complicated optically and often have superior performance and extremely large apertures as a result. Some specialty lenses, called **macro lenses**, allow for focusing on very close objects, such as insects and jewelry. Most professional photographers, such as wedding photographers, carry an assortment of lenses for different situations or types of photos.

Photo Temperature and Tint

In addition to a photo being properly exposed, which represents all of the light and dark values of an image, the image also requires interpretation of the color scale. When a photo is taken, it captures the available light within an environment, which may be mostly green if the photo is outdoors or too warm if it is taken in particularly orange light. There are two spectrums that must be accounted for to make a photo look correct color-wise. The first and more important is called **temperature**, and refers to the blue to orange spectrum. When a photo is too blue, it is referred to as cold, and when a photo is too orange, it is referred to as being too warm. The **tint** refers to the green to purple spectrum and is usually more difficult to notice. Usually an editor will judge the temperature and tint by looking at the colors that should be white and by looking at skin tone to make sure people don't look too orange, blue, or green in the end photo.

Digital Editing

In digital photography, the files produced are saved into a file format on the camera that can be modified using computer programs or mobile applications. Cameras are often able to save multiple formats, including uncompressed forms called RAW files that are highly editable, but are relatively large, or compressed formats, such as .jpg or .png files, which reduce the amount of information stored, limiting the ability to edit further, but which contain enough information to look good and are able to be printed or displayed. There are many programs available on which to edit photos, most notably the adobe platform, including lightroom and photoshop. Editing often includes cropping and correcting camera angle, color correction, exposure correction, and removal of distractions or flaws.

Common Digital Editing Methods

Digital images can be edited using many different methods. They can be edited on a smartphone or a computer, but many of the techniques are the same from one device to another. **Cropping** an image involves removing some of the outer area of an image to improve the composition. This is usually done by dragging the corners of the image to reframe the subject. When an image is **resized**, the image becomes larger or smaller without removing any part of the image. Images might be resized to reduce their file size for transfer or online use. Resizing should maintain the width to height ratio. It does change the pixel information since sizing an image smaller causes some of the pixels to be discarded. Resizing to a larger size will also affect the resolution, making the image blurry or pixelated since the editing tool will need to add pixels.

Images also can be **color-corrected** by changing the hue or saturation, adjusting the white balance, or even changing the brightness. The artist might want to change the colors to make them more realistic or add a desired effect by emphasizing or changing colors. Image **filters** use predefined settings to add effects or change the mood of the photo. A filter might add a blur or grain or change the colors to make it look vintage.

Procedures for Uploading/Downloading/Transferring Digital Image Files

Digital images can be **uploaded** to an online image gallery or to a file storage cloud or site, like Dropbox or Google Drive. When uploading digital images, it is important to consider how much space is available in the storage site or gallery. The artist should also consider how the image will be used. If it is to be used online, the resolution does not have to be high. However, if the image is to be printed, the artist will need to upload a high enough resolution to print.

When **downloading** image files, the artist should make sure he or she is downloading from a reputable and safe site to avoid getting viruses or spyware on their computer. The artist should download the file into a folder or location on the computer where he or she will be able to locate it and should give it a file name that is descriptive and recognizable.

Files can be **transferred** by a USB or thumb drive, a file upload site, or even by email. Many email clients will have a file size limit. If a digital file is particularly large or multiple images are being transferred, the artist can compress the files into one zip file for easier transfer.

When uploading, downloading, or transferring a file, it is important for the artist to know and use the correct size, resolution, and ratio for the image file.

Printing Methods for Images

There are several things to keep in mind when **printing digital images**. Artists should choose the paper that works best for their image. Photo paper is glossy and thick, and it can show vibrant colors and sharp details. Matte paper is not coated with a glossy finish, so colors might soak in and look less vibrant.

The image should be prepared so that it has the same aspect ratio as the paper. It will need to be at a resolution of at least 300 dpi for detail and sharpness. The artist should not attempt to enlarge an image while printing it; it should be printed at 100%, meaning it prints at its actual size. A lossless file format does not lose information such as color values when it is saved. TIF and EPS are examples of lossless formats, while GIF and JPG are lossy formats. Each edit made to an image saved in a lossy format will make it less clear.

When printing, the printer settings should be adjusted for the type of paper and the desired type of print. The photo printer should be set for the most detailed, high-quality print. The settings can be changed to color or black and white based on the desired outcome. The printed image should be allowed to sit for a few minutes before handling so that the ink does not smear or transfer.

Videography

Videography is built on the same principles as photography. The cameras essentially work the same, relying on shutter speed, ISO, and aperture to create a proper exposure. In addition to the fundamentals of photography, video incorporates movement of either the subjects or the camera to dramatic effect. Sound also plays an important role in videography, whether that be sound captured by a microphone or on camera, or added in editing. The types of shots employed by a videographer are heavily informed by the type of video they are making, whether that be informational, tutorial, documentary, short story, cinematic movies, or music videos. Each of these may use different arrangements of shots, cuts, effects, and editing styles to arrive at an appropriate product.

Video Art

Video art began in the 1960s, and artists used mainly analog videotape as their medium into the 1990s. Nam June Paik is known as the pioneer of video art. The first instance of video art is when Paik used a Sony Portapak video recorder in 1965 to tape Pope Paul VI's procession in New York City, and then he played the tapes in another location. The availability of consumer video equipment such as the Portapak allowed artists to begin experimenting with this new medium. Artists experimented with the capabilities and limitations of the equipment by combining, layering, and distorting the signals. In the 1980s and 1990s, video editing software became more readily available and allowed video artists much greater flexibility and control over their work. With the advent of digital video technology, equipment has become increasingly compact and portable, as well as more easily available.

One of Paik's most famous works is *Electronic Superhighway* (1995), which includes a 51-channel video installation, along with neon lights. The scale and images represent the enormity of the United States as seen by this artist who came from Korea at only nine years old.

Videography Processes and Tools

Videography involves filming an event for the purpose of capturing footage rather than creating a film for artistic purposes. It can be used for capturing events, creating promotional material, or even streaming social media content. The process is often more spontaneous than filmmaking since the footage is captured as it is happening. The videographer may be responsible for the entire process, including capturing the video and editing it for production. The process involves coming up with an idea or concept and deciding how and where it will be shot. The videographer may make a list of shots they want to include. He or she can also capture B-roll, which is supplemental footage to fill in for parts of the video.

Videographers will need some sort of video camera, but they can use anything from a high-end camera to a cell phone camera. They can use lighting to enhance the subjects and a microphone to capture audio. A tripod can be used to hold the video camera steady. They might need a boom mic to capture audio from a distance. They will also need editing software to edit the video and music to add to the video for the final product.

Filmmaking Overview

Filmmaking is a way for artists to tell stories for different purposes, such as education or entertainment. The artist follows a process to produce a film. This process includes picking characters, writing a script, finding actors, choosing filming locations, setting up and directing the scenes, adjusting or creating lighting, and capturing the scenes on film. It also includes editing the captured film to create the sequence of events desired by the artist and adding effects, music, sounds, and more to fine-tune the final product. A simple filmmaking process might be accomplished by just the artist and the cast. A bigger and more complex production might include a director, a producer, and a crew, such as those doing the filming, lighting, and audio. The director chooses the angles of the shots and how the video will be filmed. The producer oversees the process by selecting a script and cast, finding and hiring a director, managing the budget, and releasing the final product.

Filmmaking Processes/Tools

The **process** of producing videos for **filmmaking** involves several steps. Filmmaking differs from videography by having a cinematic intent. In the pre-production step, the artist will plan the logistics and the artistic vision that will be used for filming. He or she will decide on the budget, script, talent, goals, equipment needs, and location for the video. Next, in the production step, the artist will set up the equipment and record the audio and video. For the post-production step, the artist will edit the video, add music, sound, and video effects, review the final product, and finalize it for delivery.

Common **tools** used for filmmaking are as follows:

- A video camera, which can range from an expensive, high-end camera to a cell phone camera
- A microphone, audio cables, and batteries, depending on the camera used
- A tripod to keep the video camera steady
- Lights to help illuminate the scene
- Memory cards to capture and store videos
- Different lenses to help create different effects while filming
- A mounting rig such as a shoulder rig, a jib and crane, or a dolly to stabilize the camera when a tripod is not a good choice

The Rule of Thirds

The **rule of thirds** is a compositional technique used for not only photography, but also for other two-dimensional art forms. The rule of thirds involves dividing an image vertically and horizontally into three equal parts. This divides the image into nine equal parts. The subject or focal point of the image should then be placed at one of the intersections of these lines. Doing this creates tension and imbalance in the image, and it creates a more interesting composition than placing the subject or focal point squarely in the center of the photograph. This image illustrates the rule of thirds and the lines associated with it. In this image, the center of the nearest object is placed on the lower right intersection of lines and the tower in the background is aligned along the left vertical line. The horizon also falls along the lower horizontal line, rather than being placed in the center of the image.

Aperture and Focal Length

A video camera's **aperture** is the opening in the lens, and it is measured in f-stops. Moving from one f-stop to the next doubles or halves the size of the opening. A larger f-stop number means a smaller aperture. Adjusting the aperture will change the depth of field of your photograph, which is how much of the image is in focus. A shallow depth of field is a result of letting more light in or a larger aperture (a smaller f-stop). A shallow depth of field means that only a part of the image is in focus and the rest is blurry. A large depth of field results in most of the image being in focus, and this is done with a smaller aperture (larger f-stop).

The focal length of a camera lens determines the magnification of the image, and it is usually expressed in millimeters. The field of view and focal length are inversely proportional. A 24–35mm lens will give a wider angle and capture more of a scene from the same distance as a 50mm lens.

Photography Used to Document Events

Early photographers attempted to record the events of war, but limitations of the process prevented them from recording movement and action. Instead, they photographed the still aspects, and they even recreated scenes to attempt to convey their impressions of the battles. During the Civil War, photographers staged scenes of battles to heighten the emotional effects of their images. They would even move and rearrange dead bodies. These images were used to convey the atrocities of war to the public.

During the Great Depression, the Farm Service Agency sent photographers out to document American life, especially rural America. These photographers, including Dorothea Lange, captured images of life during this difficult time. These images serve as a reminder of this era, as well as documentation of how Americans persisted through their difficulties. One of the best-known images from this time is *Migrant Mother*, by

Dorothea Lange. She skillfully captured the worry and fear on the face of a mother dealing with raising children during a time of extreme poverty.

Acceptance of Photography as an Art Form

Since the invention of the camera, photographers have struggled with acceptance in the art world. They questioned the role that photography would play in art and whether they should be confined to the aesthetics of other art forms or explore ideas and characteristics of the new medium. Photography has taken many forms, including photojournalism, but it has historically mostly been accepted as a craft.

In the early and mid-1900s, Alfred Stieglitz, Edward Steichen, and Ansel Adams were critical to advancing photography from a craft to the acceptance as a fine art. In Adams' case, his beautiful photographs of nature scenes were used not only as artistic expression, but also to promote the conservation of nature. His work *The Tetons and Snake River* is an example of this. It wasn't until after the 1950s that it was thought acceptable and unpretentious to frame a photograph for a show or exhibition. Until the 1970s, the main genres of fine arts photography were portraits, landscapes, and nudes.

Cindy Sherman

Cindy Sherman is a photographer whose work has been an inspiration for contemporary portrait photographers. She began her photography work in the 1970s. In her first self-portrait series, *Untitled Film Stills,* she plays the role of "everywoman," dressing up and characterizing herself in many different clichéd feminine roles including housewife and pinup girl. Sherman changed the perception of portrait photography to a depersonalized method of critiquing social issues. She used an antinarrative approach to photography, discarding notions of documentary realism and creating works that left unresolved ideas and emotions.

Sherman used her photography to examine assumptions and stereotypes, and her work is often associated with feminism. Her work has highlighted the objectification of women, as well as obsessions with youth and beauty. She explored identity and representation in new ways and opened the door for creative and conceptual photographic portraiture. In the 1980s, her work helped to drive photography into acceptance as high art.

Digital Art

Electronic Art as a Medium

Electronic art is an art form that uses electronic media, including digital art, video art, and interactive art. Digital art is created using a computer, and it started when artists began to experiment with computers in the 1960s. As computers have become more affordable, digital art has grown as a medium.

Photoshop was first developed in 1987 at Industrial Light and Magic, a visual effects company, and it was later sold to Adobe. Many versions and related programs have followed, including a touchscreen version for tablets.

Nam June Paik is regarded as a pioneer in **video art**, which emerged as a medium in the late 1960s as video cameras became available to consumers. As time has passed, prices have dropped, and video cameras have become increasingly portable and more versatile.

Interactive art involves the viewer participating with the artwork. This could include the viewer walking into or onto the artwork, or even becoming part of the artwork. Currently, these works generally include some computer or motion sensor components, but the earliest examples of interactive art date back to the 1920s.

Digital Art

Digital art is a broad category of media, including any type of composition made up of digitally produced or modified works. Below is a list of examples of types of digital art:

- **Pixel Art** - Art made by placing individual pixels on a digital canvas to create low-resolution images, often in the form of 8-bit or 16-bit style artwork.
- **Vector Art** - Art made with mathematics-based lines to compose shapes and compositions.
- **Digital Painting** - Art made by physically painting onto a digital canvas, often using a pen-and-tablet-style input device.
- **3D Modeling and Animation** - Art made by producing 3D objects in a digital space that can be viewed and interacted with in three dimensions. These are often printable with a 3D printer.
- **Photo Manipulation** - Art made by modifying photos or scans to improve the original image or render a new composition using components of the original.
- **Digital Collage** - Artwork made by digitally combining or stitching photographs or other artwork together into a new, complex image.
- **Generative Art** - Artwork made using a visual modeling program and computations or algorithms that produce images, often including highly patterned and abstract designs.
- **Interactive Art** - Artwork that a second party can interact with using input devices or sensors to allow for experience in the real world.

Graphic Design

Graphic design is the process of composing images, colors, text, and shapes to share information visually. A graphic designer uses knowledge of visual hierarchy to arrange elements on a digital or printed medium to meet the needs of clients and users and to convey the target message. The term originated in the print industry of the 1920s. A graphic designer must understand typography, color theory, and gestalt principles so that they can match the mood of the piece or the organization while effectively sharing information. In addition to these considerations, a graphic designer follows the same principles of art that are used for other mediums. Graphic designers create logos, print materials, online graphics, and websites to help businesses and clients achieve marketing goals and reach their target audiences. Effective graphic design can elicit an emotional response from the audience or motivate them to take action.

Materials and Processes for Graphic Design

Graphic designers create designs that convey messages and evoke emotions. To begin the design process, they must become familiar with the design's goal so they can effectively convey those necessary messages or emotions. The designer will first gather the project requirements and research both the client's goals and the audience of the project. The designer will then brainstorm designs that will share the message both creatively and clearly. He or she will send the ideas to the client and discuss how to proceed. Once the design is finished, the graphic designer will either prepare a high-resolution digital image if it is a digital project or prepare the project to be printed. The graphic designer works with printers to gather quotes for the project, then chooses the appropriate printer and sends the project for printing. The designer is responsible for checking the colors, fonts, layout, and graphics before it is printed, so he or she will often receive a proof to review before signing off on the final printing.

Graphic designers use different software that suits the needs of the projects, like Photoshop, Illustrator, CorelDraw, Adobe InDesign, and QuarkXPress to create digital designs. They use Adobe Photoshop to edit photographs and Adobe Illustrator and CorelDraw to make and edit vector graphics. Adobe InDesign and QuarkXPress are used to lay out designs that include both text and graphics, like brochures, posters, or books. Pantone color swatches help the designer to match and verify colors throughout the process.

Digital Art: Supplies

Supplies used for digital art include computers, tablets, video cameras, scanners, and digital cameras. The computer can be used to generate art, for example, with fractals or algorithms, in which data are put into the computer and the computer uses the data to create an image. The computer can also be the tool that the artist uses to create their artwork. The artist can use a mouse or a stylus to draw and edit images on the screen. This can also be done on the touchscreen of a tablet. The final product can be printed on papers of various thicknesses, colors, and surfaces. An inkjet printer blends colors smoothly and is cost effective. Laser and LED printers are more expensive and faster but are best with solid colors and black text.

Video cameras can be used to capture video, which can be edited on a computer to produce the final product. Another part of digital art includes using an electronic display in an art installation. The artist can include TV screens or projector screens to display their videos.

Techniques Used in Digital Art

To create digital art, the artist can use the computer to manipulate found images, images taken with a digital camera, or images scanned with a scanner. The computer can also be used to automatically generate images such as fractal or algorithm art. Once the artist has images in the computer, they can use editing software such as Photoshop to alter those images. Illustrator is another popular software used to create images, but it is used to create vector-based illustrations and text that can be enlarged or shrunk without losing quality. Photoshop is used to edit photographs and raster (pixel)-based artwork. If a raster-based artwork is enlarged too much, it loses quality and becomes pixelated.

To create artwork that includes an electronic display, the artist can use a projector and a screen to project a large video or can include TV or computer screens within their work to show their video art.

Creating Digital Images: AI

Prompt engineering is an important part of creating **artificial intelligence (AI) images**. These images are generated by AI based on an input prompt. It involves giving specific instructions to the AI image generator so that it will create the results that the artist desires. These specific instructions can include an artist or artwork to style the AI image after, colors to include, lighting to use, or even media styles to employ, like watercolor, pen and ink, or oil paint. By using these specific instructions, an artist can get the AI image output to look like what was envisioned. The artist might need to experiment with these instructions, wording them in different ways or including more details to get the image output they desire.

There are free image generators and paid image generators, and the paid generators often give better results. Some AI image generators may allow more customization of images or more options for prompting, including using negative words to exclude items or colors from an image. Free AI image generators may have a cap on images that can be created, create low-quality images, or limit the available aspect ratios. It is important that artists remember to use AI ethically and that they do not claim AI work as their original work.

File Formats for Digital Art

Common image file formats include JPG, GIF, TIFF, and PNG. JPG is the most commonly used image format, and it stands for Joint Photographic Experts Group. JPG images are highly compressed; this has the benefit of a small file, but the compression is lossy, meaning it sacrifices quality for a smaller size. A GIF file uses lossless compression, but it is limited in its display of colors. It is better for graphics than photographs. A TIFF file is lossless and is considered the best quality format for graphics work. It can be saved in red, green, blue (RGB) or cyan, magenta, yellow, and black (CMYK). A PNG file will be smaller than a TIFF but larger than a JPG, and it is also lossless. It is the newest of these formats. A GIF or PNG file will support transparency or animation.

Videos are saved as Audio Video Interleave (AVI), Flash Video Format (FLV), Windows Media Video (WMV), Apple QuickTime Movie (MOV), or Moving Pictures Expert Group 4 (MP4) formats. AVI is one of the oldest video formats. FLV files are created with Adobe Flash. WMV was originally intended for streaming content online. MP4 is a newer format becoming popular for sharing videos online.

Advantages and Disadvantages of Digital Art

Digital art can be saved in an image or video format, and it can be shared and reproduced multiple times. A digital image can be printed, and this artwork can be shared with multiple people or shown in multiple locations. Many traditional art methods produce only one artwork, and if this artwork is damaged, there is not another copy saved elsewhere. Digital art can be created quickly, and it can be edited, erased, and changed until the artist is satisfied. As technology evolves, new techniques and possibilities emerge.

Because digital art can be reproduced and shared endlessly, it is not held in as high regard as other art forms. Digital art is thought to require less skill than other art forms, and because anyone can create digital art, it is thought of as a lesser art form. It does not require the knowledge of traditional art media or practice involved with drawing, painting, sculpture, and other media.

Performance, Site-Specific, Installation, and Environmental Art

Performance Art as a Medium

Performance art began in the early 20th century with the futurist, Russian constructivist, and Dada art movements. Performance art is a scripted or unscripted performance that is presented live in the context of fine arts. The performance is usually conceptual and not just for entertainment. The artist seeks to break away from the traditions of art and can even include audience participation if desired.

Performance art involves four components: the performer, time, space, and a relationship with the audience. It can be experienced live or through media, with no specific venue or length of time required. The artist might stick to a script or improvise as the performance goes on. Unlike some performing arts, performance art does not create a fictitious drama with a linear script. Performance art is often satirical or will make the viewer think about art in unconventional ways.

The Evolution of Performance Art

Performance art has become accepted as an art medium in the past 30 years. It differs from theater and performing art by its lack of a clear narrative. Inspired by the abstract expressionism movement, artists wanted to include the body's role in artmaking into the actual artwork. The act of creation, not just the final product, was seen as important, like Jackson Pollock's action paintings. His movements and process played a big role in the creation of his paintings. Performance art emphasizes the time and space in which art exists, as well as the actions of the artist. Artists sought new ways to express themselves, and museums have sought ways to display these works. In a way, this is opposite to the idea of performance art existing in a finite time and interacting with the viewers. New strategies of performance art have sought to create interactions between people who would not have interacted otherwise. Artists have even begun to reenact performance pieces from the past, attempting to recapture those experiences.

A Happening

A **happening** is a performance or event created in the context of fine art. Happenings include audience participation as a main component, and although some parts are planned by the artist, there is often also room for improvisation as well. Every time a happening was performed, it would be different due to the unplanned and improvised parts. This is in stark contrast to static, unchanging works of art, which provide the same experience to each viewer. Happenings exist as a fleeting moment, something that cannot be preserved and shown in a museum. A major difference between happenings and other types of art is that each happening is unique. They could be elaborate and large or intimate and small, depending on the artist's intentions.

Allan Kaprow first used the term "happening" in 1957 to describe art events that he experienced at a picnic on George Segal's farm. Kaprow's 1959 work was titled *18 Happenings in 6 Parts*. A happening could include any combination of elements of dance, music, performance, poetry, and theater, as well as art creation.

PERFORMANCE ART: MATERIALS

Performance art involves the presence of the artist as the performer, the involvement of the audience, time, and a space for the performance. It includes the actions of the performer or performers as the artwork. The actual work requires live performance, but the artwork can reach a wider audience afterward by documentation through photography and videotaping. The documentation can affect how the viewer understands the work, and it can be different than experiencing the work firsthand.

In Marina Abramović's work *The Artist Is Present*" (2010), she sat silently at a wooden table, and people took turns sitting across from her, silently engaging her gaze. Abramović was experimenting with people's perception of expected time of a performance, stretching it out to eight hours a day for three months. She sought to push limits of the time of a performance piece, while engaging thousands of participants.

PERFORMANCE ART: TECHNIQUES

Performance art involves many techniques and materials, all depending on the artist and the messages that they are trying to convey. One example is Yoko Ono's *Cut Piece* (1964), in which she sat on a stage while viewers took turns cutting her clothing off of her with scissors. This was a commentary on voyeurism and a voyeur's participation and responsibility in objectifying women.

Another example is Chris Burden's *Shoot* (1971), which involved a friend shooting him in the arm while another friend documented the performance with a camera. This work touched on the second friend's desire to intervene, ideas of gun control, and even the Vietnam War.

For *Art/Life: One Year Performance* (*Rope Piece*), begun in 1983, Linda Montano and Tehching Hsieh were tied to each other by an eight-foot piece of rope for an entire year but did not touch each other. For this work, the rope represented people's struggle to connect to each other socially and physically.

SITE-SPECIFIC ART

Site-specific art is created to be displayed or erected in a certain location, and it loses meaning if it is removed from that location. The term was first used in the mid-1970s. Site-specific art includes sculptures, land art, or even a dance or performance created for and performed in a specific location. Christo and Jeanne-Claude are known for their large-scale, site-specific artworks including wrapped bridges and surrounded islands.

INSTALLATION ART

Installation art is a large-scale construction created with mixed media, for a specific location and a set length of time. An installation can take up an entire room and is sometimes referred to as an environment. They often fill a gallery room or large space that the viewer walks through or stands in to experience the artwork. They are usually placed in an interior room and are designed specifically for the space in which they are constructed. The term "environment" was first used for these types of artworks in 1959 by Allan Kaprow, and the term "installation" was later used in 1969 and onward. This type of art became popular in the 1970s. Today, it can include interactive electronic or digital-based installations or even immersive virtual reality installations.

MATERIALS/TOOLS/PROCESSES FOR INSTALLATIONS

An **art installation** is created to occupy a specific space. To create an installation, the artist must first assess the available space to decide the best way to install the artwork. The process begins with checking the dimensions, lighting, and temperature of the space. The artist will need to plan the layout and how it will be installed. To install the artwork, the artist will need to gather tools, such as levels, drills, nails, screws, hammers, mounting hardware, string, cable, or adhesives. The necessary tools will depend on the artwork being installed. For a large-scale installation, the artist might need scaffolding or a lift.

The artist should protect the artwork by handling it safely during installation and consider how to protect the artwork using security measures and climate control. If the installation includes electronics and needs power, the artist will need to ensure there is a power source and make sure all cables are out of the way of foot traffic to prevent tripping. After installing the artwork in the space, the artist should assess the installation from different angles to ensure it is positioned correctly. He or she will also need to check that the art is mounted securely. After this, the artist will clean the area and the artwork to remove any debris from the installation process.

An installation is often multimedia and can include a variety of materials. Traditional materials like the following lend different textures and structural elements to a sculpture.

- **Wood** is a versatile material that can be used for structure and texture.
- **Paper** is lightweight, easy to manipulate, and it might be used for temporary elements.
- **Textiles** can connect elements or be draped over them. They can provide texture or be used to create soft sculptures.
- **Glass** is reflective and transparent, and it can be used for light installations or for fragile elements.
- **Stone** is heavy and solid, and it might be used for architectural or large-scale elements.
- **Metal** is malleable and durable, and it can be used for large-scale elements, structural components, or reflective surfaces.

Plastics, organic materials, and found objects are more contemporary materials. Plastics might be used for modern elements. Found objects could comment on consumerism. Organic materials can change over time.

Electronic and digital materials can include LED lights, monitors, sensors, projectors and screens, and sound systems. Viewers can sometimes interact with electronic and digital installations so that the art changes in real time. Soundscapes and projections can create an immersive environment.

Christo and Jeanne-Claude

Christo and Jeanne-Claude are artists known for some of the largest and most ambitious site-specific artwork created. Whereas landscape art uses natural materials to create artwork, Christo and Jeanne-Claude used manufactured materials to contrast with the environment in which they created the artwork. Part of their process included negotiating with and gaining permits from the owners of the land or structure they wished to use. Each artwork created was large scale and required a lot of time and work to construct. They have insisted that the artwork was created for aesthetic value alone, and not for any deeper meanings. Some well-known artworks include wrapping the Pont-Neuf, the oldest bridge in France, in a sand-colored fabric, and surrounding several Miami islands in a bright pink fabric. *The Umbrellas* involved placing more than 1,000 umbrellas in Japan and the United States at the same time. In their project *The Gates*, installed in Central Park in New York City in 2005, visitors could walk through and around these 7,503 fabric gates throughout the park, which changed the look of the familiar landscape.

Environmental Art

The **environmental art movement** began in the 1960s and consisted of site-specific sculptures. Environmental art can use part of the environment to create aesthetic artwork, or it can create a statement on environmental, social, or political issues relating to the natural world. It can highlight and celebrate the artist's connection with the natural world, and it can use natural materials within the environment. The movement began in rural areas, but in the 1970s and 1980s, environmental art was also created in public and urban areas. It can be created to blend in with nature or highlight environmental issues, but sometimes environmental art actually damages the environment, like Robert Smithson's *Spiral Jetty*, shown here. The creation of this work permanently damaged the land it was created on, and it has been criticized for such.

Another criticism of environmental art is the fact that it either has to be experienced on site or displayed as a photograph of the art, posing a challenge to gallery exhibitions.

EARTH ART

Earth art, or Earthworks, is a genre of art that seeks to use materials taken directly from nature. This is a subgenre of environmental art, but it focuses on the use of local and natural materials to create sculptural forms. Artists would use water, stones, gravel, soil, and sticks, paying homage to the specific site by using local materials. Earth art shares some characteristics with minimalism, using a simplicity of form to express ideas. Earth art highlights the beauty and aesthetics of the natural world while rejecting the traditions of art creation and exhibition. Earth art can be categorized as invasive or noninvasive, with invasive Earth art making significant alterations to the environment. Noninvasive Earth art is thought of as being more respectful to the environment, preserving the integrity of the landscape. Because Earth art is site-specific, it is not accessible to the average viewer, cannot be displayed as is in a museum, and cannot be bought and sold.

ENVIRONMENTAL ART: TECHNIQUES

Environmental art seeks to challenge traditional notions of sculpture and bring sculptural elements to the natural environment. Some environmental art uses elements of the natural landscape to create the artwork, including sticks, sand, rocks, stones, and moss. The artwork is intended to disappear back into the landscape as time and weather affect the sculpture.

In the 1980s, artists began creating environmental art in public spaces, including vacant lots and other urban locations. Artists sought to bring their artwork closer to people, to engage them in the dialogue about art, the environment, and conservation. One artist planted cabbages in a pattern in an empty lot. Another made the particulates in the air visible for viewers. Yet another artist marked possible flood lines in at-risk cities that could result from climate change.

For environmental art to be shown in a gallery or museum, the artist must provide photographs, which do not give the full experience of the art.

ENVIRONMENTAL ART: MATERIALS

Environmental art can incorporate materials from the natural environment, or it can introduce new and surprising materials into the natural environment. Some environmental art will include leaves, branches, rocks, moss, logs, vines, and other materials found in the local environment, changing the environment and emphasizing the local materials. Other environmental art will include nonnatural materials such as nylon fabric, spray paint, or metal.

This example by Robert Smithson, *Broken Circle and Spiral Hill*, was created in 1971 in the Netherlands. Smithson listed his materials as green water and white and yellow sand flats. Smithson used the local materials to create something different and recognizable as something not created by nature, but rather created with nature. Smithson had begun the "land art" movement, desiring to create art out in the open and not inside a studio. The life span of this type of artwork is finite, meant to be eventually reclaimed by nature.

Environmental Art: Motivation

Environmental art, or land art, sprung partly from artists' desire to work outside of the studio and create artworks that could not be contained in a gallery or exhibit. Depending on the artist, it can be created to raise awareness of environmental issues such as erosion or conservation. It can explore humans' relationship with nature or the human-built world with the natural environment. It can capture how we are polluting the environment or how man is affecting the natural world. It can even highlight the artist's love of nature and the beauty of our world. Environmental art is created as site-specific artwork that will eventually be reclaimed by its surrounding environment, so its existence is usually short-lived. Photography is an important component of these works, capturing the scene for those who cannot view it in person before it is gone.

Material Handling, Storage, and Safety

Identifying Dangerous Materials and Their Effects

Hazardous Substances in Art Materials

There are several **art materials** that can be **dangerous** to the user, and it is important to understand the hazards associated with them.

- **Toxic pigments**, including cobalt, cadmium, mercury, chrome, and manganese, are used in several paints and inks. Repeated exposure to these pigments can cause a cumulative effect on the user, especially if the artist inhales a powdered pigment.
- **Silica dust** is used for or is a byproduct of ceramics and plaster, and it is hazardous when inhaled.
- **Metals and metal oxides** like copper or lead, soda ash, and silica are harmful to inhale and can be found in some ceramic glazes.
- **Chemicals used in a darkroom**, such as the developing bath, stop bath, and fixer, are often toxic upon skin contact or inhalation, especially in concentrated amounts.
- The **volatile and toxic substances** such as acetone or turpentine in lacquers and varnishes are dangerous to inhale.
- **Permanent marker fumes** are dangerous to inhale, particularly when concentrated.
- Some **adhesives** that are not water-based can be toxic for someone to inhale.
- The **metal** used to make stained glass pieces usually contains lead.

Categorizing Dangerous Materials and Their Effects

Some **art materials** are toxic to touch, while some others are dangerous to inhale or can be fire hazards. It is important to know the **hazards** of these items.

Heavy metals in paints and pigments, such as lead, cadmium, chrome, and cobalt, are hazardous when absorbed through the skin. The styrene in polyester resin can cause skin issues and even cancer with frequent exposure. Fiberglass causes skin irritation, and darkroom chemicals are dangerous to absorb through the skin.

Several media are hazardous to inhale and can pose a fire risk. Clay dust, chalk pastels, powdered pigment, aerosolized pigment, and spray fixatives are dangerous to inhale. Certain permanent markers contain xylene, which is hazardous to inhale. The fumes from zinc chloride flux are also an inhalation hazard. Metal forging furnaces can release toxic fumes from the metals. Rubber cement and other solvent-based glues are inhalation hazards and are flammable. Solvent-based spray paints are also flammable and are inhalation hazards. Some varnishes, solvents, and paint strippers are hazardous to touch and inhale, and they can be flammable.

Water-based paints like watercolor and tempera, washable markers, graphite and color pencils, oil pastels, water-based ink, oil-based clay, and water-based glue are all safer choices of media.

Mechanical and Chemical Hazards

When handling materials and tools, one must be aware of the potential safety hazards involved. Hazards can affect the people involved in the process, people in the area, or even tools and the environment. **Mechanical hazards** are safety concerns surrounding the tools and materials that can cause direct physical harm when the appropriate precautions are not followed. Examples include straining a muscle by lifting too much weight or receiving cuts from something sharp or abrasive. Other results of mechanical hazards include breaks, cuts, crush injuries, and burns. **Chemical hazards** are safety concerns mainly dealing with reactive or toxic substances. These can include explosive, flammable, acidic, corrosive, and toxic or poisonous materials. Where mechanical hazards are usually immediately apparent, chemical hazards can be less obvious and can cause serious short and long-term health effects.

Storage of Materials and Equipment

Materials must be stored in a way that protects both the supplies and the users. Improperly stored materials can go bad or become a safety hazard. Principles of **proper storage** include ensuring proper labeling, including dating of materials to ensure they are not expired, keeping materials out of excessive humidity or moisture and sunlight, proper sealing of containers, and ensuring there is adequate ventilation. Some materials should not be stored together as they can produce dangerous chemical reactions. **Material storage cabinets** should be lockable and inaccessible to children and should ideally be made of a durable, corrosive-resistant, and heat-resistant material, such as painted metal to help prevent deterioration over time and to reduce risk in the event of a fire. **Ventilation** is particularly important when it comes to storing volatile materials that off-gas. Without proper ventilation, flammable, combustible, or toxic fumes can build up to produce unexpected reactions. Objects in storage should also be organized in a way which minimizes **physical risk**. For instance, items should never be stored in precarious positions and sharp objects should not be loose but should be in well-labeled containers.

Ventilation, Storage, and Disposal Procedures Based on the Medium

Different media require different methods of ventilation, storage, and disposal.

Non-water-based paint, including oil thinners such as turpentine or mineral spirits, should be used in a well-ventilated area with an exhaust fan in a window. Flammable solvents used for thinning or cleaning oil paints should be stored in a cabinet made to hold flammable materials. These should be disposed of at a hazardous waste collection site, not poured down a drain. Rags used for oils, such as linseed oil, should be kept in tightly closed metal containers for cleaning or disposal. For disposal, the metal container with rags should be filled with water and treated as hazardous waste.

Photography chemicals require proper ventilation with an exhaust duct near the chemical trays. Developing powders should be mixed in a fume hood or glove box. Chemicals should not be stored in a breakable container or one with a lid that fits loosely. They can be disposed of in small quantities down a drain when a sewer system is used, but the artist should contact their local municipality for proper disposal of larger quantities.

Media that create dust, such as plaster, pastels, charcoal, and carving stones, should be used in a well-ventilated area while the artist wears a NIOSH-approved respirator.

Safety in the Immediate Area

When working with materials or tools, the area must be secured in such a way that all people entering the area will be **aware** and **protected** from **immediate hazards**. Active work zones should be obvious and not have too much foot traffic. PPE such as hearing protection may limit the awareness of people working near one another, so a clear line of sight is important to maintain. All people in the immediate area should have clear access to first aid and other emergency response devices, such as fire alarms, wash stations, and fire extinguishers. Flammables, toxic materials, and aerosols should be used away from other people and require adequate ventilation. Ventilation requires access to fresh, clean air, and not just airflow alone. Blowing a fan in a closed area while using volatile chemicals can actually increase the buildup of harmful or dangerous chemicals and lead to a worse outcome than a closed room with no ventilation.

Safety Procedures for Art Processes

An artist should understand the **safety procedures** for **cutting**, **etching**, and **spraying.** Several media involve cutting, including printmaking, sculpting, and paper crafts. Cutting should always be done in a direction away from the body. A bench hook should be used to hold the material in place for relief printing. Safety goggles or a shield should be worn when cutting glass or plastic to protect the artist from particles.

Since chemicals used for etching can contain concentrated acids, artists should wear goggles, gloves, and an apron to protect themselves. They should also have an eyewash station available. The area should be properly ventilated to protect against harmful fumes.

When spraying, the artist should use a spray booth that has ventilation to the outside. Another alternative is to spray outdoors. To avoid inhaling pigments or chemicals, the artist should use gloves, goggles, and an appropriate respirator. Combustible sprays should be kept away from an open flame.

Safety Procedures for Art Materials and Tools

When working with **art materials and tools**, it is important to follow proper **safety procedures**.

- **Flammable materials** should be stored in a fireproof cabinet away from ignition or heat sources. There should be a fire extinguisher on hand, and the artist should know the fire evacuation routes.
- Since **rags soaked in solvents or oil** can spontaneously combust, they must be kept in an airtight metal container.
- **Toxic materials** should be stored in a locked cabinet, and any reactive materials should be stored separately. Hazardous materials should be bought in small quantities and kept in a location away from children's reach.
- Since solvents and some pigments can be **toxic** if absorbed through the skin, the artist should avoid touching them and should have gloves and aprons readily available. It is important to read labels to properly understand the risks.
- A **brush** should not be pointed toward the artist's mouth, and artists should not keep drinks or food nearby when working with art materials.
- **Spills** should be cleaned up immediately, and the floor should be kept clear. Tools should always be put away when they are not being used.
- Safer versions of materials should be considered as substitutes whenever possible.

- The artist should know what chemicals are present in each material and know the appropriate actions to take if there is an accident. This could include handwashing, using an eyewash station, or calling Poison Control.

Material Handling and Protective Equipment

When handling materials, one must be sure to use the appropriate protective equipment. Generally protective equipment refers to personal protective equipment (PPE), which generally means clothing used to protect the body. Common PPE includes the following:

- **Gloves** – Various types and uses ranging from protecting the hands from material exposure to protection from sharp, abrasive, hot, or cold objects.
- **Eye protection** – Generally recommended for any time a material might be introduced into the air or flung by a process.
- **Aprons or smocks** – Protects the body from exposure to materials that can cause abrasions, stains, burns, etc. Generally recommended when handling liquids.
- **Closed-toe shoes** – Necessary when handling chemicals, sharp objects, or heavy objects that could harm the feet if dropped.
- **Helmets** – Used primarily in construction where heavy materials are hoisted.
- **Hearing protection** – Necessary to protect against loud or sustained noises.
- **Respirator or Dust Masks** – Protects against fumes and dust exposure. The type of filtration needs to be sufficient for the materials in use.

The equipment used for protection, including PPE must be **sufficient** to handle the specific materials in use, such as using the appropriate type of gloves and apron to protect against the hazards on hand. For instance, workers' gloves may protect against minor abrasions, but they do not resist the penetration of chemicals. Likewise, the PPE must not be so restrictive that it actually causes greater risk. For instance, spinning tools are unsafe to use with most gloves as the gloves can be pulled into the machinery, creating a greater potential for injury.

Disposal of Materials

When disposing of materials, it is always important to follow federal, state, and local laws to prevent unnecessary environmental damage or risk to others. Many materials should not be placed in the general waste due to chemical or physical hazards associated. Likewise, chemicals should never be poured down sinks as solvents and volatile chemicals can either eat at the infrastructure or cause buildup of harmful gases that could be toxic, flammable, corrosive, or explosive. Many of these types of chemicals can be taken to a designated facility, or even recycled. Other materials, such as glue, concrete, paint, or adhesives should simply be set aside to continue curing until they become solids and are safe to dispose of in the trash. This can prevent unnecessary and harmful spills of liquids that are challenging or impossible to clean up.

SDS (Safety Data Sheets)

Safety Data Sheets (SDS, formerly Material Safety Data Sheets, MSDS) provide information on the physical and chemical properties of a substance as well as potential health and environmental concerns. OSHA requires that all chemicals be labeled appropriately and that SDS be readily available in the workplace. The hazard communication standard also requires employees to be trained, and for the employer to maintain records of the training given. The format for SDS includes sixteen sections. The required sections are as follows:

I:Identification
II: Hazard Identification
III: Composition/Information on Ingredients
IV: First Aid Measures
V:Firefighting Measures
VI: Accidental Release Measures
VII: Handling/Storage Requirements

VIII: Physical/Chemical Properties
IX: Exposure Controls/Personal Protection
X:Stability/Reactivity
XI: Toxicological Information
XII: Ecological Information
XIII: Disposal Considerations
XIV: Transportation Information
XV: Regulatory Information
XVI: Other Information

Chemically Protective Clothing

SDS often recommend the usage of chemical protective clothing (CPC). Protective eye goggles with splash guards and air vents should be used when handling chemicals. Face shields should be used when working with large quantities of a substance and are most effective when used in conjunction with safety goggles. If the mode of possible hazard is through contact and/or absorption on skin, appropriate gloves should be worn. Gloves are chosen based upon their permeability to and reactivity with the chemical in use. Personal respiratory equipment may be indicated if fume hoods do not provide adequate ventilation of fumes or airborne particulates. Body protection depends on the level of protection needed and ranges from rubberized aprons to full suits that are evaluated for their permeability and leak protection. Closed-toed protective shoes should always be used when working with chemicals.

Requirements for Labels

The term *label* under the Globally Harmonized System (GHS) of Classification and Labeling of Chemicals refers to the label on the container. Under GHS, it's required to contain certain elements; these requirements apply whether the label is affixed by the manufacturer or whether the chemical is placed into a smaller, secondary container in the workplace. The label must include the identification of the chemical, the manufacturer's name and contact information, the applicable GHS pictograms, the applicable signal words (either *danger* or *warning*, as applicable), and precautionary statements (measures to reduce risk from exposure to the chemical).

Pictograms

The pictograms used in the GHS system are simple pictures used to convey hazards posed by the chemical. They are meant to be universally understandable by people with diverse language and reading fluencies. They are as follows:

 *Health Hazard*	 *Flammable*	 *Sensitizer/ Irritant*
 *Gas Under Pressure*	 *Oxidizer*	 *Corrosive*
 *Reactive*	 *Environmental Hazard*	 *Poison*

Signal Words

Under the GHS hazard communication and safety data sheet system, the term **signal word** is used to describe one word that summarizes the degree of danger posed by the substances. There are only two signal words: *danger* and *warning*. The word **danger** is used for more hazardous substances that present immediate hazards such as flammability, reactivity, poison, and so on. The word **warning** is used for lesser hazards such as irritants, environmental hazards, and less toxic substances. The signal word is used on the label to provide a quick and easily understandable indication of the degree of hazard posed by the substance.

Health Issues Related to Art Materials and Tools

There are several **health issues** that can occur from using art materials and tools.

- Toxic art materials containing **heavy metals**, like cadmium or lead, pose dangers through skin absorption and inhalation. Repeated exposure can increase a person's risk of cancer as well as liver or kidney issues. They are also dangerous to inhale when used in a spray or powdered form.
- The inhalation of **solvents** like turpentine or mineral spirits can cause respiratory irritation, headaches, dizziness, and even brain damage in the long term. They can also cause dermatitis and skin irritations.
- **Aerosolized paints** are dangerous to inhale, and they can cause nausea, breathing difficulties, and headaches.
- The **xylene** in permanent markers can cause several issues, including dizziness, headaches, loss of muscle coordination, and even death in high enough amounts.
- The inhalation of **clay dust** containing silica or asbestos can cause lung diseases like silicosis or asbestosis. Asbestos in clay dust can cause cancer.
- Firing glazes and clays in a **kiln** can pose a risk of inhalation of fumes, including carbon monoxide, fluorine, sulfur, and metallic vapors. Some glazes will emit barium, manganese, cobalt, or lead fumes, which are highly toxic to inhale. Materials containing lead can cause peripheral nervous system damage as well as brain, kidney, or chromosomal damage.

Chapter Quiz

Ready to see how well you retained what you just read? Scan the QR code to go directly to the chapter quiz interface for this study guide. If you're using a computer, simply visit the online resources page at **mometrix.com/resources719/osatart** and click the Chapter Quizzes link.

Art Elements and Design Principles

Elements and Principles of Art

The Elements of Art

The seven elements of art are **color, texture, shape, form, line, space, and value**. **Color** has three characteristics: hue (such as red, yellow, or green), intensity (how bright or dull the color is).

- **Colors** opposite each other on the color wheel are considered complementary. Examples include red and green or blue and orange.
- **Texture** is how something feels, or appears to feel, and it can be real or implied. Examples of textures include smooth, rough, or bumpy. A real texture is one you can actually feel, whereas an implied texture is two-dimensional yet appears to have texture.
- **Shapes** are categorized as geometric or organic. Geometric shapes include named mathematical shapes such as circles, ovals, squares, and triangles. Organic shapes are asymmetrical and are often found in nature.
- **Form** is used in three-dimensional art such as sculpture, and it describes the shape of the artwork.
- A **line** is used to define a shape, and it is the path between two points. A line can be straight, curved, broken, implied, or free-form. Lines can be used to create movement or to lead the viewer's eye around the artwork.
- **Space** can refer to the foreground, middle ground, and background of an artwork. It can also refer to the positive and negative space created by the artist. Positive space is the subject of the artwork, and negative space is the area that surrounds it. An artist can create the illusion of three-dimensional space within an artwork.
- **Value** is the lightness or darkness of a color. An artist can use value to provide visual interest in an artwork, to create a mood, or to draw the viewer's eye to a certain focal point. Contrast is the difference in value or the difference in the lightness and darkness.

Color Wheel

The color wheel is a representation of the color spectrum and is made up of twelve colors arranged in a circle. The **primary colors** are red, yellow, and blue and are considered primary because they are not made up of any combination of other colors. The **secondary colors** are green, orange, and purple, which are made up of combinations of two of the primary colors. For instance, green is the resulting color when blue and yellow paint are mixed in equal parts. The **tertiary colors** are the colors between a primary and a secondary color, such as red and orange, which together make red-orange. The color wheel helps to organize and understand the spectrum of colors and guides color theory, resulting in several common color schemes. Colors are often described as being warm or cool and the careful selection of colors can amplify the mood of composition.

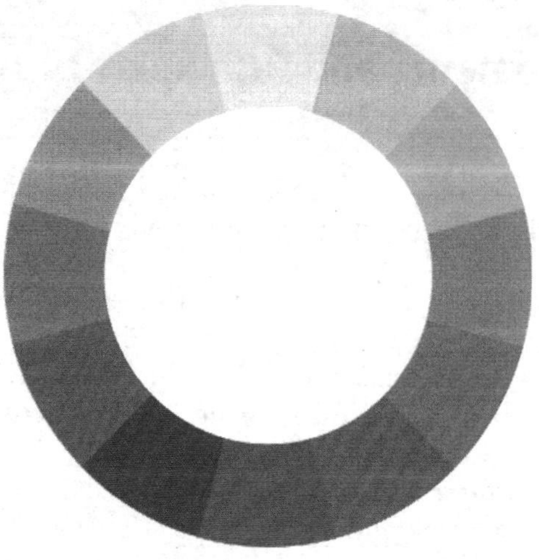

Color Schemes

- **Monocromatic** – made up of one color base, such as blue, used in various values or tones to produce an image.
- **Analogous** – a color scheme similar to monochromatic, but using only colors that touch each other on the color wheel. For instance, one might use blues and greens and colors in between to form a particular mood in a painting.
- **Complementary** – a color scheme that uses colors that are opposites on the color wheel, such as blue and orange. This often produces a dramatic effect in a composition.
- **Split Complementary** – a color scheme based on the complementary scheme, except instead of two colors that are opposites, split complementary schemes use three colors, one color that stands as the primary, and two that stand in as the complementary color. For example, a composition might use purple as the primary color. Then, to select the split complementary colors, the artist must first find the traditional complement of purple, which is yellow. Instead of using yellow, the artist would use colors that are on each side of the complementary color, which would be yellow-green and a yellow-orange. The two split complementary colors must be very close to the traditional complementary color on the color wheel, or the scheme will shift from being a split complementary to a triadic color scheme.
- **Triadic Color Schemes** – a color scheme that uses three equally-spaced colors, such as red, yellow, and blue.

Principles of Design

The principles of design include balance, contrast, movement, emphasis, pattern, rhythm, and unity. An artist can use multiple principles of design in their artwork, or they can focus primarily on one principle.

- **Balance** is how an artwork's visual weight is organized, and it can be symmetrical or asymmetrical. Symmetrical balance has the same weight on both sides, whereas asymmetrical balance is visually weighted more on one side. Asymmetrical balance gives the artwork more visual interest and leads the viewer's eye around the artwork.
- **Contrast** is when an artwork's elements are juxtaposed against each other to create interesting differences. This could include a difference in warm and cool colors or a difference between organic and geometric shapes.
- **Movement** is using the elements to lead the viewer throughout the piece. One example is a repetition of shapes that moves the viewer's eye through the artwork.

- **Emphasis** creates a focal point in the artwork by using a bold color, asymmetrical balance, or a strong contrast. Pattern and rhythm consist of a repetition of elements.
- **Pattern** is repeating elements in the same order, whereas **rhythm** is repeating elements without a specific order.
- **Unity** is harmony throughout the artwork created by elements working together. This can be achieved by a repetition of an element, similarity of elements, or even a rhythm of elements.

The Relationship Between Elements and Principles of Design

The elements of art are the building blocks of visual art, and the principles of design are ways to organize these elements of art. An artist can use multiple elements and principles in their artwork, or they can focus primarily on certain elements and principles. By using the principles of design to organize the elements of art, the artist can decide what the focal point of the artwork is and where they want to lead viewers' eyes. An artist can use the principles of design to arrange the elements of art in their artwork, and they can use the terminology of these elements and principles to explain their artistic decisions. They can also use them to analyze another artists' artwork. The elements of art and principles of design are both sets of established criteria that are used to objectively judge artwork rather than using personal preferences.

Many of the elements of art and principles of design can be found in both two- and three-dimensional artwork. **Texture** can be real on a three-dimensional work, whereas it will be implied on a two-dimensional work. A marble statue might be smooth, whereas a steel sculpture could have a rough texture. **Space** in a two-dimensional work will be created by how the artist uses the elements and principles to arrange the artwork and even to create a foreground, middle ground, and background. **Space** in a sculpture or three-dimensional work is how the artist uses the space in three dimensions. In three-dimensional artwork, **form** has width, depth, and height. The form can be viewed either from all sides, which would make the sculpture in-the-round, or it can be viewed from one side, which is a relief work (built from a solid background). Form describes the shape of the artwork.

Applications of Principles of Design

Two-Dimensional Artwork

This painting, *Composition with Red, Yellow, and Blue* (1927), is by Dutch artist Piet Mondrian. It is a product of the de Stijl art movement, which began in Holland. He eliminated any representational forms in his artwork and pared it down to a few elements. The main elements of art used in this painting are color, line, and shape. Mondrian used planes of pure color in this painting, separated by thick black lines. Here you see the primary colors — red, yellow, and blue — along with black and white. He used black lines to create geometric shapes throughout the canvas. The geometric shapes and the parallel and perpendicular lines give the work a solid and stable feel. Mondrian placed the planes of color in an asymmetrical way and balanced them with panes of white.

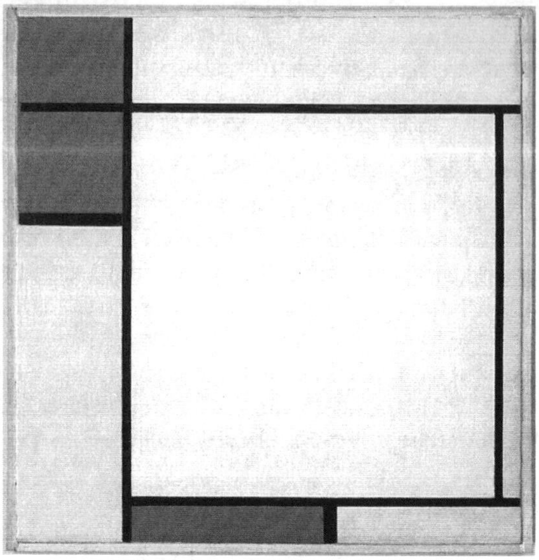

Three-Dimensional Artwork

This sculpture is titled *Embrace IV*, by Emilia Glaser. The main elements evident in this sculpture are color, value, shape, line, and texture. The sculpture is mainly one color of red-orange, with a darker value of the color on part of the sculpture and a different color and value for the base. This use of warm color can invoke a feeling of happiness or excitement, and it can draw the viewer closer to the sculpture. The sculpture appears to be a combination of different shapes, and strong lines visually separate the borders of these shapes. The lines have mostly upward movement, giving the sculpture a strong, uplifting feel. The sculpture appears to have a rough and bumpy texture, which in this case would be real texture because it is a texture that could actually be felt.

The Starry Night

This painting is called *The Starry Night* (1889) by Vincent van Gogh. The artist used several principles of design, including contrast, emphasis, balance, and movement. There is contrast in the values used throughout the painting — the darker blues and grays and the lighter whites and yellows. There is also a contrast of warm (yellow) and cool (blue) colors, in which the warm colors advance and the cool colors recede in the artwork. The bright yellow moon in the top right shows emphasis, being the largest portion of this light value and the brightest color in the painting. The large dark shape on the left of the painting is visually balanced by the smaller, bright moon and glow on the right. Van Gogh's brushstrokes look like wind blowing through the sky, and they provide movement in the painting, which leads the viewer's eye around the artwork.

Screwarch

This sculpture by Claes Oldenburg and Coosje van Bruggen is called *Screwarch* (1978–1984). It appears to be an oversized screw, bending to create an arch. The main principles of design evident in this sculpture are balance, pattern, contrast, and movement. The sculpture is asymmetrically balanced, being much visually heavier at the thicker end on the left. The threads of the screw show a repeating spiraling pattern, which follows the arch to the pointed end on the right. The larger, bulkier end of the screw is smooth and sharply contrasts with the rest of the screw, which tapers slowly to a point and has a spiraling pattern and texture. The sculpture shows movement with its arched form, leading the viewer's eye from the heavier end of the screw to the tapered point on the other end.

ORGANIC SHAPES

The elements of art and principles of design can all be found in nature, but it is likely that you will find more organic shapes than geometric. The natural environment contains many textures, such as rough bark, smooth petals, or gritty sand. Many colors and values can be found throughout landscapes, as well as a depth of space and varied forms of plants, trees, and rocks. Bright flowers contrast against dark leaves, providing a focal point or emphasis against the green. Wind creates movement in the natural world, and the repetition of plants or trees creates rhythm. The edges of objects in nature can create implied lines between each other, and lines can be found in the veins of a leaf. The repetition of greens throughout a spring scene or reds and oranges in a fall scene can create unity throughout the landscape.

COMPOSITION

Composition is how an artwork is organized, and the principles of design help an artist decide how to arrange the elements of art in their artwork. An artist can use the principles of design to decide what will stand out in their artwork and where they will lead the viewer's eyes. An artist could focus on the use of color as an element in their artwork but then use a pattern to repeat the colors in a certain order or use emphasis to draw attention to a certain color in a certain part of the artwork. They could create unity in the work by repeating a certain color throughout. An artist could focus on certain shapes in their artwork, but then they could use contrast by putting different shapes next to each other. They could use the shapes to create a rhythm by repeating them without a specific order. The artist could even focus on using lines in the artwork, but then they could use movement to guide the viewer's eyes around the artwork with the lines.

Chapter Quiz

Ready to see how well you retained what you just read? Scan the QR code to go directly to the chapter quiz interface for this study guide. If you're using a computer, simply visit the online resources page at **mometrix.com/resources719/osatart** and click the Chapter Quizzes link.

Art and Culture

Purpose and Role of Art

Purpose of Art

A common perception of art in the modern era is that artwork serves only to entertain. Historically, this has not been so. Art has historically served to recreate reality as a historical medium. Especially before the advent and popularization of the camera, artforms like drawing, painting, and sculpture were sometimes used as a means of recording what people looked like. Some forms of art embody only a decorative purpose, such as jewelry. Others, such as clothing, furniture, and architecture, have their roots in utility, but over time have morphed into elaborate or decorative forms as an expression of beauty.

Fine Art vs Applied Art

Fine art is art with no purpose other than being aesthetically pleasing or for expressive purposes. This can include drawing, painting, sculpture, and other media. **Applied art** is art that serves a purpose. Applied arts are useful objects with artistic design applied to their creation. This includes graphic design, interior design, fashion design, decorative arts, and architecture. Graphic design and illustration are also categorized as commercial arts, which fall under applied art. Decorative arts is the creation of jewelry, metalwork, ceramics, embroidery, carpets, furniture, and more. Sometimes applied arts are used in fine art works, so the line between fine arts and applied arts can be blurred, depending on the creator and their intent. In the 1960s, artists such as Andy Warhol began to blur the division between the two, which had been clear in previous years. Warhol used commercial art techniques to mass-produce works that were considered fine art.

Various Roles of Art

Storytelling vs Documentation

When art is used for **storytelling**, the artist creates a narrative that tells a story, expresses a theme, or communicates a message. The artwork guides the viewer through the narrative with composition, characters, and symbols. Art for storytelling often engages the viewers' emotions while connecting with them on a cultural or personal level. This type of art has historical and cultural significance because it passes down stories, legends, and myths while preserving cultural identity. Egyptian hieroglyphs are an example of art with the role of storytelling. This art gives stories of pharaohs, gods, and the afterlife. Renaissance artwork like da Vinci's *The Last Supper* expresses a religious narrative through its composition.

When art is used for **documentation**, it attempts to accurately show an event, a moment in time, or the likeness of a person or place. Art for documentation can serve as a historical record. It helps to ensure that details, people, and events are preserved so that future generations can see and understand them. This type of art is realistic and focuses on the accurate representation of perspective, proportion, and likeness. It avoids the use of symbolism, and the artist avoids adding his or her interpretation by maintaining accuracy and objectivity. Portraits of significant historical figures are examples of art for documentation. Da Vinci's illustrations of human anatomy are another example.

Decoration vs Utility

Art with a **decorative** purpose is intended to enhance a space aesthetically. It is created with the goal of pleasing the viewer's eye or adding color or texture to a space. This type of art shows the personal, social, or cultural tastes of an individual or society. It can influence a person's mood by creating feelings like calmness, agitation, or inspiration. This type of art can be found in a variety of forms, including drawings, paintings, tapestries, mosaics, and sculptures. It increases the visual appeal of a place but does not serve a practical function otherwise.

Art that is **utilitarian** is created to serve a functional purpose while also being artistic. This art combines function with beauty and can enhance the user's everyday life. Many cultures have traditions of making finely crafted utilitarian objects that are also symbols of their cultural heritage. These include furniture, textiles, and pottery. Even though this type of art is pleasing to the eye, it is made primarily to serve a practical purpose. These types of art are often durable enough for regular use so that they will last over time.

Purposes and Origins of Art

Art is used to record **history**. It gives a viewer insight into the political, cultural, and social conditions from different periods of time. Historical events and figures inspire artists to create art that depicts or comments on them. Art is used to help historians understand past civilizations.

Art can be inspired by **literature**. Literature and art converge with book cover graphics and illustrations. Both art and literature use symbolism and narratives to convey meanings and emotions to the reader or viewer.

Advancing **technology** helps to reshape art practices. Technologies like photography, digital media, and virtual reality have expanded what is possible when creating art. New forms and mediums have been created from the advancements of technology. Art can be displayed in online galleries and social media, and some artists create art digitally. Art is also used to comment on or critique technology and its impact on society.

Scientific advances have influenced art. Art created during the Renaissance shows an increased understanding of human anatomy. Art is used to depict complicated concepts visually, such as medical diagrams and scientific illustrations.

Artists have been led to explore dreams and the unconscious mind because of theories from **psychologists** like Jung and Freud. The psychology practice of art therapy helps people improve their mental health by expressing themselves through artwork. Psychological principles help people understand how artwork is perceived.

Some **philosophical** ideas have influenced artists and art movements. For example, some artists focused on absurdity in modern art due to the philosophical movement of existentialism. Art can help people express and explore philosophical concepts. It can challenge the viewer to contemplate deep ideas.

Sociology has led to artworks that highlight or critique social issues. Social realism and protest art influence and reflect changes in society. Sociology can help the viewer understand the cultural values and collective identities depicted in artwork.

Both **anthropology** and art explore the practices, beliefs, and cultures of humans. Anthropology has helped people to understand indigenous and traditional artwork. Art is a cultural artifact that gives the viewer insights into the values and rituals of the societies that created it.

Value and Role of Art in Modern Society

Art serves many roles and values within **society.**

- The various cultural groups that make up the society in the United States use art to express parts of their identity. The art shows their history and traditions, and it is used to celebrate the heritage of communities. This art helps others appreciate cultural diversity.
- Art can help promote activism and social change. It provokes thoughts and emotions in the viewer while also inspiring public discussions and social movements.
- Art education helps students with their cognitive, emotional, and social development. It promotes critical thinking, creativity, and problem-solving while helping students learn empathy and self-expression.
- Public art increases the aesthetic appeal of public areas. It creates spaces that a community can be proud of. Installations, sculptures, and murals are accessible to all people. The art helps give neighborhoods unique identities and can revitalize urban areas.

- Art industries within the US help contribute to the economy. They generate jobs and drive tourism to areas. Museums, festivals, and galleries stimulate economic activity and attract visitors from other places.
- Iconic artworks created by American artists reflect the values, struggles, and triumphs of America. They remind people of the nation's values.

Social Themes in Art

Themes

Themes are universal ideas explored and represented in artwork. One popular recurring example is identity. Identity includes the characteristics and behaviors that put an individual in a certain group. Some of the factors for identity include race, religion, culture, and language.

Photographer Cindy Sherman explored identity by photographing herself in different roles and costumes, essentially erasing her own identity and taking on the identity of other people. In doing this, she focused on the stereotypes of these female roles, addressing feminism, youth, aging, and obsession with status, ultimately questioning identity.

Kara Walker, an artist working with silhouettes, explores ideas of identity through race and gender. She portrays racism and historic scenes of slavery, getting past the romanticized notions of the past and exploring its reality. Her silhouettes simplify forms and focus on the topic at hand. She seeks to get past misconceptions and portray the true nature and identities behind tough subjects.

Realism

The **realism movement** began in France in the 1850s, and it attempted to document people and ordinary life faithfully, rather than avoiding unpleasant subjects or romanticizing them. Realist artists depicted laborers and ordinary people engaged in everyday life activities, realistically documenting and preserving life and culture at that time.

This example by Gustave Courbet is called *The Grain Sifters* (1855). It shows a mundane scene of workers sifting grain, using dark and natural colors to portray the scene realistically. Courbet led the realism movement in France. The realism movement challenged the narratives and depictions of history paintings, which was an academic style with posed action scenes. Realism artists documented manual labor and the plight of everyday people, using dark, serious tones to show serious-looking people. Realism artists were not interested in depicting history or anything that they did not personally see or experience; they were only documenting the present-day struggles of the common man.

Emotions and Ideas

Emotions and ideas can be expressed through artwork in many ways, including the imagery, subject matter, or colors used. Frida Kahlo is a Mexican artist who used the subject matter and imagery in her artwork to express her physical and emotional pain and frustration. Throughout her life, Kahlo experienced abuse as well as a near-fatal bus accident that caused many physical problems. She began to paint self-portraits and explore ideas related to her pain and injuries, including emotional pain from her divorce from artist Diego Rivera. In her paintings, she often depicted her physical problems as well as open wounds to portray her pain. She sometimes included imagery of roots, to symbolize growth and a feeling of being trapped. Kahlo would also depict issues of childbirth and miscarriage, to communicate her frustration over her own failed pregnancies. She would often mix reality with elements of fantasy and paint scenes relating to pain and death. She used self-portraits to communicate her emotions and ideas relating to her pain as well as to explore her identity.

Political Ideas

Artists can use their artwork to support or criticize **political ideas**. Political protest is an often-used theme in artwork. The imagery in artwork can show the devastation caused by political decisions and the harm they can cause to innocent people. Pablo Picasso's *Guernica* (1937) is one of the best-known antiwar paintings in history. Picasso created this to depict the violence, chaos, and suffering of war. Picasso focused on how war affected innocent civilians, and he depicted this in his work, showing the pain and suffering inflicted by the Spanish Civil War. The imagery and title reflect the bombing of the town Guernica by German and Italian war planes. *Guernica* was painted in black, white, and gray, and it depicts a wounded horse, a woman holding a dead child, and a woman with her arms raised in horror, among other imagery. The woman's hand suggests the shape of an airplane. The color scheme allows the viewer to concentrate on the imagery without being distracted by other colors. To many, this painting has become a symbol of the devastation and horrors of war.

Social Ideas

Artists will often reflect the social climate surrounding them through the subjects that they portray in their artwork. They can choose to portray marginalized populations, bringing social issues to the attention of a larger population. Romare Bearden is an African-American artist known for capturing the social and cultural climate of African-American neighborhoods in his collages. During the civil rights movement in the 1960s, he began to use cut paper and magazine clippings to portray the culture and community in African-American neighborhoods and to celebrate themes such as jazz music, the rural South, blues musicians, religion, and spirituality. He focused on unity and cooperation within the African-American community.

Another example of art reflecting society and culture is the social realism movement. Social realism artists sought to highlight the "forgotten" members of society, such as the poor, immigrants, and racial minorities. During the 1920s and 1930s, these artists portrayed the common worker as the backbone of society, and their artwork showed political corruption, materialism, joblessness, and poverty, among other social and political issues at the time. This example by Ben Shahn is a mural called *The Meaning of Social Security*, and it is an attempt to depict Franklin D. Roosevelt's speech on the upcoming social security legislation and the ambitions of the New Deal programs.

Women's Emerging Role

During the medieval era, women would work with men to create manuscript illuminations and embroideries. During the Renaissance, though, some women artists gained international reputations, thanks to shifts in culture such as humanism. Humanism emphasized the value of all people. During the baroque period, women began depicting women as strong figures, and they also began painting still-life artworks. In the 18th century, women began to be accepted as students by famous artists and two women founded the Royal Academy of Arts in London. In the 19th century, women began to gain access to formal art education and more women began to exhibit their artwork. Photography was an accessible medium for women, with no formal training or traditions to constrict their creativity. In the 20th century, particularly the 1960s onward, feminism played a role in increasing the focus on women artists as well as their presence in formal training and prominent exhibitions. In 1985, the anonymous female artist group the Guerrilla Girls spoke out strongly about gender inequalities, especially in the art world.

Reflecting the Current Economy

Artists can use their artwork to show how the economy is affecting certain populations and bring this awareness to a wider audience. One example of this is the visual depiction of the economic ruin caused by the Dust Bowl. In the 1930s, dust storms swept through the American West and wiped out many farms and ranches. The land was ravaged by drought and rolling clouds of dust. Farmers lost everything and had no way to make a living. The Dust Bowl, as it was called, was reflected in the artwork of the time. The artists who depicted this event attempted to show how it affected farmers and the economy. Below is Thomas Hart Benton's lithograph *Prodigal Son* from 1939, which shows the desolate and wasted land as well as the farmer mourning it. The farmer is meant not to represent one single man, but all farmers who were affected by this tragic event. Benton approached the topic symbolically, showing the ruined land and home, animal carcass, and the man who will have to move on from his land.

Another artist who depicted the Dust Bowl was Alexandre Hogue. Whereas Benton saw this event as something happening to passive victims, Hogue saw it as something created by man's effect on nature. Hogue showed the slashes and furrows made in the land and the ruined green plains.

Influences in Popular Culture

Pop art served as both an art movement and a cultural movement. Pop art used images and objects from popular culture and blurred the line between "high art" and mass-produced cultural objects. This movement elevated common items to fine art, rather than sticking to traditional art themes. Andy Warhol took mundane Campbell's soup cans and Brillo boxes, creating repeated images and objects based on them, and showing them as artwork. Many pop artists, including Andy Warhol and James Rosenquist, began as commercial artists.

Warhol began to mass-produce his artwork, much like the products he was depicting were also mass-produced. In doing this, he equated artwork to a commodity that can be bought and sold, just like these products. Warhol would use bright colors, high contrast, and multiple prints of the same image, as if you were seeing the product repeated on a store shelf. The repetition, bright colors, and contrast of pop art are still used today in advertisements, perpetuating the link between art and culture.

Technology and Art

Technology is used in conjunction with art in many different ways. Some artists use technology within their art, such as video artists. Others use computers, digital cameras, and scanners to create art, such as electronic artists or graphic designers. This art can be printed repeatedly, and multiple copies can be shown or sold. For those who do not use a form of technology to create their art, they might use it to compose a scene. An artist can use digital photography to capture images to work on, or he or she could use computer software to compose the artwork before drawing or painting it. An artist might draw or paint from life with no assistance from technology, but then he or she may use technology to document the work and put it online on a website for others to view. Technology can also be used to keep records of work or to submit artwork to art competitions across the world.

Architecture

African Architecture and Its Purpose

The **architecture in Africa** is diverse, and its structure and materials depend on the region. Architecture in North Africa is largely influenced by Islamic architecture, with intricate tilework, domes, and courtyards. West African architecture is earthen, using sunbaked mud bricks and plaster. East Africa has a blend of influences like Persian, Indian, and Arab shown in the Swahili architecture along its coast. The architecture of central Africa is not as well documented but is known to use local materials like bamboo, thatch, and wood. In southern Africa, architecture is often made of stone.

Buildings are designed to stand up to local conditions, such as insects, heavy rains, or intense sun. Many African structures have repetitive patterns and geometric designs. They are designed with aesthetics in mind as well as the cultural identity expressed by the unique ethnic groups. Many societies live in communal compounds with extended families, where the architecture supports interaction. Houses are made to be cool in hot climates and to guard against cold temperatures. Religious buildings like churches, mosques, and spiritual huts serve as points for community gatherings. Marketplaces and town halls are central areas for trading and holding meetings.

Examples of African Architecture

The **Great Mosque of Djenne** in Mali was built in 1907 on the Bani River's floodplain. It is made of adobe and was the second mosque to be built. The first was constructed around the 13th century and was found to have fallen into ruin by a French explorer in 1828. It is built on a raised platform to prevent flooding. It is the main worship site in the city and the biggest mud and brick building in the world.

The **Kasubi Tombs,** built in 13th century Uganda, are a burial site for four Bugandan kings and their families. It's an important political and religious site for the community and is known for its plant-based construction materials. The site includes a main building with surrounding smaller buildings. Some buildings were destroyed by a fire in 2010, but the remains are still intact.

The **Pyramids of Meroe** in Sudan are a group of steeply sloped Nubian pyramids that served as burial sites for Kushite monarchs, royal family members, and officials. There are three cemetery groups. While there are around 1,000 total graves, around 150 of the gravesites are pyramids. They were constructed from the third century BC to the fourth century AD and are the best relics remaining of the Kush kingdom.

Asian/Eastern Architecture and Purpose

Eastern and Asian architecture includes a wide range of styles and purposes depending on the region. Some architecture has a religious or spiritual purpose, like Hindu temples in India, Buddhist temples throughout East and Southeast Asia, mosques in the Middle East, and Shinto shrines in Japan. Other architecture has a political purpose, like Imperial palaces in China and Japan or some of the fortresses throughout India and other regions. Some notable examples of Eastern architecture include the Great Wall of China, which is a defensive wall; the Taj Mahal, which is a mausoleum in India; and Angkor Wat, which is a temple complex in Cambodia.

Asian architecture often includes decorative elements that are intricately ornamented and contain symbolic meaning. Islamic architecture uses calligraphy and geometric patterns to show the infinite nature of Allah. Hindu and Buddhist structures contain statues and carvings of deities and myths. Colors are often symbolic as well. Chinese architecture often includes red and gold, which are associated with prosperity and luck.

Mesoamerican Architecture and Purpose

Mesoamerican architecture was created from 1500 BC to the early 16th century AD by pre-Columbian civilizations like the Aztec, Maya, Olmec, and Teotihuacan cultures. They commonly created pyramid-shaped structures out of stone with flat tops for altars or temples. They also made large, open plazas, elaborate palaces, and ball courts for playing a sport.

The architecture had a variety of purposes. The pyramids and temples were built for religious and ceremonial use. They made sacrifices and astronomical observations. Palaces were centers for political power, where rulers lived and governed. They symbolized the power of the ruler's authority. Ball courts were used for playing a ritualistic ball game. Plazas and markets served as a hub for both social and economic dealings. The Teotihuacan culture created the Pyramid of the Sun and the Pyramid of the Moon, which were massive religious centers. The Mayan civilization made the Tikal, which is a complex of 3,000 structures that includes pyramids and palaces. The Aztecs constructed Tenochtitlan, a capital city with a major religious temple.

Examples of Mesoamerican Pyramids

El Castillo is the best-known pyramid located at the Chichen Itza archaeological site. Chichen Itza was a large city built by the Mayans between the 8th and 12th centuries AD. This step pyramid in the center of the ancient city is a set of square terraces with steps going up the center of each side. With 91 steps on each side, plus another step at the top, there is a total of 365 steps, which is the same as the number of days in a solar year. There is a temple on top of the pyramid. The building was constructed as a temple to Kukulcan, the Mayan feathered serpent deity.

Teotihuacan is an ancient Mesoamerican city in Mexico that is the site of several prominent pyramids. The Pyramid of the Sun was constructed around 200 AD, and the Pyramid of the Moon was constructed around 250 AD. The pyramids were built on top of earlier structures. They served as the focal point of the city. The Pyramid of the Sun was the largest structure built in Mesoamerica at the time. A tunnel-like cave has been found under the Pyramid of the Sun, and the chambers at the end were used for rituals. Since the temple on top of the pyramid has been destroyed, it is unknown what the purpose of the pyramid was. The temple at the top of the Pyramid of the Moon was built to honor the Goddess of Teotihuacan, who was the goddess of fertility, water, and the Earth.

Egyptian Architecture and Context

Ancient Egyptian architecture was mainly created along the Nile. It was designed to reflect the world's perfection at its moment of creation, as well as reflecting the relationship between the king, humankind, and the gods. Art and architecture in ancient Egypt were not meant to show the artistic creativity of individuals. Iconic examples of ancient Egyptian architecture include the pyramids and the Sphinx.

The **Giza Necropolis** is a complex of pyramids consisting of three main and several smaller pyramids. These were constructed during the Fourth Dynasty, between 2613 and 2494 BC, and served as grave sites for pharaohs. They show the great power of the pharaohs as well as the incredible engineering skills of the Egyptians. The Great Pyramid of Giza is the oldest and largest pyramid in the world. It is the only monument left standing of the Seven Wonders of the Ancient World.

The **Great Sphinx of Giza** is a monument of a mythical creature reclining near the Giza Necropolis. It was built during the Old Kingdom of Egypt between 2575–2150 BC. It was created for the builder of the Khafre pyramid, one of the three large pyramids at Giza. This monolith was carved from bedrock, which also served as material for the pyramids.

Classical Architecture

Classical architecture includes buildings that employ the principles and aesthetics of Greek and Roman architecture. This style includes a post and beam system with columns bearing the load. The pediment (shown) is the triangular part of a building above the columns. It might include elaborate sculptures within. Greek architects used the golden mean, or golden ratio, to create their ideal proportions for some of their buildings.

Columns were units of measurement in human scale, and several styles, orders, were developed over time. Caryatids were stone carvings of females, used as support pillars, which functioned as columns in Greek architecture. Greek architecture often used marble and stone, but the Roman discovery of concrete enabled the construction of arches, domes, and vaults, as used in the Pantheon in Rome. Whereas Greek temples were invariably oriented east to west, Romans would orient their temples with respect to the other surrounding buildings.

Greek and Roman Column Orders

Ancient Greek architecture has three distinct column orders. These styles are distinguished by their proportions and their unique characteristics. The Doric order is the simplest design, with a flat and unadorned design for the top and bottom of the column. This order is four to eight times its diameter. The Ionic order consists of spiral scrolls, or twin volutes, at the tops of the columns. This column's height is nine times its bottom diameter. The Corinthian order is much more ornate, embellished with floral designs. This column is taller, at 10 times its diameter.

The Romans adopted all of these column styles, and they later added two of their own. Their Tuscan order is very plain, and it is a simplified version of the Doric order. The composite order is a blend of the Ionic and Corinthian orders, using the scrolls of the Ionic order and the floral motifs of the Corinthian order.

Byzantine Architecture

Byzantine architecture is the architecture of the Byzantine, or later Eastern Roman Empire. This style was highly influenced by Greek and Roman architecture. Buildings became more complex, geometrically; in addition to stone, bricks and plaster were used in some instances. Mosaics were used in place of carved stone decorations, and many domes were used at this time. The architects used pendentives to support a circular dome over a square space, or they used an elliptical dome over a rectangular space. Prior to this, domes were used over circular spaces. Most of the surviving examples of Byzantine architecture are sacred in nature.

The greatest surviving example of Byzantine architecture is the Hagia Sophia in Constantinople (shown). A huge dome was constructed over a square space. The interior of the church included colored marble and other stones, and the vaults and domes were covered with elaborate mosaics.

ROMANESQUE ARCHITECTURE

Romanesque architecture is a style of medieval Europe beginning around the 11th century. This style is characterized by semicircular arches for doors and windows, and barrel or groin vaults. Many castles and churches were built in this style. Romanesque churches had large, thick walls and piers with few windows, a large tower where the nave and transept cross, and smaller towers at the western end of the church. An arcade, or row of columns, was constructed in the center of larger churches, separating the nave from the aisles. These buildings, both secular and sacred, give a feeling of solidity and strength by their massive size, thick walls, and masonry construction. Instead of relying on columns for support as in Greek and Roman architecture, this style, like the Byzantine style, relies more on walls. This example shows the few small arched windows that exemplify the Romanesque style.

Gothic Architecture

The **Gothic architecture** style in Europe spanned from the mid-12th to the 16th century. Architects sought to solve problems created by simple, dark, damp buildings from previous styles and instead create light, airy, beautiful structures. Gothic architecture is characterized by grand tall designs with upward visual movement. New building techniques allowed builders to create taller towers. The flying buttress is a defining element of this style, and it helped to allow these new heights. The pointed arch is another characteristic of medieval architecture, along with the advent of vaulted ceilings and gargoyles. Gargoyles serve a practical purpose as a drainage spout, but they also serve as decorations with evil or menacing features. The medieval style is known for being ornate, as seen in this example of the Amiens Cathedral in France. Beauty and aesthetic considerations are shown in the designs for these highly decorative buildings.

Balustrade, Pediment, and Flying Buttress

A **balustrade** is a series of pillars, or balusters, that support a rail to form a low wall or barrier. This could also be used for an ornamental parapet or balcony.

A **pediment** is the triangular gable used in classical Greek temples, as well as Renaissance and neoclassical architecture. It is found under the roof of the building and above the entablature. This would usually be on top of a portico or columns. The triangular area within the pediment is called a tympanum, and this was usually decorated with relief sculptures.

A **flying buttress** (shown) is a masonry support that transmits the thrust of a vault or a roof into the outer support. This is usually an inclined bar on a partial arch that extends, or flies out, from the wall and carries the weight of the vault or roof. This architectural element developed in Gothic architecture, from prior hidden supports in previous styles. This helped architects create the high ceilings characteristic of Gothic-style churches.

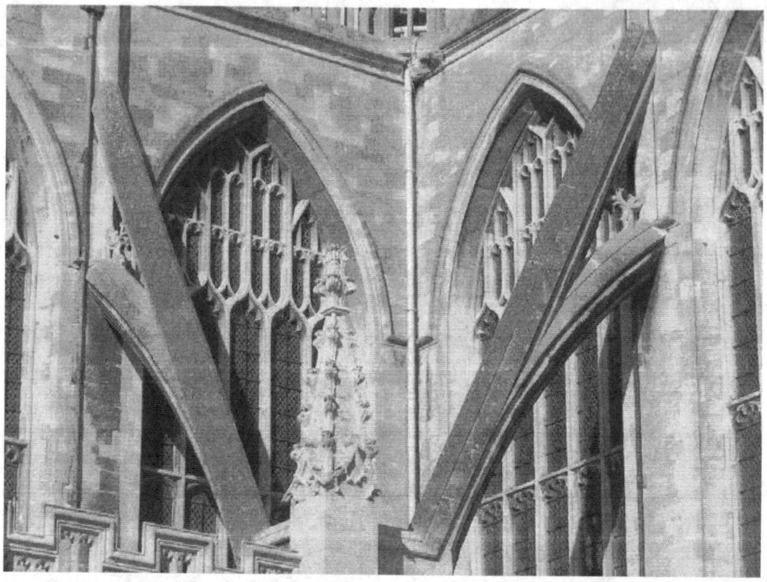

Spire, Facade, Caryatid, and Entablature

A **spire** is a tapering structure that comes to a point at the top of a building. These are often found on skyscrapers and church towers. A spire can function as a symbol of the power of religion, giving a sense of strength and reaching toward heaven.

The architectural term **facade** comes from a French word meaning "face." The facade of a building is its front or face, and this is often the most important design aspect when planning a building.

A **caryatid** is a stone carving of a female figure, draped in clothing, used to support an entablature. This caryatid, as shown, was used in place of a column in a Greek building. The entablature is the upper section of a classical order, and this is divided into the architrave, frieze, and cornice. The architrave is the lowest section of the entablature, which rests on the columns. The frieze is the middle section, in which relief sculpture might be found. The cornice is the crowning molding that will be found directly under the pediment.

Basilica, Apse, Nave, and Transept

A **basilica** was originally a type of Roman building, but this later became the basis for the design of the Christian church. In ancient Rome, a basilica was a public building in which courts were held, and other public functions were held there as well. The basilica would be centrally located in town, near the main forum. It is a rectangular building divided by rows of columns, or colonnades, into three aisles. The center aisle is called the nave. The nave runs from the entrance or vestibule of the church to the apse. The apse, or chancel, is the vaulted semicircular structure at the end of the center aisle. This is where the altar would be located. The transept is part of the church that lies across the main body and forms the cross shape. In this illustration, it is just before the apse.

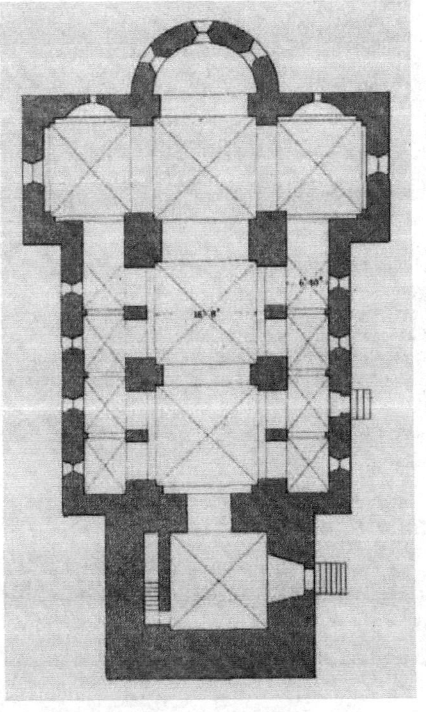

Obelisk, Oculus, Pilaster, and Rotunda

An **obelisk** is a tall, four-sided structure that is freestanding and tapers to a pyramidal point. These were often found at the entrances to Egyptian temples, and they continue to be used in Western architecture. One well-known example is the Washington Monument in Washington, D.C.

Oculus is the Latin word for "eye." In architecture, it is a circular opening in the center of a dome, and it is a feature in Roman, Byzantine, or neoclassical buildings. An oculus can also be found in a wall. The oculus in the Roman Pantheon is open and allows rain in, which leaves the building through drains in the floor.

A rotunda is a building that is round inside and out and is topped with a dome. A rotunda can also be a large interior space topped with a dome.

A pilaster (shown) is a flat, upright architectural element that projects from a wall, giving the appearance of a column inset in the wall. A pilaster only functions as decoration, not as support.

Renaissance Architecture

Renaissance architecture occurred in Europe between the 14th and 17th centuries. This style followed Gothic architecture, and was itself followed by the Baroque style. The Renaissance style emphasized proportion, geometry, and symmetry, and it included orderly composition of the columns and pilasters they used. These architects used semicircular arches, as well as hemispherical domes. The building plans are square and symmetrical, and facades are symmetrical as well. Church facades would usually be topped by a pediment, as shown in this example of St. Peter's Basilica. Renaissance architecture used the Greek and Roman orders of columns, either as structural objects or as purely decorative pilasters. The dome was used often as a large external feature or as a structural internal dome. Doors would have square lintels, and openings without doors would have arches with a decorative keystone. The keystone is the top center stone in an arch that carries the load of the arch structure. Moldings and decorative details were created with great attention to detail because they found it critical to master the techniques of the ancient Romans.

Baroque Architecture

Baroque architecture originated in Italy in the late 16th century, and it was prevalent in areas including Germany and South America until the 18th century. The baroque style is characterized by complex architectural plans often based on an oval design, with broader naves in an oval shape. Other characteristics include purposely fragmented elements, dramatic lighting and contrast, large frescoes on the ceiling, trompe l'oeil paintings, sumptuous colors and decorations, pear-shaped domes, and marble or faux finishing in the interior. The interior might also include bronze gilding, sculpted angels, and twisting columns. Baroque architects sought to explore new forms and styles as well as methods of lighting. They were using this architectural style to express the wealth and power of the Catholic Church during the time of the Counter-Reformation, a movement in response to the Protestant Reformation.

Rococo Architecture

The **rococo** style of architecture began in Paris in the early 18th century. It then spread throughout France and other countries. The rococo style first developed in interior design and decorative arts; then it expanded to architecture and other arts. This architectural style is characterized by pastel colors, serpentine lines, and excessive, elaborate ornamentation. The exterior of a rococo building will be simple, and the interior is filled with ornament and decoration, with the intent to wow the viewer. Floor plans of churches were complex, sometimes with interlocking oval shapes, and the stairways of palaces became ornate, central focuses. This style was meant to be highly theatrical and have something for a visitor to see at every turn. One example of rococo architecture is St. Andrew's Church in Kiev, Ukraine (shown). This facade shows a simplicity with a pastel blue and some ornamentation, but in keeping with the style, the interior is much grander and more elaborate.

Neoclassical Architecture

Classical architecture of ancient Greece and Rome was revived later with neoclassical architecture in the mid-18th century. This style began as a reaction to the excessive ornamentation of the rococo style. This international movement was characterized by a return to the clarity, restraint, and balance, as well as subjects and motifs, of classical styles. Neoclassical architecture used columns, especially the Doric order, and it showed a desire for blank walls rather than decorations. The roof would be flat, sometimes with a pediment, and the facade would be flat and long, with a wall of columns across. No domes or towers were used in this style. Examples of this style include the National Mall and the Lincoln Memorial in Washington, D.C. (shown). The

Lincoln Memorial exemplifies the long, flat facade with a row of columns and the flat roof used in this style of architecture.

Art Nouveau Architecture

The **art nouveau style of architecture** was popular in the United States and Europe beginning in the 1880s, and it declined around 1910. Architects using this style sought to express modern ideas and use nontraditional forms in their buildings. This is sometimes referred to as the first modern architectural style. It is characterized by curved, graceful lines and decorations influenced by nature including leaves, vines, peacocks, and dragonflies. Ironwork and glass were used as sculptural elements as architects tried to embrace what was then possible because of the industrial revolution. These buildings also might contain mosaics, stained glass, and Japanese motifs. The architectural detail was often colorful and decorative, helping bring in the new, modern era.

This example, the Casa Batlló in Barcelona Spain, was remodeled and redesigned by Antoni Gaudi in 1904. It has the irregular shapes and flowing stone sculptural work that is characteristic of the art nouveau style. The facade is decorated with a mosaic made from broken tiles, and the roof is arched and rounded.

Beaux Arts Architecture

The **beaux arts architectural style** was taught from the 1830s to the end of the 19th century at the École des Beaux-Arts in Paris. From there, it strongly influenced architecture in the United States. Beaux arts architecture drew from Greek and Roman styling and included arched and pedimented doors, arched windows, flat roofs, columns, and symmetry. Beaux arts may also include sculptural details as well as classical details such pilasters, garlands, and balustrades. Interiors often have grand stairways and marble floors, with arched doorways and large rooms. Government buildings may have domes and high, vaulted ceilings.

The San Francisco Opera House (shown), built in 1932, is an example of the beaux arts style in the United States. The bottom floor is rusticated, with rough-cut stones. The top floor features columns and archways, as well as a low-pitched roof.

Neo-Gothic Architecture

Neo-Gothic architecture, also known as Gothic Revival or Victorian Gothic, is a style that occurred in the late 18th century in England. The use of this style increased in the early 19th century as architects sought to revive the Gothic architecture style. This style follows the original Gothic architectural style, with pointed arches for doors and windows; steeply pitched roofs; decorative ornamental patterns; spires; leaded glass, quatrefoil, or clover-shaped windows; pinnacles; grouped chimneys; stone carvings of gargoyles, leaves, and birds; and sometimes patterned brick or multicolored stone. A Gothic Revival building will emphasize vertical elements, leading the eye up to the sky. The style was often used in church architecture and also in the construction of colleges.

This example is the Salt Lake Temple in Utah, and it exhibits many of the Gothic architecture characteristics, including the emphasis on vertical elements. The spires are also reminiscent of the Gothic style.

ART DECO ARCHITECTURE

The **art deco style of architecture** began in Paris in 1903. This style was applied to apartment buildings and public structures, but rarely to private homes. Art deco architecture used rectangular, block-like forms, arranged geometrically, with these elements broken up by ornamental and curved decorative motifs. This style was sleek and linear, with a modern feel. Buildings were embellished with repetitive designs, such as chevrons or geometric shapes, and these decorations might be machine made rather than hand-crafted. Art deco emphasized the horizontal rather than the vertical, and for practicality, a simple geometric box-shaped building could be embellished in this style to create a modern fashionable design on a budget. Materials used in art deco architecture were smooth stone, terra-cotta, stucco, steel, aluminum, and glass blocks.

The Chrysler Building, built in New York City in 1928, is an example of this architectural style. It includes ornaments protruding from the corners, as well as contrasting brickwork and emphasis on horizontal elements.

Bauhaus Architecture

Bauhaus architecture developed from the Bauhaus School of Art and Design in Germany beginning in 1927. The Bauhaus School sought to connect art with design and technology. The director of this school was Walter Gropius, who was a German architect known as a pioneer of modern architecture. The architectural style is simple and straightforward, following the Bauhaus minimalist and industrial aesthetic. Bauhaus architects sought unadorned functionality rather than aesthetics, and they often used a limited palette of neutral colors. This style favored function over form. Gropius designed door handles that became a well-known component of Bauhaus architecture and design.

The Bauhaus Building in Dessau, Germany (shown), built in 1926, is attributed to Gropius and embodies the Bauhaus style. The building is simple, with a clean design and geometric styling, and it uses a limited palette other than the red doors. This building is an example of Bauhaus architecture valuing function over aesthetics.

The Prairie School Movement

The Prairie School was a style of architecture prevalent in the Midwestern United States in the late 19th and early 20th centuries. Most architects associated with this movement were employed by Frank Lloyd Wright or Louis Sullivan, but Sullivan himself is not considered an architect of this style. The Prairie School style was used on some public buildings, but it is mostly known for home design. Common features include an emphasis on horizontal lines, overhanging eaves, low pitched or flat roofs, an open floor plan, clean lines, strings of windows in a row, built-in cabinetry, and the use of natural materials such as stone and wood. Wright favored geometric shapes as decorative designs in his buildings, whereas some other Prairie School architects used floral and circular geometric decorations. This example, Wright's Frederick C. Robie House in Chicago, Illinois, shows the clean lines, horizontal emphasis, overhanging eaves, and emphasis on geometric shapes prevalent in this style.

Skyscrapers

Architect Louis Sullivan is known as the "father of skyscrapers" and is considered the originator of the modern skyscraper. The name skyscraper was first used in the 1880s as the first skyscrapers were built in the United States. Originally this referred to buildings containing 10 or 20 stories, but later it came to describe buildings higher than 40 or 50 stories tall. After the first safe passenger elevator was created in 1857 and a need for more business space arose in cities, it became desirable to build buildings more vertically than horizontally. The refinement of the steel process in the 1860s also allowed for taller buildings to be constructed. These buildings had a steel skeleton rather than load-bearing walls, and this steel construction allowed these skyscrapers to rise to greater heights. This load-bearing steel frame was developed by architect William

Jenney. Sullivan's Wainwright Building (shown), built in 1891, was the first building with a steel frame and vertical bands to emphasize its height. It is considered the first skyscraper.

The International Style of Architecture

The **International style of architecture** developed after World War I in the 1920s and 1930s, and it emphasized modern design. This was the dominant style of architecture until the 1970s, and it was influenced by the de Stijl and Bauhaus movements. This style is characterized by industrial materials, linear or geometric forms, and an absence of ornamentation. Glass, steel, and reinforced concrete were the main building materials. The style grew from a desire to get away from eclectic and mixed architectural styles and decorations, the development of new construction technologies, and a growing need for office buildings and other industrial structures. These architects took advantage of the inexpensive mass-produced iron and steel, and sheathed the buildings in glass, creating a new, modern look for the era. Prominent architects of this style include Walter Gropius, Ludwig Mies van der Rohe, Le Corbusier, and Philip Johnson. A notable example (shown) is van der Rohe's Seagram Building in New York, built in 1958.

Grotesque, Plinth, Keystone, and Stringcourse

- A **grotesque** is a carved mythical creature that is used for decoration on a building. Grotesques look similar to gargoyles, but gargoyles have a functional purpose as a water spout that carries water away from the side of a building.
- A **plinth** is the square slab at the bottom of a column. This term can also refer to a flat block at the base of a door, or a projecting course of brick or stone at the base of a wall.
- A **keystone** is the wedge-shaped stone at the top of an arch. This stone locks the arch pieces in place; it is the last piece placed in the arch to give stability to the structure.
- A **stringcourse** is a projecting horizontal course, or band, of bricks or stonework on a building. It can be thin and undecorated or larger and ornate. This stringcourse, above the window, runs along the building horizontally and has a decorative pattern.

The Principles of Form and Function

The principle "form follows function" is associated with modernist architecture and design. It suggests that the design of a building should be led by its function, or purpose. This quote is attributed to American architect Louis Sullivan, who is known as the "father of skyscrapers," as well as America's first modern architect.

Sullivan saw the purpose of the building as determining the form, reflecting the activities that will happen inside, instead beginning with a design and fitting the function to it. This became a maxim of modernist architects in the 1930s, who thought that decorative elements were inessential and should not be used in the design of modern buildings. Sullivan, however, continued to use some decorative art nouveau and Celtic elements in his designs, including green ironwork that became a recognizable hallmark of his work. Sullivan was a mentor of Frank Lloyd Wright, who later altered the saying to "form and function are one."

Art from Around the World

Prehistoric Art

Prehistoric art is art that was produced in preliterate times, prior to writing or recordkeeping. The first known art is from the Paleolithic era, and it consisted of petroglyphs, cave paintings, and sculptures and carvings in bone. Humans were making art to express ideas and to represent their beliefs and surroundings visually. One of the earliest representational artworks from prehistory is the *Venus of Willendorf* (shown), from roughly 28,000 BC.

In China and Japan, prehistoric pottery has been found, as well as bronze figures. In Europe, cave paintings were found in Lascaux and Chauvet, France, and in parts of Spain. Aboriginal painted rock art has been found in Australia, and engravings and paintings on stone and walls have been found in African caves. A large percentage of known prehistoric art is attributed to hunters and foragers. Repeated motifs include animals, humans, tools, maps, and symbols. Portable objects, such as rocks and bones, and stationary surfaces, such as cave walls, were used for art creation.

Characteristics and Purpose

Whereas some think that cave art was purely decorative, others think it was created for other reasons. Some of the cave walls used were remote and inaccessible, so it is thought that they were used for religious ceremonies, perhaps to summon better hunting conditions. Animals and other figures were generally depicted from a simplified side view. Artists painted and drew animals, hunting scenes, landscapes, maps, and many different symbols.

Petroglyphs have also been found, which are prehistoric rock carvings created by removing parts of the rock. Some show real subjects, whereas others are abstract. They might have been used to convey information or for religious purposes. Some might even be a form of prewriting, or a way to map the stars.

The Venus figurines from prehistory are women with exaggerated features, and they are thought to be fertility idols, good luck statues, or a symbol of a mother goddess. The *Venus of Willendorf* is one of the earliest examples of a female nude.

Materials

Paleolithic artists used five main colors: black, white, yellow, red, and brown, as shown in this example from the Lascaux cave art in France. Color pigments were used for body and face decoration long before creating artwork. Some would mix earth or charcoal with animal fat for blacks and browns, and many paintings like this most likely vanished over time. Later rock art that has been discovered used materials such as iron oxide, kaolin, hematite, and manganese. Crayons were developed from solid pieces of pigment, and brushes were formed from animal hairs. Artists would also apply paint with their fingers or a pad made from lichen or moss.

Later in the Stone Age, artists used ochre for yellows, browns, and reds and used manganese or charcoal for black. White was ground calcite or kaolin. The artist would grind the pigment into a powder and mix it with water, blood, animal fat, juice, or other materials to help the pigment stick to cave walls or other surfaces.

Examples of Prehistoric Art

There are several notable examples of cave paintings from prehistory. The **Lascaux** cave paintings in France date back to 15,000 BC. These Paleolithic paintings include detailed depictions of horses, bison, and deer. The large animals depicted in the paintings are ones that were native to the area. Although reindeer were a source of food, they are not depicted in the art. Among the more than 6,000 figures painted are not only animals but also people and symbols. Theories suggest that the artwork depicts successful hunting or possibly a ritual to improve the yield of future hunts.

The Cave of **Altamira** in northern Spain also contains Paleolithic art. This cave complex includes both charcoal and multicolored paintings from between 35,000 and 11,000 BC. The well-preserved petroglyphs, pictographs, and paintings show bison, bulls, and horses, among other animals. This was the first European cave system with prehistoric paintings discovered within.

The **Chauvet-Pont-d'Arc** Cave in France contains artwork from the Upper Paleolithic time. The art is thought to date back to 30,000 BC. This cave was inhabited by humans during two separate periods. The cave's floor includes impressions of cave bear prints and of where the bears slept. The artwork includes animals not seen in other paintings from the time, like hyenas, leopards, bears, and rhinoceroses.

African Art

African art includes painting, sculpture, pottery, masks, textiles, body decoration, jewelry, and rock art. Some African art is aesthetic, some is political or ideological, and some is used for rituals. Characteristics of African art include stylized realism, an emphasis on sculpture, geometric forms, and a focus on the human figure. African artists will tend to visually abstract, or stylize, figures rather than represent them in a naturalistic way.

Sculpture is a preferred art form rather than working in two dimensions. The human figure has often been a main subject for African art, depicted in masks, paintings, and sculptures. Human figures tend to show youthful characteristics because of an emphasis on health and physical strength as well as youth. African artists use geometric forms and symmetry, with repeated geometric shapes throughout an artwork. This example of a mask is symmetrical and includes several geometric shapes.

Context and Purpose

Some African art was created for religious purposes. In addition to regional religions, Christianity and other religions have been practiced there. Some art objects were created for display on an altar or shrine. Other artworks could be used to present sacrificial offerings, to commemorate leaders, or to contact spiritual ancestors. African art objects could also be used to connect with spirits through religious rites or by a religious specialist. These spirits could be summoned for healing or for communicating with ancestors.

Masks were used in performances and rituals with the participation of musicians, dancers, and the audience. When the masked dancer put on the mask, they took on the role of a powerful spiritual being. Many African societies have names for their masks, and these names are connected to the dance, the meaning of the mask, and the spirits associated with the mask.

Examples of African Art

The **Great Zimbabwe birds**, a set of soapstone sculptures created between the 11th and 15th centuries AD, were discovered at the archaeological site of Great Zimbabwe, the capital of the Kingdom of Zimbabwe. The purpose of the birds is unknown, but they are thought to have had religious significance and to have possibly represented a link between the rulers and gods. The Zimbabwe Bird is now a national symbol for the country. It is shown on the country's coat of arms and flag.

The **Benin Bronzes** were created by the Edo people in the Kingdom of Benin, which is modern-day Nigeria. They date back to the 13th century, and they decorated the king's royal palace. The bronzes are plaques and sculptures that show scenes of historical events and important figures. They glorified the king and documented the history of the kingdom. The craftsmanship and intricate designs show high skill in metalworking.

The **Nkisi Nkondi** figures are wooden figures made by the Kongo people in the Democratic Republic of Congo. They have sharp objects, such as nails and blades, driven into them. These figures were used for spiritual and magical intervention and to cure illnesses, settle disputes, and protect villages. They were believed to contain spirits that were capable of punishing people or bringing about good outcomes.

Egyptian Art

Painting, sculpture, and jewelry created in ancient Egypt from 3000 BC to 30 AD has largely been found in monuments and tombs. The artwork is mostly formal, and it follows specific guidelines for depicting figures. The stone statues are rigid and formal, whereas wood figures are more expressive. Ancient Egyptians' two-dimensional art is a combination of people, animals, and symbols. The organization of this artwork depends on the context: For more formal, organized scenes, they are sorted with the more important figures at the top. For a chaotic scene, such as a battle, this organization is not used.

The art we are most familiar with was found in the tombs of wealthy leaders; however, items of lesser quality are found in the burial sites of people of lower status. Statues were used as a conduit for people to interact with their gods. A ka statue is a statue intended as the resting place for a person's life force. Certain conventions were used for the creation of these, such as the sky god Horus always being represented with a falcon head. This consistency gave the figures a timeless quality.

Characteristics and Purpose

Much of the artwork created in ancient Egypt was not meant to be seen; rather, it was mostly created for tombs, and it emphasized life after death. Tombs in ancient Egypt were packed with furniture and food, as well as art and jewelry. The more important and wealthy the person, the more precious artifacts were found in their tomb. These items were meant for the person in their afterlife.

Egyptians used a hierarchy of scale to depict people, leaders, and gods: The larger the figure, the more important they were. Kings and deities might be shown on the same scale. Another common element of Egyptian artwork was hieroglyphs, or images that were symbols for sounds and words. These were the writing system of ancient Egypt, and they often accompanied the artwork.

Two-dimensional scenes were organized in registers, or parallel lines that separated scenes and served as ground lines. People were depicted with a simultaneous profile view and front view.

Materials

Ancient Egyptians used soft stones such as limestone, sandstone, and calcite for sculpture. Copper chisels and stone tools could be used on these softer stones, and ancient Egyptians used copper alloys on harder stones such as quartzite, basalt and granite. Most statues were painted, as evidenced by traces of paint left on them. For wood carving and sculpting, a variety of native woods was used, including acacia, fig, fir, and cedar.

For metalwork, Egyptians used copper, bronze, gold, and silver. Many metal statues were melted down, and the materials were reused. They were able to cut stones for jewelry with precision. They used many stones in jewelry including lapis lazuli, feldspar, jasper, amethyst, and quartz.

The pigments used for painting came from local minerals. They used carbon for black, gypsum for white, iron oxide for reds and yellows, azurite and malachite for blues and greens, and orpiment for bright yellow. Paints were applied directly, or they were layered to create other effects.

Examples of Ancient Egyptian Art

Ancient Egypt created many well-known examples of artwork. One is the bust of Nefertiti, which was created in the 14th century BC. This bust is made of limestone, coated in stucco, and painted decoratively. Nefertiti was the wife of a pharaoh and may have been a pharaoh herself after his death. The bust exemplifies a classical style of Egyptian art. While the purpose of the bust is unknown, it is thought to have been used for creating official portraits of her.

Tutankhamun's Golden Death Mask is an iconic symbol of ancient Egypt. This funerary mask was created around 1323 BC and was made in the likeness of the god Osiris, who is the Egyptian god of the afterlife. The mask was made of copper and covered with a thin layer of gold. It was decorated with semiprecious stones like turquoise, lapis, and obsidian. Tutankhamun's burial chamber in the Valley of Kings contained his sarcophagus, which was opened in 1925 to reveal this mask.

Asian Art

Eastern art does not follow the same aesthetics of the elements and principles as Western art. Asian art does not have a hierarchy of fine arts versus crafts; rather, the skill of craftsmanship is valued, and all types of arts and crafts will be exhibited simultaneously. The crafts of creating porcelain or textiles, for example, have a long and respected history in Asia. Calligraphy, or the art of writing, is also a valued art form, and it has included many different scripts from different times and cultures.

Eastern art focuses more on landscapes and spiritual ideas, rather than representational subjects or realism. It will often be shown on more of a flat plane, instead of showing traditional perspective that is used in Western art. Some common forms of traditional Asian art include silk painting, woodblock printing, and batik, as well as painting with ink on rice paper.

Context and Purpose

Buddhism has had a great influence on Asian art. Mandalas, which are geometric artworks representing the universe, and Buddha statues are examples of this influence. Asian art has sought to depict man's understanding of natural forces and the pattern of nature. The creation of artwork, including calligraphy, could refresh the spirit of the artist. Portraits would attempt to highlight the subject's moral character rather than just faithfully depict the subject. Art showed inspirational themes, and it often stayed away from subjects such as war, violence, death, and nudes. All objects in nature were seen as "alive," and rather than depicting nature realistically, Asian artists would try to capture the inner essence of these things. The artwork is full of symbolism, such as a dragon representing an emperor, or a pine tree symbolizing endurance. In the 1800s, Asian artists began to experiment with Western artistic traditions but turned back to Eastern traditions and began to combine Eastern and Western ideas.

Examples of Ancient Far Eastern Art

Ancient China has a rich history of artwork dating back to Neolithic pottery and jade art. This early art included decorated, unpainted pottery made without the use of pottery wheels. In early Imperial China in 211 BC, more than 8,000 life-sized terracotta warriors and over 500 horses were created to be buried with the First Qin Emperor in his mausoleum. The figures of this **terracotta army** are lifelike and show several different poses. The original colors faded over time, but some are still visible. Each of the figures was created with a uniquely formed head.

The **Jomon art** of **ancient Japan** was created by the Jomon people, who were some of the first settlers of the country. The art and vessels were decorated with cord markings. Some of the early figurines were thought to be fertility figures based on their size and proportions. **Dogu** figurines were created in the late Jomon period, and they were small humanoid and animal earthen figures that were mostly between 4 and 12 inches high. The majority of the figurines were women, and they were thought to be used as a form of sympathetic magic, similar to voodoo dolls.

Examples of Eastern Asian Art

The Great Wave off Kanagawa, by Katsushika Hokusai, was created in 1831. This color woodblock print was part of a series called "Thirty-six Views of Mount Fuji." It is an example of *ukiyo-e* or floating world woodblock prints. This Japanese style flourished from the 1600s to the 1800s and showed scenes from life, theater, and landscapes. The artwork has a limited color palette, and the wave takes up much of the composition, capturing the raw power of nature and the Buddhist theme of impermanence.

Mughal miniatures were small paintings created during the Mughal Empire in South Asia between the 16th and 18th centuries. They include Central Asian, Persian, and Indian techniques. These miniatures had vivid colors and meticulous craftsmanship. They were often only a few square inches and were used for illustrating manuscripts and books. Some lines were so fine that they needed to be painted with a brush made of one hair.

Middle Eastern Art

Middle Eastern or Islamic art includes artwork created by countries in the Middle Eastern region by Muslim and non-Muslim artists. This includes architecture, mosaics, calligraphy, manuscript illumination, metalworking, textiles, and more. Religion is the most important aspect of Islamic art, and the artwork will often include patterns that could be repeated into infinity. This concept is important to Muslims, contrasting the experience of infinity with man's finite existence on earth and disregarding this temporary presence. Another important concept is the dissolution of matter, which can be achieved by applying patterns and decoration to surfaces. Floral patterns were often used for patterns and decorations, and they could be highly intricate and ornate. Calligraphy was integrated into artwork and decorations as an important element, and the inscription is often a quote from the Qur'an.

This image is an example of a repeated infinite pattern as well as dissolution of matter by covering it with a pattern.

The Ardabil Carpet, created between 1539 and 1540 in the town of Ardabil in Iran, is the oldest dated carpet in the world. It is made of wool with silk highlights and has a high knot density. The precise weaving technique shows the artisans' skills. This Persian carpet, made during the Safavid Dynasty, was intended for a major religious shrine and demonstrated the wealth and power of the Dynasty.

South Pacific Art

South Pacific artwork from areas including Polynesia, Melanesia, and Micronesia often uses natural materials that are readily available. Carving wood is a main technique of this artwork, as well as textile work and weaving. Some of the common forms of art include statues and figures carved from stone or wood. These often represent ancestors, gods, or spirits. Elaborately decorated masks are another commonly found form, as well as tall wooden totem poles. Canoe prow ornaments decorate the prow, or front, of canoes.

Some of the regional variations include the tattoos, wood carvings, and tapa cloth designs of Polynesia, as well as their Moai statues and tiki figures. Melanesian art uses complex patterns for carvings and features both masks and totem poles. Micronesian art focuses on weaving and art related to navigation like stick charts, canoe prow ornaments, and paddle decorations.

Purpose and Context

South Pacific artwork showcases the traditions of cultures from Polynesia, Micronesia, and Melanesia. Religious Polynesian art from regions like Hawaii, New Zealand, and Easter Island includes tiki figures used in ceremonies to honor ancestors and deities. The artists often served as priests since making art required adding spiritual powers to the work. Ancestor figures were made of wood and housed the spirits of those who had died. Polynesian tattoos and carvings show lineage and rank within the society. Their navigation-related art reflects their seafaring culture.

Melanesian art from countries like Papua New Guinea, Vanuatu, and Fiji includes figures and masks used for spiritual ceremonies to channel ancestors and other forces. Each object was created for a specific purpose or ritual and was not designed to last. Body painting and elaborate costumes were used in New Guinea, and totem burial poles honored significant family members after they passed.

Micronesia, which includes Palau and the Marshall Islands, has created art relating to navigation, including stick charts and weather charms. Few of their sculptures or paintings were intended to last. The stick charts show where the region's islands were and were used for navigation. Weather charms protected travelers against evil spirits. Canoe prow decorations showed the importance of canoes in their society.

Examples of South Pacific Art

The **Moai statues** of Easter Island are a well-known example of Polynesian art. The monolithic carvings were created between 1400 and 1600 AD. There are more than 900 of them, and they have oversized heads and no legs. The majority were carved from compressed volcanic ash called *tuff*. They are thought to be religious and political symbols, as well as vessels for sacred spirits.

The wooden figures found in Micronesia, called **Nukuoro sculptures** after their origin in Nukuoro, are deity sculptures that represent ancestors and gods. They were created in the late 18th and early 19th century. They were used in homes and temples to ward off bad spirits and ill fortune. These sculptures were made from breadfruit wood and were made smooth using pumice. Their faces are devoid of features, and they are mostly unornamented, but some have carved tattoos.

Bisj poles (also called Bis or Mbis) were created in Vanuatu and New Guinea. They have been created from about 1900 AD to the present. They are made from mangrove trees and are carved for memorial feasts honoring those who passed away recently. Each pole is carved from one piece of wood, and all the roots are removed except for one. The tree is then inverted so that the root projects out from the top. The carvings feature figures of those who have died, and the poles are thought to help the dead pass on to the afterlife.

Aboriginal Art

Early Aboriginal art from Australia included rock paintings (shown) and carvings now found throughout the country, and many are protected in national parks. The rock art is thought to be for decoration or ceremonial purposes. Indigenous art is still created today in Australia and has become popular again since the 1970s.

The European colonization of Australia had a large impact on its artwork. Since the 1700s, Europeans began depicting Australian scenes, landscapes, and natural history illustrations. They attempted to capture the difference in lighting and scenery from the European landscape to the Australian landscape. The Victorian gold rush of the 1850s prompted wealthy landowners and merchants to commission landscape paintings. A distinctly Australian style of painting arose in the late 1800s, focusing on idealized landscapes and plein air painting. The main themes included working and conquering the land, the Australian outback, and the rural pioneer.

Latin American or Precolonial/Mesoamerican Art

Latin American art, from Central and South America, begins with the indigenous people. The first art objects were utilitarian, but eventually they began to produce artwork that represented the values and religions of the different regions. When South America was colonized by Europe, the art forms began to merge and blend. Latin American art is a blend of three cultures: Native American, African, and European. Prior to colonization, many Native Americans lived in Latin America, but then European settlers arrived and brought African slaves. During colonial times, art was usually religious, and it resembled traditional European artwork.

In the 1800s, artists began to develop their own regional styles that departed from European styles and traditions. One important artistic movement is muralism, which began in the 1920s. Hundreds of murals were painted in public places, with social and political messages, ideas of identity, and a theme of unity.

Characteristics

Mesoamerican artwork used a lot of natural materials. Stone was used for sculptures, feathers were used to decorate ceremonial attire, and stones like jade and obsidian were used for carving masks, figures, and tools. Some of the artwork was very colorful, such as the Aztec Portrait of Moctezuma II. Metals such as gold, copper, and silver were used for jewelry and ceremonial items, but not as extensively as in some other ancient cultures. They also created ceramic pottery that was decorated with elaborate designs.

The artwork included themes of mythology and religion with images of gods, scenes from mythology, and religious rituals. It also included plants, animals, and celestial bodies, as well as portraits of people in power. Skeletal figures and underworld scenes highlighted a focus on the afterlife.

Mesoamerican artwork used a mix of realistic depictions of human figures as well as idealized representations. They included stylized geometric patterns and abstract motifs on pottery, textiles, and architecture. They also used artwork to show sequences of events or stories in codices, which were a form of book, and murals.

PURPOSE AND CONTEXT

Mesoamerican artwork was created for a variety of **purposes**. One such purpose was ceremonial and religious. Sculptures, masks, and ceremonial items were created for religious practices. Some objects were used for sacrifices and rituals to appease deities. Some art showed significant astronomical events.

The art showing rulers was used for political propaganda. It showed the divine right of rule and legitimized those in power. It was also used to show the history of the ruling dynasties. Art was used to document legends, myths, and historical events, as well as observations of astronomical events. Art also helped to keep genealogical records of significant families.

These materials and themes were influenced by the diverse environments of the regions, including rainforests and plateaus. Artistic motifs spread through trade and alliances, allowing the cultural heritage to be shared while regional variations were maintained. Mesoamerica's complex system of beliefs and gods remained a central theme throughout the artwork.

EXAMPLES OF PRECOLONIAL/MESOAMERICAN ART

The **Maya Stelae** are tall stone slabs created by the Mayans during the Classic period, which was from 250 to 900 AD. They were carved from limestone, sandstone, or volcanic tuff. These structures are rectangular and measure anywhere from several feet to over 30 feet high. They include elaborate carvings of gods, rulers, and scenes of events. They have hieroglyphic text that explains the events with dates and names.

The **Olmec Colossal Heads** were created from 1400 BC to 400 BC by the Olmec civilization. This area is now the Gulf Coast of Mexico. The heads are carved from basalt boulders and are anywhere from 4.8 to 11 feet high. Many have helmets, and each head is unique. They are considered to be portraits of important figures or rulers. They show the civilization's skill at carving and transporting large stones.

The **Aztec Calendar Stone** was found under the main plaza in Mexico City. It is thought to date back to the early 16th century. The stone is about 12 feet in diameter and has detailed carvings showing elements of Aztec mythology and cosmology. The sun god Tonatiuh is in the center, and the outer rings show the 20 days in the Aztec month as well as other astrological and mythological symbols.

Western Art through the Ages

RELATIONSHIP BETWEEN WESTERN TRADITION AND NON-WESTERN TRADITION ART

Western art is created in America and Europe, while **non-Western** art is the artwork created in other regions of the world. Western art has historically valued individualism and realism, while non-Western art has valued communal identity and symbolism. Despite their differences, both Western and non-Western art have been used for religious ceremonies, to record historical events, and to portray important people. Both types of art have been enriched by their exposure to each other. However, questions about Western art appropriating non-Western artwork and issues of cultural power have also arisen.

Thanks to trade, like through the Silk Road and colonial expansion, Westerners were exposed to non-Western forms of art like Chinese silk painting. Certain Western art movements were influenced by non-Western art, like the influence of Japanese woodblock prints on Impressionists and Post-Impressionists. Modern artists in the early 20th century found inspiration in the stylization and abstract forms from Oceanic and African art.

Large museums like the Louvre include diverse collections that juxtapose non-Western and Western work. The internet has facilitated the exchange of ideas across the world, and virtual exhibitions now allow audiences to easily engage with both Western and non-Western art.

EUROPEAN ART

European artwork began with prehistoric rock painting and carving, and it has developed over the centuries through many different artistic movements. Beginning in the Middle Ages, art would be commissioned by a patron, usually by the church or state. This artwork mainly showed historic, biblical, and religious scenes and religious and political leaders. Secular artwork included landscapes and still lifes. Academies trained artists in methods, materials, and anatomy. They attempted to elevate art from a craft to fine art and began to exhibit artwork. Art was created in workshops by master artists and their apprentices. As the importance of the church and royalty declined, the subject matter changed. The industrial revolution brought changes in technology that included premade, portable paints. Artists became independent and could use their own creativity. Because the academies resisted these changes, innovative artists became avant-garde while academic art stuck to traditions.

NORTH AMERICAN ART

Traditional Native American art flourished in North America prior to colonization. **Early colonial** art was based on European traditions, and artists mainly painted portraits and landscapes. In the 18th century, artists such as Benjamin West, John Singleton Copley, and Gilbert Stuart became some of the first significant American painters. Starting in 1820, the Hudson River School produced romantic landscape painting artists. The American Revolution brought a demand for patriotic artwork, and artists began to document rural America. Prominent 19th-century painters created portraits and painted a wide range of subjects including pioneers, soldiers, and sailors. American impressionism flourished in the 19th century, and in the 20th century, European art continued to impact America. This influence gave rise to the abstract art scene. Many art genres have risen in North America since the beginning of the 20th century, including pop art, minimalism, and photorealism.

GREEK AND ROMAN ART

The great classical art period began in Greece, and this art later greatly influenced Roman artwork. Romans borrowed many elements of their religion from Greece, and they also borrowed art and architectural styles. Ancient Greeks used art to express noble ideas and emotions. They wanted to highlight the great accomplishments of man and honor their gods through their artwork. Sculptures included nude athletes in realistic poses, as shown, as well as gods and goddesses. The artwork was mostly sponsored by the government and made for the public to see, and it was a great source of pride for the people. Art from ancient Greece includes stone and wood statues and pottery in red figure and black figure styles. They also painted on panels and pottery.

Ancient Romans used their artwork more for aesthetics and decoration, rather than for lofty ideals like the Greeks. In Rome, art lost its spiritual quality and was used more to adorn homes. They did copy the Greek statues of gods and goddesses, but they also created skillful and realistic portrait sculptures. In addition to sculptures, they created paintings and mosaics for homes, showing scenes of daily life.

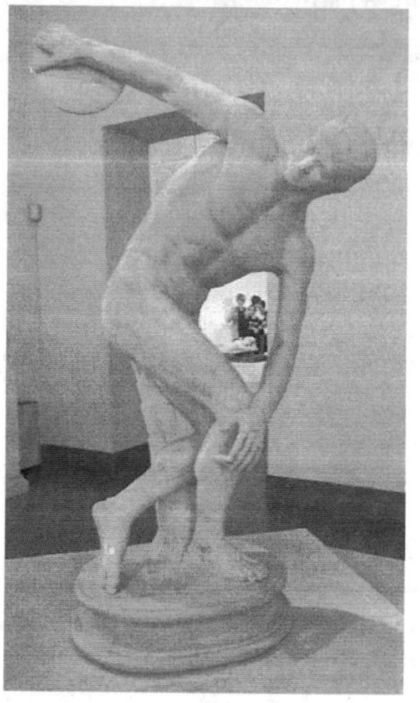

MATERIALS

The Greeks and the Romans used marble and bronze for sculptures. Roman artists used encaustic (pigment mixed with hot wax) and tempera for painting scenes on panels, and they created fresco paintings on architectural surfaces. For mosaics, Romans used small cut pieces of glass, tile, pottery stone, and shells. The pieces were called tesserae, and they were stuck to the surface with mortar.

The ancient Greeks also created wood sculptures in their early period, although few of these have survived. The preferred sculpture materials were marble and limestone, as well as cast bronze. They created figurines from terra cotta and bronze. The Greeks also painted on panels with encaustic and wax, and they painted their sculptures as well as parts of their temples. Most of the paintings that have survived are on pottery. Their pottery had a high iron oxide content, giving it a red color. This example is of the Greek red figure pottery.

CHARACTERISTICS AND PURPOSE OF ANCIENT GREEK/ROMAN ART

While the art of **ancient Greece** and **ancient Rome** include some similarities, their purposes and characteristics differ. The art of ancient Greece was intended to celebrate the philosophical ideals of beauty, the divine, and heroism. Greek art and sculpture emphasized proportion, beauty, and balance. It featured mainly gods, athletes, and mythological figures. The Greeks paid attention to details of the human form, including posture and musculature. The artwork was lifelike and made gods more relatable.

The art of ancient Rome mainly commemorated individuals, especially those in power. The sculptures and busts included people's imperfections in their realistic portrayals. The artwork was more utilitarian and individualistic, showing age as well as unique features. The artwork communicated the achievements and power of Roman leaders. The artists adapted their style from the art of ancient Greece, associating themselves with the prestige of Greek artwork and culture while changing it to make it their own.

Examples of Ancient Greek and Ancient Roman Art

The **Discobolus**, or Disc Thrower, is a well-known example of **ancient Greek** sculpture. This bronze sculpture by Myron was created during the Classical period, around 450 BC. It shows a nude male athlete throwing a discus, standing in a twisted pose. The face shows the Greek ideal of athletes with calm, controlled expressions.

Venus de Milo was created by an unknown sculptor between 130 and 100 BC. This marble sculpture portrays Aphrodite, the goddess of love, in a contrapposto stance with the weight shifted onto one leg. The arms of the statue are missing, and it is unknown what pose they had or what they might have held. She is partially draped in a cloth with her upper body exposed. It was designed to show the divine beauty of the goddess in a human form.

The **Colosseum** of ancient Rome is an iconic piece of architecture located in the center of Rome. Also known as the Flavian Amphitheatre, it was built between 70 and 80 AD and was made from mainly concrete and sand with a limestone facade. The elliptical building was used for public events and had tiered seating that reflected the hierarchy of society.

The statue of **Augustus of Prima Porta** was made of marble and created around 20 BC. This statue portrayed the first Roman emperor, Augustus, in a detailed military breastplate and cloak. His face shows idealized eternal youth, much like Greek tradition, and his right arm extends as if addressing his troops. This powerful piece of political propaganda presented Augustus as an ideal ruler.

Early Christian Art

Early Christian artwork was created from the late second century to the sixth century. It shows the formation of religious identity and theological ideas of early Christians. Since Roman authorities often persecuted the early Christians, much of the art was created secretly. Once Christianity was legalized, Christian art became more visible. The spread and public presence of its artwork accelerated when Christianity was adopted as a state religion of the Roman Empire under Theodosius I in 380 BC.

The purpose of this artwork was to educate faithful followers, most of whom were illiterate, about biblical narratives through visual storytelling. They used allegories and symbols to convey ideas and maintain secrecy during the times they were persecuted. Art was used to adorn worship spaces and to honor martyrs and saints. It helped Christians to develop a distinct identity and fostered a sense of unity.

Medieval and Byzantine Art

The period of medieval art spans more than 1,000 years, from the fall of the Roman empire to the Renaissance period. Subjects explored during this time include mythology, Christian themes, and biblical stories. The medieval period can be separated into Byzantine, Romanesque, and Gothic. Byzantine art was from the Eastern Empire called Byzantium, and it was highly stylized. Byzantine art favored symbolism over realism, and the subject matter included imperial and religious subjects. This example of Byzantine painting shows religious subject matter.

Romanesque art included massive churches built with stone arches, similar to Roman architecture. Romanesque painters created frescoes and used encaustic on panels. Gothic art began in Paris and spread throughout Europe. Its greatest contribution was the cathedral and elaborate architecture with complicated decoration. Painting during the Gothic period included animated figures and expressions, painted small in relation to their backgrounds.

Examples of Medieval and Byzantine Art

There are several notable examples of **medieval art**. The **Bayeux Tapestry,** from the 11th century, is an embroidered tapestry almost 70 meters long showing the events leading to the Norman conquest of England and the Battle of Hastings in 1066. It was commissioned by Bishop Odo of Bayeux, William the Conqueror's half-brother, to serve as a record of the conquest. It legitimized William's claim to the throne of England.

The **Ghent Altarpiece**, from the 15th century, is a polyptych altarpiece made by Hubert and Jan van Eyck for the Saint Bavo Cathedral located in Ghent, Belgium. It was the centerpiece for liturgical ceremonies and meant to inspire devotion by depicting Christian themes in a detailed and symbolic way.

The **Hagia Sophia**, constructed in the sixth century under Emperor Justinian I, was built in Constantinople as a Christian cathedral. It served as the central church of the **Byzantine** Empire as well as a symbol of religious devotion and imperial power. Notable aspects include a massive dome and intricate mosaics.

The **Icon of Christ Pantocrator**, an icon created in the sixth century, is one of the earliest icons of Christ. It is now found in Mount Sinai, Egypt. Icons were used in worship, serving as a focal point for prayer.

Byzantine Characteristics and Purpose

Byzantine art is influenced heavily by Christian themes. This style is a subset within the broader medieval art movement, and it is the artwork specifically of the Byzantine Empire from the 4th to the 15th century. It often shows scenes from the Bible, scenes of the lives of saints, and other Christianity-related events. Icons were the main focus of Byzantine art. An icon is usually a painting of Jesus Christ or another holy figure. They were painted on wooden panels and used for both private and public worship.

Byzantine art is stylized and abstract. It focuses on conveying ideas rather than showing realistic representations. Figures in Byzantine art are shown on a hieratic scale, with more important figures depicted as larger than others to show their significance.

Byzantine art was created mainly for the Eastern Orthodox Church and was used in rituals and religious services as well as private devotional practices. The artworks were focal points for prayer. They were also used as teaching tools to educate people about biblical stories. The saints and holy figures depicted in artwork served as models of virtuous behavior for others to follow.

Medieval Art Characteristics and Purpose

The medieval period of art covered over 1,000 years and several styles from the 2nd century to the 16th century when the Renaissance began. Medieval art mainly depicts Christian subjects, including images of Christ, the saints, and biblical scenes. Much of the art was created to decorate churches, including stained glass, frescoes, altarpieces, and illuminated manuscripts. The art contains allegories and symbols that convey moral and spiritual meaning. It uses symbols or icons for subjects, such as a lamb for Christ, to convey complex ideas. Medieval art lacks linear perspective and often appears flat. Objects and figures are stylized, and they often have vibrant colors and bold outlines. Figures are shown using a hieratic scale, with important figures being larger than those that are less important. Figures placed centrally are more significant than those placed on the sides.

Medieval art was used to educate people on Christianity and convey ethical and moral lessons. The artwork showed the consequences of sin and the benefits of piety. The art was an important part of religious services and was used for personal devotion as well. Artwork in churches and cathedrals inspired awe and helped bring the soul closer to the divine. Some of the tapestries and manuscripts served as a visual record of historical events.

Renaissance Art

The **Renaissance** was a revival of classical learning during the 14th, 15th, and 16th centuries in Europe. Renaissance artists sought to capture the value of the individual and the beauty of the natural world. This revival of drawing, painting, sculpture, and architecture was partly driven by humanism, which is a philosophy that attached importance and worth to the individual. Artists looked to the past for inspiration, while innovating and producing some of the best-known art in history. Artists used naturalism, attempting to portray figures realistically rather than exaggerating or stylizing them. Renaissance artists studied anatomy and perspective, as well as light and shadow, to use them accurately in their artwork. They took ideas from the mythology of classical civilizations and used them as a starting point to create their own monumental works.

During the Renaissance, the ambition of classical civilizations was rediscovered, boundaries were pushed, and artists innovated to capture the beauty of humanity. The Greek idea of humanism was used to celebrate the accomplishments of man. Renaissance artists saw the classical period as the height of humanity and attempted to recreate and build upon this movement.

Increased prosperity during this time led to an increase in commissioned artwork from wealthy patrons (especially the Medici family). At the same time, the church was conflicted on spiritual and secular issues, which helped the spread of humanism. The church was also a big patron of the arts, and it spent a great deal on art and architecture at the time. In addition to the wealth of Italy, Italy also contained a lot of Roman architecture and artifacts, which contributed to the beginning of the Renaissance in this area.

Characteristics and Purpose

The ideas of humanism brought greater attention to detail and greater realism, as well as a focus on virtue. Artists began to use linear perspective foreshortening, bringing a natural realism to faces and figures. Sculptures, drawings, and paintings showed increased knowledge of anatomy. Most painters began to use oil paint rather than tempera at this time, which contributed to this realism.

Christianity was still the main subject of artwork at this time, reflected in the paintings and sculptures of many prominent artists including Michelangelo, Leonardo da Vinci, and Raphael. Stories from mythology were depicted, too, to promote the idea of humanism. During the Renaissance, artists were creating artwork for patrons and their status was raised to a level above craftsman. Because of the Renaissance movement, Western art developed from the ideals of classical artwork.

Altarpieces were commissioned often, and these would be the focal point of the space they occupied. Frescoes were often created in churches and in private buildings. This painting method was time consuming, with a prominent example being Michelangelo's Sistine Chapel ceiling (shown). Patrons also commissioned portraits of themselves and artworks for their homes.

MATERIALS

Frescoes, that is, murals painted onto plaster walls, were painted during the Renaissance period. The pigments were mixed with water and applied to wet plaster, and once the plaster dried, the pigments were visible on the wall. This was a time-consuming process, but it was used for large works of art including the Sistine Chapel ceiling.

Artists also painted with oil paints, which became available in the 15th century. The slow drying time allowed artists to blend and paint with greater realism and detail than before. More colors were available, and the transparency allowed artists to use glazing techniques, layering transparent colors for greater depth and richness. Artists during this time also still painted on wood panels or rigid supports with tempera.

For sculpting, the most common material was marble. Michelangelo's famous sculptures, including *David*, *Moses*, and other notable works, were carved from marble.

LEONARDO DA VINCI, MICHELANGELO, AND RAPHAEL

Leonardo da Vinci, Michelangelo, and Raphael are a few of the best-known artists of the Renaissance period. Leonardo was a "Renaissance man," with knowledge of math, astronomy, architecture, art, inventing, literature, anatomy, and more. His well-known works include the *Mona Lisa* and *The Last Supper*. He pioneered a technique called sfumato, which uses subtle gradations to create a smoky look.

Michelangelo showed a mastery of anatomy in his artworks. His best-known works are his *David* statue and his painting of the Sistine Chapel ceiling. Unlike many artists, he achieved fame as an artist during his lifetime. He was accomplished in art, sculpture, and architecture, and he inspired the artist Raphael.

Raphael is known for his skillful composition, as well as his serene depictions of the greatness of human nature. One of his best-known works is the School of Athens, a monumental work from 1509–1511 depicting many ancient Greek philosophers (shown). This artwork also shows a mastery of perspective, as well as natural poses and lighting.

THE MANNERISM STYLE

The **mannerism** style of art and architecture emerged as a reaction to the high Renaissance. From the end of the Renaissance in the 1520s to the beginning of baroque art in 1590, mannerism focused more on style and technique than the meaning of the subject. Mannerism arose partly from new scientific discovery that man was not the center of the universe, but, rather, the earth revolves around the sun. At the same time, the Reformation movement highlighted a need for church reforms, bringing turmoil and religious uncertainty.

Mannerist artists reflected this uncertainty, attempting to solve artistic problems by changing proportions and portraying people in new and strange ways. These included elongated limbs, small heads, and dramatic, unnatural, contrived poses. Departing from the linear perspective and depth used in Renaissance art, mannerists flattened the composition and arranged the figures on a flat plane, as shown. Mannerism artists experimented with form, portraying emotions, and bright and unusual colors.

El Greco and Tintoretto

El Greco, a nickname meaning "the Greek," painted in the mannerist style, using elongated and strange proportions and portraying strong, dramatic emotions. The poses are strained and unnatural, heightening the emotion conveyed by the subjects. Rather than using accurate lighting, the lighting in his works seem to come from within the figures or from an unseen source. In his later works, he elongated figures even more, especially on altarpiece works. This work from 1600 shows his odd use of lighting and forced, strained poses that illustrate the mannerist style.

Tintoretto, another mannerist painter, created monumental religious works and emphasized the mystical nature of religion. He also used elongated forms and forced poses, but his works show a mastery of lighting along with a better idea of spatial depth. He sought for viewers to experience the divine through his religious depictions. Through lighting and composition, he created a supernatural atmosphere, portraying scenes not from this world.

BAROQUE ART

Baroque art dominated Europe in the 17th and 18th centuries. The style was propagated by the Catholic Church, often in the form of monumental works of public art. This style was meant to counter the rationality and simplicity of the Renaissance style and inspire a sense of awe. Many baroque artworks illustrated Catholic ideas, within biblical or mythological depictions. Architecture, painting, and sculpture all reflected these ideals successfully. Baroque sculpture also used a dramatic sense of movement, contrasting with the comparatively still and calm Renaissance sculptures.

Baroque paintings would often include allegories, which are stories with hidden meaning and messages. The educated viewer was expected to recognize and understand symbols and hidden meanings in the artwork.

The *Trevi Fountain in Rome* (1732, shown) is an example of the overly ornate baroque style in sculpture. Some of the major artists of this time include Rembrandt, Caravaggio, and Peter Paul Rubens.

CHARACTERISTICS AND PURPOSE

The **baroque** art style is characterized by exaggerated motion and attention to detail. The scenes are created to enhance a sense of drama and grandeur. The chiaroscuro technique is often used in baroque art. This is the use of strongly contrasting tones of light and dark, usually in a dramatic, high-contrast scene. Another technique used is tenebrism, which consists of keeping an area black, while a portion of the subject is brightly illuminated, as shown in this painting from 1636.

To set their artwork apart from the Renaissance artworks, artists departed from tranquil scenes and expressions of that time and instead showed intense emotion and movement in their work. Instead of the even lighting of Renaissance artwork, they used more dramatic lighting and they used asymmetry to enhance the sense of instability and movement. Clothing would be moving by wind or the motion of the person instead of draped and resting motionlessly.

Neoclassicism

Neoclassicism occurred during the late 18th and early 19th centuries. This movement in art and architecture was an attempt to revive the classical Greek style and depart from the highly ornate baroque style. It also came about partly from the discovery of Roman ruins at Pompeii and Herculaneum. Neoclassical artwork was serious, stoic, and heroic. Artists portrayed moral narratives of ethical superiority, returning to classical subjects and motifs from Greek and Roman art. This art is characterized by somber colors, shallow space, balance, clarity, and restraint. Artists sought to show smooth paint surfaces with no brushstrokes visible in their artwork.

This movement coincided with the Age of Enlightenment, or Age of Reason, which was an intellectual and philosophical movement focused on reason as the main source of authority. These ideas were also reflected in the art at the time, as artists moved from ornate and frivolous art to more serious, classical subjects. Neoclassical artists had few surviving Greek paintings to model their work after, but they had many more examples of sculpture to follow for their work.

Jacques-Louis David and Jean-Auguste-Dominique Ingres.

One significant artist of the neoclassical style is Jacques-Louis David. His painting *Oath of the Horatii* is a prime example of the neoclassical movement. This painting (shown) tells a story from classical times, from a Roman legend in which the Horatii brothers take an oath to defend Rome. In this carefully organized composition, three arches with columns span the background, whereas all the figures and action are pushed into the foreground as if creating a sculptural relief.

Jean-Auguste-Dominique Ingres was a student of David, and he also created works in the neoclassical style. Unlike David, he began to favor more sensuous subjects and became known for portraits. His work *Oedipus and the Sphinx* (1808) was completed while Ingres worked in Rome. This scene is from the Greek myth of Oedipus, when Oedipus was guessing the riddle of the Sphinx. Ingres won the prestigious Prix de Rome for this painting. Keeping with classical standards, Oedipus is depicted as a beautiful and ideal young man.

Romanticism

The **romanticism** movement began in 1770 and encompassed art, literature, music, and culture. The term romantic refers not to love, but to intense emotion. This movement emphasized emotion and individualism, and it was a reaction against the rationalism of neoclassicism. Romantic artists often illustrated literary themes. They emphasized and depicted emotions such as terror, awe, and apprehension, and they attempted to capture the beauty and sublime feel of nature. This painting by Thomas Cole from 1836, *The Course of Empire: Destruction*, embodies the focus on nature and destruction in a romantic artwork.

This style first manifested in landscape painting, and artists challenged the previously low status of landscape art by painting monumental works. History painters also created large works, portraying disaster, divine wrath, and natural catastrophe. Artists portrayed vast spaces with people dwarfed in comparison, mystical landscapes, and nature's triumph over man. No traditional religious art came from this period, but artists continued to portray small villages and the wilderness, despite the increase of urban spaces.

Eugène Delacroix, Theodore Gericault, Thomas Cole

Several significant artists worked in the romanticist style. Eugène Delacroix was at the forefront of the French school of romantic artwork. In *Liberty Leading the People*, he depicted the female figure of Liberty leading the French Revolution of 1830. It is a history painting, showing a violent, dramatic, catastrophic scene.

Theodore Gericault was another French romantic artist. His work *The Raft of the Medusa* is a significant romantic painting. This work is larger than life size, and it shows the aftermath of the wreck of a French naval frigate, with people escaping on a makeshift raft. It shows men dying and struggling to survive against nature, with strong emotions and an unfolding drama.

Thomas Cole was an American painter who portrayed the American wilderness in the romantic style. One of his well-known works is called *The Oxbow*, which shows a bend in the Connecticut River, in a valley after a thunderstorm. There is a juxtaposition of broken trees, violent cliffs, and dark rain clouds beside blue skies and a tranquil bend in the river.

REALISM

The **realism** movement began in France in the 1850s, as a rejection of the ideas of romanticism. Rather than exaggerated scenes and heightened emotions, realism sought to portray ordinary scenes with accuracy and truth. The artists attempted to show people from all walks of life and social classes accurately and not smooth over or avoid unpleasant subjects. Realist artists did not portray people heroically or sentimentally; instead, they wanted to treat all subjects with equal seriousness. The advent of the camera helped to increase the desire to show subjects realistically.

The realism movement is thought to be the first modern art movement, because the artists rejected traditions and expanded the definition of what is considered art. They examined the political, cultural, and economic structure of society, and they used earthy tones to show what was happening in all parts of society. Realist artists painted real-life events, workers, street life, cafés, peasants, and nightclubs, rather than grand landscapes or posed scenes with extreme emotions.

GUSTAVE COURBET, JEAN-FRANCOIS MILLET, AND HONORÉ DAUMIER

The main realist artists in France were Gustave Courbet, Jean-Francois Millet, and Honoré Daumier. Courbet would paint ordinary scenes on vast canvases that were normally used for history paintings. Two of his well-known works include *The Stonebreakers* (shown) and *A Burial at Ornans*. *The Stonebreakers* was painted in 1849, and it shows ordinary workers in his native region of France. He uses natural color and lighting to portray his subjects.

In the United States, Thomas Eakins and Winslow Homer were significant realism painters. Winslow Homer began as a commercial illustrator, but then he was inspired by Courbet, Millet, and Daumier and began to paint ordinary subjects in America. Eakins painted his friends and local people in outdoor sports, including his work *Max Schmitt in a Single Scull, from 1871.* His most well-known work is *The Gross Clinic*, which showed a scene from a surgical operation, and this was received unfavorably by critics due to its subject matter.

IMPRESSIONISM

The **impressionism** movement began in the late 1800s as artists in Paris began to practice plein air painting together. The artists included Claude Monet and Pierre-Auguste Renoir. Impressionists departed from a faithful depiction of a scene, and instead they attempted to capture their impression of it, or the momentary effect of lighting on the scene. Artists used small brushstrokes and pure color. They tried to capture the optical effects of light, and the differences that weather and sun position create in a scene.

The recent invention and availability of paint in a tube helped spur on this movement. Artists were able to paint outside more easily and capture scenes as they saw them. The emphasis in the painting was as much on the artist's perception of the scene as it was on the scene itself. The painting by Claude Monet, *Haystack. End of Summer. Morning.* from 1891, shows how Monet used color and brushstrokes to capture the lighting of a summer morning on the haystack.

CLAUDE MONET, EDGAR DEGAS, MARY CASSATT, AND AUGUSTE RENOIR

Claude Monet is the most well-known impressionist painter, and some of his subjects include cathedrals, haystacks, landscapes, water lilies, and his garden in Giverny, France. The paintings of his garden included a Japanese footbridge that spanned over water lilies. His paintings became increasingly abstract in later years due to his failing eyesight.

Edgar Degas was an impressionist painter best known for his paintings of ballerinas and dancers. He captured his impression of dance lessons and performances, showing the movement of the moment with visible brushstrokes. This example from 1873–1876, *The Dance Class*, shows a dance class being instructed by the man in the center. He did not capture outside light like other impressionists, but he still captured fleeting moments in time.

Mary Cassatt was the best-known female impressionist painter, and she often painted domestic scenes with a child and mother as the subjects. Cassatt was invited to exhibit with the impressionists by Degas, and she began to be influenced by their work.

Auguste Renoir captured stunning landscapes and beautiful portraits in the impressionist style. The visible brushstrokes, soft edges, and pure colors follow the patterns of impressionist painters, and he shows a masterful understanding of how light affects his subjects.

Postimpressionism

Postimpressionism was a French art movement from 1886 to 1905 that followed impressionism and preceded fauvism. Postimpressionism sought to explore the emotional response of the artist and depart from the naturalism of impressionism. These artists still used bold and pure colors as well as real-life subject matter, but they also leaned toward more geometric shapes, distorted forms, exaggerated or arbitrary colors, and sometimes heavy outlines.

Neoimpressionist Georges Seurat departed from the spontaneous nature of impressionism for a more planned approach that included the optical blending of spots of color. This is now known as pointillism, but it falls under the postimpressionist movement. Paul Signac carried on Seurat's ideas; he helped Seurat develop the pointillism style.

This work by Henri de Toulouse-Lautrec from 1889, titled *Monsieur Fourcade*, shows several major ideas of postimpressionism. Although the artworks and artists of this period are fairly varied, this work does show the bold, arbitrary colors and outlines used in postimpressionist artwork.

Vincent van Gogh, Paul Gauguin, and Paul Cézanne

Vincent van Gogh, a prominent Dutch postimpressionist artist, exhibited many of the ideas of this movement. He used bold colors, sometimes arbitrarily or in odd ways, as well as bold lines to express his emotion through his paintings. In this 1890 painting, *Portrait of Dr. Gachet*, van Gogh expresses emotion through the pose, facial expression, and colors. Bold colors and brushstrokes, along with heavy outlines, are visible in this artwork.

Paul Gauguin used bold and unusual colors, sometimes in flat planes and flattened spaces. This French artist's work includes many paintings of landscapes and people of French Polynesia, where he lived for 10 years.

Paul Cézanne was another French postimpressionist painter, and he is known as the father of postimpressionism. His exploration of geometric shapes and bold colors prompted Picasso and others to eventually experiment with multiple views of forms. He sought to reduce nature to geometric shapes and find new ways of modeling space and volume.

Fauvism and Expressionism

The **fauvism** movement, from about 1905 to 1908, followed the postimpressionism movement and included some similar ideas. Fauvism emphasized strong and unusual colors, using color to express mood without being representational of actual colors. Fauvism also emphasized the flatness of the canvas, and it valued individual expression over naturalistic representation. The leaders of the fauvism movement were Henri Matisse and André Derain.

Expressionism began in Germany at the beginning of the 20th century, and it spanned from roughly 1905 to 1920. Artists of this movement used strong colors and distorted forms to express their feelings in their artwork. Artwork came from within the artist, rather than being copied from what they observed. They used swirling and exaggerated brushstrokes and sought to evoke emotional responses to their works. Edvard

Munch's *The Scream* (1893) is an example of the Expressionist style, with its unusual, nonrepresentational colors, distorted form, and desire to express a strong feeling of despair or agony.

Fauvist and Expressionist Artists

Henri Matisse was a fauvist artist who pioneered the movement. He applied large, flat areas of color to his paintings and worked with bright colors directly from the tubes to convey emotions. He is also considered a leader in defining the 20th-century modern art movement. One of his best-known works of this period is called *Woman with a Hat* (1905). He used unusual colors, including green on the woman's face.

Expressionism began with works of artists such as Vincent van Gogh and Edvard Munch, and then in 1905, German artists formed a group called Die Brücke that began the main wave of expressionism. This group included artists Erich Heckel, Fritz Bleyl, and Karl Schmidt-Rottluff, and they were later joined by Otto Müller, Emil Nolde, and Max Pechstein. Wassily Kandinsky was a notable Russian expressionist painter, and he went on to work in abstract art.

Cubism and Futurism

Cubism is an early-20th-century art movement in which several viewpoints are shown simultaneously, and simple geometric shapes or interlocking planes are used to construct a scene. Cubism began in 1907 and ended around 1915. Pablo Picasso and Georges Braque pioneered this movement, influenced partly by the three-dimensional representations in works by Paul Cézanne. Cubist artists would analyze a form, break it apart, and reassemble it visually in a more abstracted format.

Futurism, an early-20th-century movement that began in Italy in 1909, emphasized movement, technology, speed, and violence. The artwork included objects such as cars, airplanes, and industrial elements. Like cubists, these artists expressed dynamic elements in artwork. They also praised originality, admired technology over nature, and sought to convey movement through space. Futurist artists praised war and valued nationalism, and they would depict urban scenes such as riots and construction in the city.

Pablo Picasso, Marcel Duchamp, Giacomo Balla

Pablo Picasso is one of the most recognizable names of cubism. His cubist works include flat planes of color, distorted forms, geometric shapes, and reassembled faces with both eyes on one side of a profile.

Marcel Duchamp's work spanned both the cubist and futurist movements. His work, *Nude Descending a Staircase, No. 2*, from 1912, shows a dynamic scene of repeated abstracted and geometric forms of a nude descending from left to right in the painting. The repetition and form convey movement and rhythm.

Giacomo Balla's *Dynamism of a Dog on a Leash* from 1912 embodies some of the tenets of the futurist movement. The painting shows the feet of a woman, plus a leash and a walking dog. Through the repetition of the feet, leash, and tail, Balla shows the dynamic movement of the woman and the dog. The dynamic elements show almost a blur of movement, conveying speed and direction.

Constructivism and De Stijl

The constructivism movement began as a Russian abstract style of art and architecture that started in the 1910s. This movement consisted of constructing dynamic three-dimensional forms from objects such as plastic, wood, glass, or iron. This movement began with Vladimir Tatlin, who was influenced by Picasso's cubist constructions and wanted to "construct" art with dynamic components. Tatlin began to make abstracted still lifes out of scrap materials.

De Stijl is Dutch for "the style," and this Dutch art movement that started in 1917 is also known as neoplasticism. This art movement promoted the reduction of artwork into geometric shapes, lines, and primary colors. Artists attempted to turn this style into a universal form of expression, departing from individual expression. Piet Mondrian is the most recognizable de Stijl artist. Neoplasticism refers to the style and ideas developed by this artist, promoting a new, abstract form of artwork for modern times.

Vladimir Tatlin, Piet Mondrian

The **constructivism** movement began with artist Vladimir Tatlin in 1913. Tatlin was a Soviet architect and painter, and he constructed three-dimensional "counter-reliefs" of wood and metal. His intention was to question the traditions of art. His main constructivist work was the *Monument to the Third International* (*Tatlin's Tower*), which joined the dynamic components of technology with the aesthetics of machines. This construction included searchlights and projection screens, and it was criticized for being a combination of functional items and art. This tower sparked an exchange of ideas between Russia and Germany on the ideas of revolutionizing art.

The main artist from the de Stijl movement is Dutch painter Piet Mondrian. He sought to create pure abstractions with horizontal and vertical lines, as well as primary colors. He wanted to reduce his artwork to the most basic elements, using them to represent the essence of the energy and forces of nature. The pure abstraction and minimal palette was meant to express an ideal and universal harmony in the art world. His idea of neoplasticism, which guided his work, relied on color, line, and form to express universal ideas. This is an example of Mondrian's work, showing his use of black lines, geometric shapes, and primary colors.

Dada and Surrealism

The **Dada** art movement began around 1915 in Zurich, New York, Germany, and Paris. The movement came about as a reaction of disgust and revolt to the horrors of World War I, and the movement was also antibourgeois. This wasn't so much of a cohesive style as it was a group of artists looking to collaborate and create art with spontaneity. This group actually mocked the established art scene, and they started debates about the definition of art. They sought to depart from so-called traditional values of art and create a new kind of artwork. Dada is considered antiart, challenging the definition and conventions of art. Dada techniques include readymades, which involves presenting a premade object as art, and the photomontage, using scissors and glue to assemble images from images printed in the press. Dada artists issued publications and created photomontages to stand up against political ideas. Dada art critiqued society, politics, and previously established rules for art, and their penchant for the strange, satirical, and irrational was later picked up and used by surrealist artists.

Surrealism began in the 1920s in France, and the movement included paintings of strange, dreamlike, and unnerving scenes with realistic accuracy. Surrealism sought to express unconscious thoughts and resolve contradictions between reality and dreams. This movement eventually affected literature, music, and film in many countries as well. This art movement drew heavily on Freudian theories of sexuality, fantasy, dreams, and irrationality.

Marcel Duchamp, Salvador Dali, and René Magritte

As part of the Dada movement, Marcel Duchamp began creating artwork called "readymades," made from items that were already created and he just declared them to be art. One well-known example is his 1917 *Fountain*, which is an already-made urinal that he signed as "R. Mutt." Another Duchamp artwork from 1919, *L.H.O.O.Q.*, shows the departure from and irreverence toward traditional artwork. He took a postcard depicting the Mona Lisa and drew a moustache and face on the portrait, then labeled it *L.H.O.O.Q.* With this artwork, he challenged artistic conventions of the past, and the value of traditional artwork.

Salvador Dali, a well-known surrealist artist, created his best-known work, *The Persistence of Memory, in 1931. The painting depicts melted pocket watches* on a dreamlike landscape.

René Magritte, a Belgian surrealist artist, created thought-provoking artwork by juxtaposing ordinary objects in unusual ways. In *The Treachery of Images* (1928–1929) he depicts a pipe with the words, in French, "This is not a pipe." The viewer is faced with the challenge of reconciling these words with the fact that this is a representation of a pipe, not an actual pipe.

Abstract Expressionism

Abstract expressionism refers to an art style from the 1940s and 1950s. The artists grouped under this style sought total freedom of expression through their artwork. They shared an outlook, rather than a specific style, and this is thought to be the first truly American art movement. Abstract expressionism is also called the New York School, because the movement was centered in New York. Its influence extended into the 1970s. Abstract expressionist artists were influenced by the surrealist idea of expressing the subconsciousness in artwork. Abstract expressionism includes color field painting and action painting, and mixes of these two, among other techniques.

Color field painting uses solid areas, or fields of color, on a large scale that extend to the edges of the canvas. The extension to the edges suggests the colors continuing to infinity, and the large scale helps to envelop the viewer in the colors. Action painting includes dribbling, splashing, and dripping paint onto a canvas using gestures and movements, while emphasizing the unconscious.

Artists of Abstract Expressionism

Jackson Pollock is known for his action paintings, or splatter paintings. The term "action painting" was coined to describe Pollock's methods of applying paint to a canvas. Pollock considered this technique to be a way to harness the capabilities of his unconscious, which expressed itself onto the canvas. He saw the drips and splatters not as random paint, but as a balance of chaos and control.

Mark Rothko, Barnett Newman, and Clyfford Still were all color field painters of the abstract expressionist movement. They were looking to get away from form and representation in artwork, and they did away with the figure/ground convention by turning the figure and ground into one. The color seemed to extend beyond the edges of the painting and was the focus of the artwork.

Helen Frankenthaler used a mix of techniques and invented the "soak-stain" technique, which involved creating large color washes by pouring thinned paint onto a canvas. She used Pollock's technique of pouring paint but also used elements of color field painting by incorporating large areas of pure color.

Pop Art

Pop art was a British and American movement in the 1960s that used items from popular culture and incorporated them into artwork. This was partly inspired by the readymades of Dadaism. The artists of this movement went against the disengagement of abstract expressionism and celebrated popular culture and consumer items. They used bright, flat colors from advertising and imagery from comic books as well. As a response to and departure from abstract expressionism, pop art used hard edges instead of painterly techniques and impersonal, everyday reality instead of personal symbolism.

Some of the significant artists of the pop art movement used commercial imagery such as Campbell's Soup cans, imagery directly from comic books, and even a direct representation of the American flag. They were inspired by everyday objects and mass consumerism, and they combined objects, text, and images to create new meaning in their artwork.

Roy Lichtenstein, and Jasper Johns

Roy Lichtenstein was a pop artist who is known for his comic book imagery. He altered images from comic books, added different text, and painted them on a large scale. He used Benday dots, the dots produced by mechanical means in printing, to create these images. One of his well-known works is *Drowning Girl* (1963), which depicts a comic image of a drowning girl and her boyfriend in a boat, along with text.

Jasper Johns was a pop artist known for his American imagery, especially the American flag. His *Three Flags* (1958) is a painting of three American flags layered upon each other. *Flag*, from 1954–1955, is a faithful reproduction of an American flag using encaustic.

Andy Warhol

Andy Warhol was a commercial artist who became a significant pop artist as he explored the connections between popular culture and art, and he gained international attention for his artwork and for himself. He created video art, installations, performance art, and paintings, and in 1961 he began producing pop art paintings, including the iconic *Campbell's Soup Cans*. He also painted portraits of many celebrities in bright and vivid colors.

Andy Warhol He used many different media types, including painting, screen printing, and even computers, to create iconic pop art. The allure and mystery of his personal life, combined with his public persona, helped to keep him in the spotlight and create interest in him and his work. He reproduced images from mass media that nobody had thought to use before for artwork, and he successfully became synonymous with pop art. His work appealed to a large audience, and he created some the most widely recognized artworks ever made. Warhol also changed the concept of being an artist by using his factory concept to produce artwork. He predicted the quick rise and fall of celebrities with his "15 minutes of fame" concept, which became the new norm in popular culture.

Warhol's Factory

The Factory refers to Andy Warhol's studio in New York City. This location became a hangout for artists and celebrities, and it was known for its raucous parties. Warhol decorated this location with aluminum foil, mirrors, and silver paint, and it was also called the Silver Factory. The Factory later occupied two other locations. Warhol's time at this Factory location was referred to as the Silver Era.

In addition to the artistic experimentation and musical performances at The Factory, an assembly-line production of artwork also occurred. Warhol questioned the idea of artist and art production by mass-producing artwork with his silkscreen method and having a group of helpers create his work for him. These helpers became known as "Warhol Superstars," and they included musicians, free thinkers, drag queens, socialites, and celebrities, among others. He paralleled and reflected the concept of mass consumerism and mass-produced commercial objects by creating his own artwork in this way.

Postmodernism

Postmodernism is a mid- to late-20th-century art movement that departed from modernism. Since the beginning of the 20th century, modernism had led art practice and theory and had promoted the ideas of progress, reason, and idealism. Postmodern artists would not recognize the authority of previous art movements, and this movement was skeptical and antiauthoritarian. This "anything goes" style cast aside all rules of style and included elements of confrontation, tongue-in-cheek humor, and ludicrousness. Postmodernist artists built on the ideas of previous movements such as pop art and feminist art, but they questioned the ideas and subjectivity, authorship, and originality in previous art movements. This movement also questioned the commodification of art production.

Postmodernism is a cross-disciplinary term with philosophical origins, and it was highly influenced by French philosopher Jacques Lacan. Lacan added a contemporary intellectual significance to the ideas of Sigmund Freud, and he suggested that the unconscious is just as complex and sophisticated as the conscious mind.

Sigmar Polke, and Gerhard Richter

Sigmar Polke, a German artist whose artwork pioneered a postmodern approach, departed from coherence in his art as well as the idea that art comes from the artist's personality. In his 12 canvases collectively called *The Fifties* (1963–1969), he portrays a combination of cynicism and nostalgia while commenting on German culture. The grouping of paintings goes against the concept of stylistic coherence because he used different styles throughout the works.

Gerhard Richter's photo paintings of the 1960s combined photography with painting. In doing this, he combined high and low art into one technique. Richter would project a photograph onto a canvas, then paint it in neutral shades of gray, leaving out the black and white tones. He then used a dry brush to soften the edges, degrading the image to give a blurry effect. He assigned neutral titles to his works. This method of mechanical reproduction took any artist style out of the equation, as well as any emotion expressed through the artwork.

Feminist Art

Feminist art came into prominence in the late 1960s as female artists sought to revise the history of a male-dominated art world and bring attention to the contributions of female artists. They sought to abolish stereotypes as well as challenge and influence cultural attitudes. Previously, female artists did not get the same publicity or status that their male counterparts did, and the art world was dominated by male artists. The feminist art movement expanded the definition and scope of art, the artists we recognize, and who is included in the conversation of art making. Feminist artists gave credit to artists before them, and they introduced new media in their artwork. These artists began to embrace and use materials in their works that were tied to their gender, such as textiles and embroidery. They also used newer styles such as video, body, and performance art that did not have such a long history as a male-dominated style. These newer types of media allowed these artists to deliver more direct and personal messages to their viewers. Whereas some feminist artists explored the objectification of women in media, or ideas of domesticity, others focused on the absence of recognition of female artists throughout history.

Due to the accomplishments of this movement, women artists no longer necessarily feel the need to identify themselves as such, or to specifically create artwork that addresses the perspective of women. Women artists began to express their individual concerns and feelings, rather than trying to address and contribute to the feminist viewpoint.

Barbara Kruger, Cindy Sherman, and Faith Ringgold.

Barbara Kruger uses mass communication and advertising techniques, pairing black-and-white photos with Helvetica or Futura text, to explore identity and gender issues. The text and slogans she uses challenge the viewer, and her phrases often include pronouns such as I, you, we, or they. She often appropriates images from magazines and adds text to frame the images in a new context to make the viewer think. This image shows her artwork *Belief + Doubt* from 2012 and its iconic and recognizable style of text.

Cindy Sherman is a feminist artist who is known for her self-portraits. She used makeup, wigs, and props to transform herself to represent various female stereotypes in her photographs. Her artworks question ideas of authenticity and identity.

Faith Ringgold is an African-American feminist artist who worked in themes of racial and gender identity and equality. She told stories through quilts, and she recognized a need for equality in the art world. Ringgold would often insist that 50% of the artists included in prominent art shows should be women.

Armory Show

The Armory Show was the first major exhibition of modern art in America. This show is also called the International Exhibition of Modern Art, and it was held in New York City's 69th Regiment Armory building in 1913. The art exhibited here was influential to American art because of the inclusion of modern art by European and American painters and sculptors. Prior to this, Americans were used to seeing realistic art, but this show exposed them to cubist, impressionist, and fauvist artworks. Marcel Duchamp's *Nude Descending a Staircase* was included in this show. This collection of more than 1,300 artworks shocked many, and it was ridiculed and declared insane and immoral by some. The inclusion of these works in this successful art show served as a catalyst for many artists to rethink their styles and experiment with new ways of creating art.

The Degenerate Art Exhibition

The Degenerate Art Exhibition was in held in Munich by Adolf Ziegler and the Nazi party in 1937. The Nazis had removed more than 20,000 artworks from state museums that had been deemed too modern or progressive. Works by foreign artists were also confiscated, including Pablo Picasso, Piet Mondrian, and Wassily Kandinsky, but these works were not exhibited. 740 of these confiscated works were shown in the Degenerate Art Exhibition to defame the artists and show the public the decay of culture. These works were thought to lack artistic skill or insult the German culture. The works were shown in the exhibition without frames and were accompanied by derogatory words or slogans. The art was divided into categories including "An Insult to German Womanhood," and "Nature as Seen by Sick Minds." More than two million visitors attended this show, and some works were destroyed after the show ended. Many other works were sold on the international market and found new homes in museums abroad.

The Guerrilla Girls

The Guerrilla Girls group formed in 1985 to speak out against sexism and racism in the art world. The group is still active today. These women wear gorilla masks to hide their identities while they speak out against powerful institutions. They also hide their identities by using pseudonyms, taking the names of deceased female artists. They have used posters, billboards, and books, as well as public appearances, to disseminate their messages. This group has gained attention for their protest art, and their first well-known poster asked, "Do women have to be naked to get into the Met. Museum?" The image on the poster was a copy of Ingres' *La Grande Odalisque*, with a gorilla head over the woman's face. This poster was in reference to the number of nude women exhibited in the museum and the lack of female artists represented. The Guerrilla Girls have repeatedly brought attention to issues of inequity through their clean designs and jarring images.

Minimalism Art

Introduced in the 1960s, the **minimalism movement** is characterized by an extreme form of abstract art. Like many other movements, minimalist artists sought to challenge the boundaries and conventions of art. By removing themselves and their feelings from their artwork, these artists distanced themselves from the work of the abstract expressionists who came before them. They were interested in creating a new kind of artwork that was unlike any other previous fine art, minimized to its simplest and barest form, not designed to represent anything. Minimalist artists used geometric shapes and challenged the previous conventions of creating and viewing artwork. They wanted their artwork to exist simply as its own form and material, not as a representational form. Minimalist artwork shows traits of simplicity, harmony, and purity.

These artists wanted their art to show no evidence of the artist who created it and stand on its own instead of having personal elements. Paintings lacked brushstrokes and had flat fields of color, and sculptures had clean, straight lines and geometric shapes. The minimalism label referred to artists using a minimal number of colors, shapes, or forms in their artwork and the artwork was stripped of decoration and refined to its simplest form.

Although minimalist art can be two-dimensional, it is often three-dimensional, using simple, sometimes repeated, geometric shapes. Early abstract ideas, as well as the constructivist ideas of reducing artwork to its simplest and most essential form, inspired minimalist artists. This example from 1991 by Solomon "Sol" LeWitt is called *Open Cubes*, and it shows white repeated geometric forms. These forms exist only as themselves and are not meant to be representational. The viewer should only accept the artwork as its purest form of geometry and simplicity.

Street Art

Street art began with graffiti, but these artists have eventually shown their work in public areas and in galleries and museums in the 1970s and 1980s. Street art initially consisted of politically charged protest slogans and graphics illegally painted in public areas. Graffiti usually refers to vandalism, and street art was initially tied to hip-hop culture and lower income areas. In the 1970s, Jean-Michel Basquiat began spray painting his form of artwork in Manhattan. Later in the 1980s, Keith Haring was creating his distinctive artwork on the subway lines in New York City, and his well-known style of outlines and vivid colors, as shown, has persisted as popular artwork even now.

Banksy is another well-known street artist, although his identity is unknown. Banksy spray paints stencils designs onto walls and buildings throughout major cities, and those works have been turned into prints, t-shirts, and more. Street artist Shepard Fairey created the iconic Andre the Giant stencil which can be seen in many locations, and he went on to make the well-known Barack Obama graphic in red, white, and blue.

The Harlem Renaissance Art Movement

Between 1920 and 1930, a new wave of artistic creativity poured out from a group of African American artists in Harlem, a neighborhood in the borough of Manhattan in New York City. This movement became known as the Harlem Renaissance, and its influence continued through and past the 1930s. This area of New York became a center of African-American immigrants, and the movement sparked a racial pride that challenged racism and stereotypes. The artwork of this time had aims to uplift African-Americans' spirits and the race as a whole. Some of the common themes represented in the artwork were racism, the effects of slavery, folk traditions, and how to convey the experience of black life or black neighborhoods.

Jacob Lawrence was the first well-known African-American artist, and his Migration series showed the migration of blacks from the rural South to the urban North.

Aaron Douglas was an artist who painted murals on buildings and created illustrations for the covers of black publications. In this work, *Aspiration* from 1936, Douglas shows the progression from slavery to the freedom of the industrialized North.

Ashcan School

The Ashcan School describes a group of American realist painters who decided to portray urban life of New York in an unidealized fashion. This was not an organized movement; rather, it was a collective desire to portray modern life in a new way. This group believed that poor and working-class people were a worthy artistic subject matter, and they sought to portray these people in an authentic way. They used a dark palette, a sketchy quality, and visible brushwork to show scenes of everyday modern life in New York City, with subjects including street kids, alcoholics, subways, crowded tenements, and theaters. These artists challenged refined and idealized artwork, moving away from American impressionism and the more polished academic realism. After the Armory Show in 1913, as well as the advent of cubism and fauvism, the work of the Ashcan School no longer seemed as radical as it initially did.

The Hudson River School

The Hudson River School was an American art movement in the mid-19th century that included landscape painters intent on painting in a romantic style. The paintings of this movement depict the Hudson River Valley and areas surrounding it. The themes reflected in these artworks are exploration, discovery, and settlement. These landscapes are detailed and somewhat idealized, often showing a juxtaposition and harmony of settlers or agriculture with nature. They were also showing their belief in nature as a revelation of God.

This movement was the first native art movement in America. Thomas Cole is credited as the founder, and the movement spanned two generations of painters. The second generation was not as tied to a geographical location as the first, but rather followed the style. Albert Bierstadt was a notable artist of this second generation. This painting by Bierstadt, *A River Landscape, Westphalia* (1855), shows the accord of man with the beauty and grandness of nature.

Folk Art and Outsider Art

Folk art is the art of peasants or a native culture. Folk art is generally characterized by simple or naive subject matter, and it is utilitarian or decorative in purpose. Folk art is not influenced by art movements or styles, and it will not include the work of professional artists. This type of art shares and expresses the values of a community as well as their cultural identity. Pottery, jewelry, paintings, sculpture, needlework, and costumes can all be folk art.

Outsider art is artwork created by untrained artists who learned their craft and methods on their own. These artists are not part of an artistic establishment and can include the mentally ill or even rural artists outside of urban areas. Outsider art is sometimes called "naive art." An increased interest in outsider art is in line with the general rejection of traditional values and methods of art by modernist artists.

Op Art

The **op art movement** of the 1960s used geometric forms to create visual effects and optical illusions. Op art is abstract and nonrepresentational, and many works were created in just black and white. Viewers often were given the feeling of movement, vibration, hidden images, or swelling within the artwork. Op artists consider how our vision works and how the planes of the figure and the ground can work with or against each other. Op artists also work with colors and how they can function together to produce different effects on the viewer's eye. As an early op artist, Bridget Riley worked in black and white and later began working in color op art. Josef Albers is another well-known op artist who worked in color, and he would nest geometric shapes of contrasting colors within each other, making visual effects of the shapes receding and advancing against each other.

Art Deco Movement

The **art deco movement**, taking its name from the Exposition Internationale des Arts Décoratifs et Industriels Modernes held in Paris in 1925, began in Paris with architecture and decorative arts in the 1920s. It later became a major style in the 1930s throughout America and Western Europe. The art deco style is characterized by streamlined forms, symmetry, geometric shapes, smooth lines, and bright vibrant colors. This movement was influenced by the geometric forms of cubism, the industrial components of futurism and constructivism, and the bright colors of fauvism. The style was used during the roaring twenties as well as the Great Depression of the 1930s. Art deco was used to improve the style of mass-produced objects, and it was also used for posters and some fine arts. This poster from 1925 is an example of the art deco style, with hard lines, streamlined forms, and geometric shapes with vibrant colors. The style was meant to be pleasing to the eye.

Art Nouveau

Art nouveau sought to distance itself from historical styles, as well as challenge the hierarchy of fine arts over decorative arts. Art nouveau was a decorative style that focused on linear contours and outlines, and it used muted, limited colors such as blues, greens, yellows, and browns. Art nouveau artists wanted to revive good craftsmanship, lift the status of crafts, and skillfully create modern designs that did not rely on past design. This international style was popular between 1890 and 1910, and it was applied to art, architecture, as well as everyday objects such as furniture, lamps, and jewelry.

One prominent art nouveau artist was Alphonse Mucha, a Moravian artist who created many illustrations, posters, paintings, and other designs. This example shows his signature style, which was considered outdated by the time of his death. His designs often showed beautiful women surrounded by a symmetrical, flowing, floral and ornate design and muted colors.

The Impressionist Movement

The impressionist movement marked a departure from the traditional notions of art. At the time, the narrow ideals of art were controlled by institutions such as the Salon and the French academy. These institutions also held control over the careers of artists. The impressionists cast the old rules aside and painted how they wanted to, capturing the changing qualities of light in new ways and scenes as they looked at a particular moment. They captured scenes as they saw them, on the spot, rather than taking sketches back to the studio to complete a painting. Impressionism also began when photography was catching on, and it served as an imitation of and reaction against it. Impressionism imitated the capturing of fleeting moments, while reacting against a faithful photographic reproduction of a scene. This art movement transformed landscape painting, and impressionism influenced artists to later express their artistic freedom and experiment with methods and media.

The Postimpressionist Movement

Postimpressionist artists rejected the ideas of depicting the world around them, as the impressionists did, and instead sought to explore their emotions and memories to depict highly personal meanings through their artwork. Instead of showing scenes from life, as the impressionists did, postimpressionist artists wanted to go further and show their feelings through abstracted forms and new uses of color. They used symbolism and attempted to evoke emotion in their viewers. Postimpressionist artists did not seek to create a cohesive style; rather, the movement was more about the departure from a faithful depiction of the world or events, and it was about beginning to relay information from the artist's subconscious mind. Postimpressionists used saturated colors and unnatural hues to express emotion in their artwork, taking a new, imaginative approach to representing their subjects. The painterly quality and distinct brushstrokes added to the notion that this was not a faithful representation, but rather an interpretation.

The Social Realism Movement

Social realism began in the early 1900s with the aim of portraying everyday life, especially that of the working class. It became an important art movement in the 1930s in the United States during the Great Depression. At this time, urban areas were growing, and slums also grew. Social realism artists were motivated by reacting against the idealism of the romantic period. These artists revealed the realities of contemporary life, and they sympathized with the poor and working class. They recorded the realities of what they saw, without glorifying scenes or heightening emotions. While documenting the realities of the poor and working class, social realists were also critical of the government and structures that created these conditions. They wanted to use this new style as a weapon to fight against the government and capitalism, as well as the exploitation of workers, while transforming society.

Chapter Quiz

Ready to see how well you retained what you just read? Scan the QR code to go directly to the chapter quiz interface for this study guide. If you're using a computer, simply visit the online resources page at **mometrix.com/resources719/osatart** and click the Chapter Quizzes link.

Aesthetics, Art Criticism, and Interdisciplinary Connections

Design and Production Processes

Modeling Process

The **modeling process** is an additive process that involves adding material to an artwork to create the desired piece. It is a sculptural process that is used with soft materials like clay, wax, or plaster. The end result of the modeling process might be the finished form, or it might be the first step in a process to create a form for casting. Modeling often includes the use of an armature, or some sort of frame, inside the model to support the work. An armature can be wire, mesh, wood, or any other material that can be left inside the modeling material that will not cause the piece to crack if it shrinks upon drying. Shrinkage happens when water leaves a water-based modeling material like plaster or clay. Oil-based clay will not shrink. An armature that is too rigid can cause clay to crack as it dries. When clay is added onto more clay, the clays should have similar moisture content so that they will adhere properly.

Modeling for a painting or drawing is a collaborative process between the model and the artist. The model provides a subject for the artist to study, and the artist is able to capture accurate anatomy, gestures, and expressions. The model and artist should discuss the concept or mood for the artwork so that the model will be able to use poses and expressions that will help the artist create the desired work. The model will need to be able to hold the chosen pose comfortably for an extended period of time. He or she might need a chair or props to maintain the pose. The artist might want to capture a static or a dynamic pose and might ask the model to make small adjustments in order to get the desired composition.

The model might hold their pose for 20 to 30 minutes at a time and take breaks in between posing. The model will need to maintain a still pose to allow the artist to capture details. The artist will provide feedback to the model, and the model will communicate about discomfort or any need for adjustment.

Art Production: Brainstorming, Storyboarding, Researching, Sketching

- **Brainstorming** is a process that can be done by an individual or a group. It involves coming up with ideas or solving problems related to an art project or process. The individual or group may come up with multiple ideas and then narrow down those ideas and choose the best one to move forward with.
- **Storyboarding** is the process of creating sketched drawings in a series to show a story in a proposed sequence. Storyboarding can be used for art that takes place over a period of time, like video or performance art.
- **Researching** is investigating facts prior to beginning an art project. An artist might research materials, processes, art movements, similar artists, or even a location to showcase artwork. The research process can help artists reach their desired results.
- **Sketching** is the process of putting ideas down on paper or capturing a scene quickly. A sketch can be done very quickly, or it can be more detailed, but it is generally a drawing completed to decide on the composition of an artwork, record ideas, or prepare for a painting.

Organization Design Strategies

- The organization design strategy known as **hybridization** involves putting together elements from different styles, techniques, cultures, or sources to create something new. The goal is to create a new product that gains strength from the use of its original components. This strategy can also show the interconnectedness of different cultural or artistic influences. An example is merging parts from different cultural art forms, like Western and Eastern motifs.

- **Recontextualization** takes an existing concept or element and places it into a new context. By placing an element into an unexpected or wholly new setting, the artist can change the viewer's perception of that element and provoke further thought about the element. It can also create a contrast between the element and the new environment. An example is changing the background of a famous historic painting to create a modern commentary.
- **Transformation** involves changing something entirely, such as using materials to create a new form. Transforming a product is more radical than hybridizing or recontextualizing it. Transformation aims to create something surprising and new and to see the original materials or objects from a new perspective. An example is creating a new form out of recycled materials.
- **Rhythm** in organizational design is repeating or alternating elements within a design. This creates a sense of flow and guides the viewer's eye by creating a deliberate pattern. This is often accomplished with repeated colors, shapes, lines, or motifs. A regular rhythm spaces elements evenly and predictably, while a progressive rhythm changes the spacing or size gradually each time the element is repeated.
- **Disruption** of expected order is breaking up or changing an expected element or pattern in a design. By doing this, the designer introduces an element of surprise. When the designer disrupts what is anticipated, the work can engage viewers more than an expected element. This can be accomplished by changing a repetitive sequence, altering alignment, or introducing something that contrasts sharply with surrounding elements.
- **Deconstruction** and **reconstruction** involve taking apart an established element or structure and reassembling it in a new way. The designer challenges the viewer's traditional ways of thinking when they reinterpret elements. They might take traditional elements of architecture, for example, deconstruct the elements, and reconstruct them in a way that challenges what a viewer thinks they should look like.
- **Proportion** in organizational design refers to how elements in a composition relate to each other in terms of size. The sizes of the components in a composition are compared to each other, and they must also work together to create harmony, balance, or tension within the artwork. Proportion is used by a designer to guide the viewer's eye or emphasize an aspect of a design. Disproportionate elements can create surprise or visual interest. The Parthenon in Athens is an example of proportion that was used precisely to create a sense of harmony and beauty in the structure.
- **Time** is a temporal aspect of a design. The designer considers how the design will unfold over time and how it relates to other temporal contexts. This can be shown in sequential designs found in comics, performance art, and animation. It can also be used in static art forms by implying motion or suggesting a narrative in the composition. The installation art The Gates by Christo and Jeanne-Claude is an example of artists using time as an important part of their art. This installation was only displayed for 16 days. The experience was tied to the specific time it was available for public viewing.

Golden Mean and Hierarchical Proportion

The golden mean, also known as the golden ratio or Fibonacci sequence, is a geometric proportion regarded as a way to add beauty, harmony, and balance to a composition. The proportion is 1 to 1.618, and this is used throughout art and architecture as a basis for design. Sometimes this is used as a single rectangle and a single square in these proportions, but this can be divided again and again to further subdivide the composition. These proportions were used by the ancient Greeks when designing the Parthenon and by Michelangelo in many of his works, among others.

Hierarchical proportion is a technique used by artists to emphasize parts of a sculpture or other artwork. The artist would use unnatural or unusual proportions to depict his or her subjects, bringing the viewer's attention to the more important figures depicted in the art. The artist might show a person of higher status as being larger than someone who is of lower status or who is subservient. Beginning in Renaissance times, artists began to depict their subjects in more realistic proportions in relation to each other.

Juxtaposition, Appropriation, and Transformation

Juxtaposition is the placement of contrasting elements next to each other to create an effect. Artists will contrast elements in their artwork to draw the viewer's eye, emphasizing the similarities and differences of the juxtaposed elements. An artist can also juxtapose imagery or concepts to relay their ideas. René Magritte's painting, *Memory of a Journey* from 1955, juxtaposes a giant feather against the Leaning Tower of Pisa, using scale to grab the viewer's attention.

Appropriation refers to the borrowing of preexisting objects or images in artwork with little to no transformation. Marcel Duchamp's "readymades" are an example of appropriation; he used preexisting objects in his works without changing them or changing them very little.

Transformation refers to the changing of an image or object to present it in a new way. Artists might start with a preexisting idea or object but transform it and use their own style and technique to make it their own artwork.

Natural and Human-Made Subjects

Natural art subjects, such as animals, landscapes, and plants, usually have organic shapes. The forms are often asymmetrical and show the diversity of the natural world. Natural subjects have richly varied textures, like bark, fur, or leaves. The colors found in nature are often muted earth tones with subtle color variations. Subjects like flowing water or swaying grass convey movement. They can symbolically represent life, renewal, and growth, which are concepts that can be understood across cultures.

Human-made subjects feature geometric shapes like squares, circles, and straight lines. They might be symmetrical, and they show design and engineering principles. The textures of human-made items, like glass, metal, or concrete, are often more consistent than natural textures. Human-made subjects are more likely to have bold colors, and the color contrast might be more extreme. Subjects like buildings give a sense of permanence and stability rather than movement. These subjects can symbolically represent industry and human achievement while reflecting the values of a society.

Self-Critique of Artwork

Self-critique of artwork is useful for analyzing artistic processes and outcomes in order to improve the process and the final product. Self-critique involves thinking about what is successful in an artwork, as well as what could be improved. When doing a self-critique, artists can look at the composition, use of elements and principles, how they portrayed their subject, whether they expressed their ideas effectively, and their use of media. It is helpful to stop often in the artistic process and stand back to critique the work, to see how it is progressing and decide if it is going in the right direction. Sometimes it is also helpful to stop for a while and put the work away, and then look at it again with fresh eyes later. With self-critique, artists become more aware of their progress and improvements and will also learn how to critique other artists' work objectively. They will focus on improving their artwork and on finding ways to grow, rather than repeating mistakes and becoming frustrated.

Art Criticism

Purpose of Critique

Critique is when a person, referred to as a critic, evaluates artwork in a technical manner to determine the value of the artwork. While the term *critic* often connotes that a person is being harsh, critique looks to evaluate and describe both good and bad elements in a piece of work and how they work together to produce the overall effect. While artwork is generally considered subjective, there are still technical aspects of art execution and meaning that can be considered and evaluated. Art criticism seeks to be as rational and objective as possible and uses a method that looks at the artwork from a variety of perspectives to assess it.

Four Stages of Art Criticism

The **four stages of art criticism** are description, analysis, interpretation, and judgment.

- The critic first gives a **detailed description** of the artwork. The description is objective, focusing on what can be seen. The critic describes the subject matter, shapes, textures, colors, and other visual elements present.
- Next, the critic considers how the **composition** of the artwork is organized. He or she analyzes how the elements of art and principles of design are used and look at how these elements combine to work overall with the artwork.
- The critic then interprets the **meaning of the work.** He or she looks for mood, symbolism, and cultural or historical context and add his or her own personal response. This is a more subjective stage than the prior stages.
- Finally, the critic judges whether the artwork is **successful**. He or she assesses the effectiveness of the work, considering the craftsmanship, originality, and overall success in achievement of the artist's vision. This is also a subjective stage and depends on the information gathered in the prior stages.

Elements of Art

This painting, Mary Cassatt's *Young Girls* from 1867, shows effective use of the elements of art. Cassatt was an impressionist painter, and she used visible brushstrokes with soft edges to capture moments in time. Cassatt used yellows and orange-reds in the girls' dresses and greens in the background. The warm **colors** advance, whereas the cooler colored background recedes and helps the subjects stand out. The warmth of the colors in the skin tones gives life and vibrancy to the young girls. The rougher brushstrokes of the dresses, hair, and background show an implied **texture**. The implied **lines** surrounding the subjects in the foreground are softened and blurred, giving a softer feel to the subject. Cassatt used a wide range of light and dark **values** to give depth to this artwork. The darker background serves as negative **space**, whereas the subjects are the positive space. Mary Cassatt used the elements of art to successfully portray the soft, tender nature of youth and innocence in this painting.

PRINCIPLES OF DESIGN

Gustav Klimt's *The Kiss* from 1907–1908 is a painting with gold leaf added. It depicts a couple embraced and entwined in a kiss. Klimt used asymmetrical **balance** in this painting, although the figures are centrally located. The patch of meadow underneath them is mainly on the left of the painting, and the darker squares in the clothing are also on the left. This is balanced by the **emphasis**, or focal point, of the woman's face, which draws the viewer's eye. There is **contrast** throughout, with circles, rectangles, and solid areas of color. There is also the contrast of the bright gold with the darker background, causing the figures to stand out. The clothing of both figures, as well as the flowers in the meadow, show different **patterns**. The repeated yellows and golds throughout the painting give a **unity** to the piece. Klimt successfully used the elements of art to create this eye-catching painting.

Romantic Landscape

In Wassily Kandinsky's *Romantic Landscape* from 1911, he used the principles of design to successfully organize the elements of art. Although the artwork contains mainly darker and muted tones of **color**, such as darker blues and reds, as well as browns, grays and greens, he used one area of brighter orange in the top left. This small area of brighter color **contrasts** with the darker, more muted **values**, and it serves to **balance** the painting, while providing **emphasis** as a focal point to draw the eye. The **lines** and implied lines show **movement** in a triangle shape, leading the eye around the painting, from the upward sloping brown shape in the bottom left, leading up to a blue and whitish line at the top, then back down with a dark-gray line. He uses some dots of dark gray in different places to create **rhythm**, and the repeated colors throughout the painting provide **unity** to the artwork.

Using Experience to Analyze an Artwork

Using experience to analyze an artwork can help the viewer relate to and understand the artwork by relating to the context surrounding it. Experience can help the viewer feel what the artist is trying to convey. In this example, *Snap the Whip* by Winslow Homer from 1872, children are playing a game outside in a grassy field. The game is called snap the whip; the children hold hands and the main player tries to run and spin to throw the children off at the end of the chain. If a viewer has experienced this game, or even a similar game such as "red rover," they will have a greater understanding of the fun and excitement conveyed by the artist. Someone who grew up in the city without playing in grassy fields will not be able to relate as closely to this image. Relating to an artwork with experience can help the viewer decide and analyze whether the artist as successfully conveyed their ideas.

Using Observation to Analyze an Artwork

Analyzing art can be done in many different ways. By observing artwork in various ways, the viewer can get a greater overview of the artwork and its message. Viewers can begin by standing back and taking in a wide view of the entire artwork. They can observe what catches their eye and how the artwork leads their eye around. After noting their initial impressions, viewers can take a closer look, observing details such as brushstrokes, use of color, lines, and blending or glazing. Viewers should also consider the subject and messages that the artist is trying to convey, deciding whether the portrayal is successful. In a sculptural form, viewers would look closely at the materials and walk around the sculpture to observe how their view changes from all sides. Keeping in mind the elements and principles of art and how the artist is using them, careful observation of the artwork can help the viewer analyze the success of the art.

Experience, Observation, Memory, and Imagination

Artists will often use their own experiences and observations of their surroundings as sources for their artwork. An artist growing up by the ocean might use the beach as inspiration for their artwork, painting beach scenes and ocean life. A person who grew up in a crowded city might choose to portray the bustle of city life, tall buildings, or even homeless people because this is what they experienced. An artist can observe their surroundings and find the beauty in it, like the Hudson River School painters did when painting beautiful American landscapes. An artist could also draw on memories for inspiration, painting things that they remember from their past or their childhood. Imagination is a rich source of ideas too, and an artist can use their imagination to create new scenes, like surrealist painters often did. Surrealists used their imaginations to combine images in new ways, or even bend or distort ordinary objects. Experience, observation, memory, and imagination are all sources that artists use for their artwork.

Experience and Perception

A person's experiences can affect their perception of an artwork by influencing their ideas of what is, or isn't, art. This is an example of street art by Banksy, a well-known street artist whose work has become desirable to find and see. His identity is still unknown, and this mystique adds to the appeal of his art. Street art does have a negative connotation for many. Street art, or graffiti, is generally painted illegally on buildings and is often covered over. The illegal and unwanted aspect could make many people think that it is not an art form. If someone has experienced vandalism on their home or business, they would be less accepting of street art as an art form. If someone's neighborhood has been filled with unwanted graffiti, they might not want to see it on their own building or in other public places. On the other hand, people who are involved in creating street art view it as a positive experience, and they are accepting of it as an art form.

How Images/Artworks Influence Audiences and/or User Experiences

Artwork can influence the **audience's experience** by engaging their emotions, senses, and intellect.

- Artwork can evoke powerful emotional responses like sorrow or joy. Somber tones and subjects create feelings of despair, while bright colors bring about feelings of happiness. Viewers connect and empathize with the subjects in portraits, photographs, and figurative art. Artwork can remind viewers of dreams, memories, or fears and call to mind the feelings associated with them.
- When artwork includes symbolism or abstract elements, it challenges the viewer to use their intellect to interpret the meanings. The viewer engages intellectually to decipher an artist's intentions. When art serves as a window into different historical periods or cultures, the viewer reflects on the topics and gains insight into those times and cultures.
- The aesthetic experience of viewing art gives the viewer visual pleasure. An artist's use of the elements and principles of art creates an aesthetic experience that is pleasing to the viewer's eye. Artwork like sculptures or installations can change how viewers move through a space, enhancing their physical experience with the artwork.

Improving Composition

Although there are many ways to compose an artwork and lead the viewer's eye around the work, there are certain considerations that can improve the composition of a work. It is jarring to the eye to see two edges in a painting touch, but not overlap. In this case, the edge of the jug is touching the fruit, but they do not overlap. This causes a spatial ambiguity and does not make it clear that one object is in front of the other. Lines that are known, in the mind, to be straight should be made straight in the artwork. The edge of the table, in the back, does not make a straight line. From the perspective this artwork is composed, the table is tilted farther than the edges of the objects show, and this conflict makes it seem that the objects may slide off the table. The artwork is somewhere in between symmetrical and asymmetrical balance, with the objects placed in the center with similar sizes on each side, carrying similar visual weight, but slightly different. This composition could be improved by creating a purposeful asymmetrical balance, using three different-sized objects instead.

Use of Media

In this work by J. M. W. Turner from 1801, it is evident that the medium used is watercolor paint. Watercolor is by nature transparent, and painting with watercolor involves letting the white of the paper show through for lighter values. Darker colors are made by using less water for a denser color or by building up layers of colors upon each other. In this landscape painting, Turner used washes for the large areas of color in the top two-thirds of the painting. The colors are delicately built upon each other. A wet-on-wet technique, adding watercolor to already-wet paper, will yield soft edges for the colors. To achieve the edges of the mountains and cliffs, the layer beneath can dry before adding another color on top. These colors were thinned with a lot of water to let the white of the paper show through and create lighter hues. The details at the bottom of the painting would be done with a smaller brush and less water to achieve more detail and sharper lines.

Tilted Arc by Richard Serra

Richard Serra's site-specific sculpture from 1981, titled *Tilted Arc*, was installed in Manhattan in Foley Federal Plaza. This sculpture consisted of a 120-foot-long, 12-foot-high leaning plate of steel. This work, although seemingly nondescript, was actually described as ugly and an eyesore by critics. At the same time, it was deemed significant for its placement because it transformed the location it was placed in. By placing the sculpture in this plaza, Serra disrupted many people's daily routines as they walked through the area, causing them to change paths and walk around the sculpture. The sculpture was purposely located where it would redefine the space. Many people petitioned for its removal, but Serra countered that to move the sculpture would be to destroy it because it was created specifically for the site. Serra was able to successfully transform the space with his strategic sculpture placement. The sculpture was dismantled and removed in 1989.

Brushstrokes and Impasto

Vincent van Gogh often used impasto, or thick layers of paint with prominent brushstrokes, in his paintings. Using this painting technique can add texture to a painting, and it can add to the other visual elements present in the artwork. In *Starry Night* (1889), van Gogh used the impasto technique and visible brushstrokes to create movement throughout the artwork. The swirls in the sky lead the eye throughout the painting, and the circles of brushstrokes around the stars and moon accentuate their presence in the sky. The prominent brushstrokes consist of colors placed next to each other, with dashes of color repeated throughout. This creates a repetition of pattern, as well as a visual texture, in addition to the actual texture of the thick paint. The brushstrokes add a visual interest and sense of movement that would be much different if he had simply painted the background in solid colors or blended the colors gradually. The brushstrokes and impasto technique are a significant part of the artwork, transforming a night scene into a vibrant, expressive work of art.

Visual Perception Skills and Knowledge

Prior Knowledge and Perception

A person's prior knowledge can affect how they perceive things visually. Prior knowledge carries expectations and biases based on what a person knows and has experienced. We combine what we see with what we already know, and we use this information to make assumptions when viewing new stimuli. We use our knowledge and experience to interpret familiar scenes and to provide a basis for unfamiliar scenes. For example, if a person encountered a familiar street sign, but part of the text on the sign was missing or obscured, based on prior knowledge of the color, shape, and visible text, the person would still perceive the sign as meaning what they expected, such as "YIELD" or "STOP." Without this prior knowledge, someone would not know how to interpret the sign with the missing text or might interpret it erroneously. Our prior knowledge is affected by, and subsequently affects, our visual perception.

Prior Knowledge and Artwork

A person's prior knowledge can give them information to analyze an artwork differently than someone without that knowledge. Prior knowledge about an artist and their process or an art movement can help someone understand and appreciate an artwork more than someone who has no knowledge of these concepts. For example, someone not familiar with the artist Jackson Pollock and his method of action painting might dismiss his artworks as an unskilled mess. With prior knowledge of his intention and process, someone can appreciate his method of "action painting" and using his movements to express himself on canvas, moving away from figurative representation, as well as the tradition of putting his canvas on an easel. The background knowledge of Pollock's significance in art history, and the significance of his new process at the time, can affect how a viewer will perceive his artwork.

Beliefs and Perception

Our beliefs can affect our visual perception in many ways. One way that beliefs can affect visual perception is confirmation bias, which is when someone sees only evidence and information that will confirm their beliefs. Even if the visual information contradicts what someone already believes, confirmation bias can cause them to interpret visual information based on their biases and come to erroneous conclusions based on these biases. A person with strong religious beliefs might see religious symbols and religious significance in images and in their surroundings. Someone with racist or sexist attitudes could automatically view images of different cultures or races, or images of women, in a negative way, without delving deeper into what they are seeing. To avoid judging visual input based on bias and beliefs, it can help to have background information and facts about the visual input and to have objective criteria to analyze and judge the visual input on.

Beliefs and Artwork

Beliefs can affect our perception of an artwork by bringing preconceived notions to our observations of the artwork and affecting our judgement of the work. A person with strong religious beliefs could enjoy and appreciate religious-themed artworks from medieval artists and understand the symbolism used throughout. On the other hand, someone without religious beliefs may immediately dismiss the artwork, finding it uninteresting. They would not appreciate the craftsmanship and the significance of these periods of art, based on their beliefs.

The understanding of the concept of art itself can also influence perception. If people believe that artwork is strictly painting, drawing, and sculpture, they would dismiss performance art or many of the modern art genres as not actually being forms of artwork. Their beliefs about what constitutes authentic artwork would cause them to fail to examine these newer forms further, and they could not appreciate these artworks as they were intended.

Observation Methods and Perception

The way in which we observe visual stimuli can affect how we perceive them. When viewing an object from only one angle, the viewer can miss information that could be gained by looking at it from all sides. Looking at an object from high, or a bird's-eye view, can look very different from looking at it with a worm's-eye view, or from below. The distance from which an object is viewed can affect perception as well. Looking at something closely can give clues about the details of an object, whereas looking at it from a distance can give a better idea of the overall object. The length of time that an object is viewed can also affect perception. Looking at an object at a glance will give less visual information than taking the time to observe and study it.

Observation Methods and Artwork

Different observation methods can affect how a person perceives a sculpture. Sculptures are generally meant to be viewable and observed from all sides, and viewing a piece from one side, or from a certain angle can make the viewer miss information. If a large installation sculpture is viewed only from one angle, or only from close up, the viewer could miss the effect of the entire sculpture. It should be viewed from as many angles as possible, and as a whole in addition to close up.

A large painting can be viewed closely, to see the details of brushstrokes and layered color. Viewing a painting from a close distance can also show the perspective of the artist as they were creating it. It can also be viewed from a distance, to capture the entire artwork as a whole and get the effect that the artist was trying to communicate.

Multisensory Experiences and Perception

Our senses can affect each other, and they can even affect how we perceive things visually. Throughout the day, we are barraged by sights and sounds, and we must prioritize what we pay attention to and what we ignore. A sound that is recognized as alarming, such as a car horn or an ambulance siren, will take precedence over other sounds and at the same time draw our gaze. A pleasing or interesting sound can also attract our attention, encouraging us to look in its direction to see the source. If an artwork were to incorporate sound, the types of sounds and directions they are coming from can aid in directing the viewer's eye throughout the artwork and even create a focal point.

In other instances, sound can also be distracting. It will be easier to concentrate on the details of a painting in a quiet room, rather than in a noisy, crowded room. An outdoor sculptural installation near a noisy road can be more difficult to examine than one in a museum gallery.

Viewpoints and Artwork

Artwork can appear differently to different people depending on their viewpoints. Artwork can be viewed from a historical or personal perspective, or from a subjective or objective viewpoint. This painting, *Dance at Le Moulin de la Galette* from 1876 by Pierre-Auguste Renoir, can be analyzed in multiple ways. From a historical viewpoint, it is important to consider the significance of the artwork in the impressionist style, capturing a fleeting moment on a Sunday afternoon in Paris and the dappled light through the trees. From a personal perspective, someone might react favorably to the warm and inviting scene or unfavorably if they do not like crowds.

Objectively, this artwork can be analyzed using the elements and principles of art, as well as the skill used to execute the rendering. Subjectively, a person might prefer that paintings are rendered more realistically or that a subject is more posed instead of the artist capturing a casual scene.

Creating Meaning

Meaning can be created in artwork in many different ways. Sometimes the meaning of an artwork is immediately obvious and uncontested, and other times it is more complex and subject to various interpretations. Understanding the culture and context in which the artwork is created, as well as the art movement it fits into, can provide clues to its meaning.

Symbols are used to add meaning in ways that are not immediately clear, and they are usually not the focal point of an artwork. Rather, the artist relies on the viewer to see and decipher the symbols. These can have obvious meanings or rely on background or historical knowledge to understand their significance. Subject matter can be used to convey meaning in a more obvious manner. The artist's choice of subject and how it is portrayed can show meaning and intent.

An artist can also use elements and principles to create meaning in their artwork. Colors can signify feelings and moods. Size, placement, emphasis, and repetition can all convey strong ideas or the dominance of one idea over another.

Symbolism

Symbols incorporated into artwork are interpreted by the viewer based on their knowledge of these clues and the context they are placed within. This artwork, *The Ambassadors* by Hans Holbein the Younger, was painted in 1533. At first glance, this seems to be a portrait of two men, likely ambassadors based on the title, dressed in fine clothing and posing in front of a small set of shelves. The shelves contain many seemingly random objects, but they were chosen and placed for their symbolic significance within the context of the painting. The globe and maps signify the age of exploration. The gloves and dagger held by the men symbolize authority and luxury at the time. The elongated shape on the floor is a stretched-out skull, which would look more correct when viewed from the bottom left of the painting. The skull generally symbolizes death. There are also symbols throughout the painting referring to the division between the Catholics and Protestants at the time: a mostly hidden crucifix in the top left and the hymnal juxtaposed with a lute with a broken string. Symbols placed throughout the artwork add meaning and intent to this seemingly innocuous portrait.

Iconography

Iconography is a method of creating meaning through art by examining the symbols, themes, and images within the artwork. This helps critics, historians, and viewers understand art on a deeper level by decoding the symbolic language within the artwork. Symbols and motifs can include religious symbols, culturally specific items, and allegorical figures. For example, a dove might represent peace. An ankh in Egyptian art can represent eternal life. Decoding these symbols requires a contextual understanding as well as cultural knowledge. The symbols can have interconnected or complex meanings rather than many separate meanings. For example, in da Vinci's *The Last Supper*, the placement of each figure and item has meaning related to Christian theology. The apostles are grouped into threes, creating an allusion to the holy trinity. Judas holds a purse, showing that he received a reward for his betrayal. Peter holds a knife, foreshadowing his severing of a soldier's ear.

Creativity and Critical Thinking

Artistic problems can be solved through creativity and innovation by brainstorming to come up with multiple solutions. Artists solve problems involved with what media and venue to use to express themselves and how to best get their message to their viewers. They decide how to use the elements and principles to convey their message, what subject to portray, what style to use, and even how to explain their artistic process to others. Problem solving using creativity and critical thinking can occur in many ways, including creating thumbnail sketches, keeping a notebook of ideas to draw from for artwork, and experimenting with materials. Artists can brainstorm ideas and come up with the best solution for their current problem. The artist should first assess the problem and decide what they are trying to solve. They can then come up with multiple ideas through writing, sketching, experimenting, and even viewing others' artwork, and then they can choose the best solution and build upon it.

Aesthetics and Expressive Features

Aesthetics is a philosophy in art that seeks to create non-subjective criteria for the judgement of beauty. Aesthetics asks questions such as "What is art?" "What is beauty?" and "What makes art beautiful?" Aesthetics in art also questions what makes a painting good and whether a realistic painting is "better" than an abstract one. The aesthetics movement of the late 19th century favored the beauty of art over practical or moral narratives.

Expressive features in artwork include how the artists uses the elements and principles to communicate mood and feeling. An artist can communicate through the composition of the artwork, imagery, text, color, or a juxtaposition of opposing elements, among other things. These are the characteristics of an artwork that stir emotion within the viewer. The viewer could feel conflict and opposition through strong, jagged lines or contrasts of colors. They could also feel peace and harmony through the use of analogous colors and soft, flowing elements throughout the artwork.

CONTEXT

Context describes the related conditions or circumstances around which something occurs. To understand an artwork, it helps to understand its context or the circumstances in which the artist was working in at the time. This can include their environment, the historical events and traditions that were happening, their cultural values, the social movements at the time, and even the artist's personal values and commitments. Recognizing art in context includes looking at it in broad perspective; this encompasses not only of how you see it at the moment, but also how it fits into the history of art, what it was a reaction to, what movement it followed, and what it preceded. You could judge a piece of Dada art simply by its own merit and appearance, but understanding the context of it, the feelings of cynicism and sarcasm as well as their intention of creating antiart, will carry more meaning to your understanding of the artwork and give you a broader perspective of what the artist intended.

MEDIA AND TECHNIQUES

Media is the plural of **medium**, and it refers to the physical materials used by an artist to create artwork. Examples of media include paint, oil, clay, ink, metal, or any other material used to create artwork. Artistic media have changed and evolved throughout the years, with the invention and improvement of materials such as the advent of acrylic paint or the invention of tubes for paint portability.

Techniques for artwork include the ways in which an artist uses their technical skills to create artwork. This includes specialized methods for different media. Drawing techniques will differ from painting techniques, and they will also differ from the specialized methods used for printmaking or sculpting. An artist can explore new techniques, learn techniques from books, classes, or studying artwork, and use these techniques in their artwork to improve their methods or change the focus of their art.

Art Criticism Theories

THE DECONSTRUCTION CRITICISM THEORY

The criticism theory of **deconstruction** focuses on examining the many potential meanings within an artwork, including ones that possibly even conflict with each other. This theory was first used in the 1970s by French philosopher Jacques Derrida. Deconstruction involves finding and recognizing the underlying meaning and implied messages within artwork. When delving into artwork in this way, it is difficult to find and agree upon just one meaning, and it can challenge preconceived notions and previously agreed upon ideas. This aesthetic theory seeks what is hidden, omitted, or repressed to show how the initial impression is not the only interpretation nor is it necessarily the generally accepted meaning. There could be many unanswered questions within the artwork, such as the intentions of the artist, the significance of the objects or location, or the identities of the subjects, and this leads to ambiguity of meaning. Stereotypes must be set aside to look for a true meaning.

ANDY WARHOL'S MARILYN MONROE

Andy Warhol's screen printed images of Marilyn Monroe perpetuate the image of her well-known Hollywood persona. Marilyn Monroe was famous for being a beautiful and talented cultural icon, and the repeated image used by Warhol reinforces this image of her celebrity. To use the critical perspective of deconstruction to analyze this artwork, one must go past the initial impression and stereotypes, seeking what is hidden or omitted, looking for other meanings and interpretations. In addition to Monroe's exuberant celebrity personality, there was a darker, troubled side that eventually led to her suicide. The initial impression of this artwork is the superficial, smiling celebrity paparazzi image, with bright colors, repeated as it would have been seen everywhere in media. Delving further past this initial impression yields another possible interpretation, and it reinforces the idea that there is more than one possible way to view and understand this artwork.

The Representationalism Aesthetic Theory

Representationalism is an **art theory** that defines art as something that represents something else and is recognized as that by viewers. This theory does not include some art forms, like minimalist art or architecture. This theory sees art as imitating something else. A figure painting, for example, would need to be recognizably representing a figure. Realism is a form of representationalism since it closely depicts the subject without distortion. Representationalism in Classical art was shown in lifelike portraits and sculptures. In Renaissance art, linear perspective and techniques of showing light and dark further advanced representationalism. The theory evolved by encompassing Impressionistic art that intended to capture the effects of light rather than perfect details.

Critics say that representationalism is a limited theory since it values accurately depicting the subject over other ways of depicting things. Some art movements challenge the idea that art should depict recognizable subjects, like modern or non-representational art.

Examining Mona Lisa Through Representationalism

Leonardo da Vinci's **Mona Lisa** (circa 1503-1506) exemplifies the **representationalism** theory of art with its faithful representation of its subject. Da Vinci used *sfumato*, which is the blending of colors to make imperceptible transitions between them, creating a lifelike portrait that appears three-dimensional. Da Vinci used muted, natural colors that suited the subject and allowed the viewer to focus on the details of his painting. The facial expression was subtle, and he portrayed the subject's facial features as well as the landscape accurately and realistically. He used perspective to create spatial depth, and the *chiaroscuro*, or contrast between light and dark, enhances the accuracy and natural appearance of the portrayal. The emphasis in this painting is on the subject, who is positioned centrally. This supports representationalism since the goal was to realistically portray the subject. The balance is asymmetrical, which is a natural view of the subject.

By not only representing a recognizable figure but also creating a lifelike painting of the subject, da Vinci's painting is a prime example of the representationalism theory of art.

The Formalism Aesthetic Theory

The **formalist** criticism theory deals with analyzing the visual aspects of an artwork, including the elements and principles used. This theory attaches meaning in the artist's use of materials, focusing on how the artwork is made and how it looks, not the narrative it is attempting to convey or any social or historical context. Formalism is useful for analyzing nonrepresentational and abstract art, looking at the artist's use of elements, principles, composition, and media rather than trying to find meaning in the subject matter. With this approach, the critic is looking at the same things in a realistic, representational, or abstract painting, analyzing it in the same way to see if the artist successfully used media and visual elements in their artwork. An extreme form of formalism believes that everything necessary to analyze a work of art is already present in that work and no context or history is applicable to the analysis of artwork.

James Abbott McNeill Whistler's Nocturne in Black and Gold

James Abbott McNeill Whistler's *Nocturne in Black and Gold: The Falling Rocket* (1875) captures the excitement of fireworks in the night sky. This is a loosely painted, abstracted work, getting away from realistic representation. From a formalism perspective, Whistler successfully used composition, as well as the elements and principles of art, in this work. In terms of composition, he used the rule of thirds and placed the horizon line at roughly one-third from the bottom of the painting. The emphasis, or focal point, is the brightest yellow in the lower left. Whistler used strong contrast to help the bright lights and fireworks stand out from the dark background. He used repetition of colors to create a unity throughout the work and lead the eye from each colored area. The brighter and lighter colors in the lower third are balanced by the darker hues and splatters of color higher in the painting.

The Cultural Perspective Aesthetic Theory

The cultural perspective aesthetic theory looks at an artwork with consideration to the cultural and social norms that are associated with it or the artist. Instead of focusing on the elements, principles, and form, or the hidden meaning in an artwork, this theory analyzes how an artwork expresses or fits into the cultural or social viewpoint. The concept of culture includes the customs, beliefs, and traditions of a group of people during a certain time. The cultural perspective aesthetic theory could be used on an American artwork, for example, and explain the perspective that is conveyed with consideration of the origin of the artwork. An artwork from another culture will convey different messages depending on its social norms and cultural ideas and looking at the artwork in this way can reveal these messages. Artists will often express themselves and their culture through their artwork.

AFRICAN MASK

Using the example of an African mask, analyzing this from a cultural perspective of aesthetic theory is much different than using a formalist or deconstruction theory. Instead of finding hidden meanings or analyzing only the visual components, the cultural perspective looks at the connection between the artwork and the culture in which it was made, analyzing how it expresses the culture. African masks were used in ceremonies for religious and social events. The combination of human and animal elements, in this case a human face with animal horns, symbolizes the closeness of humans with the natural environment. In some cases, the person wearing the mask is thought to either communicate with or become the figure that the mask represents. They can represent totem animals, or even the deceased. Masks are an important part of African culture, and they express the significance of cultural ideas through this art form.

THE EXPRESSION AESTHETIC THEORY

The expression aesthetic theory focuses on art as the artist's expression of emotions. It sees art as a process of expressing emotion, and the artist does not necessarily know what emotions they will be expressing before creation. Expression is not a calculated process; rather, it is something that occurs from how the artist created their work. To analyze artwork in this manner, the viewer should imagine the artist's process and attempt to experience the emotion that is being conveyed. As artists create the work, they are thought to move from a feeling of oppression to a sense of clarity and freeness by expressing their emotions. They figure out their own emotions while in the process of expressing them, turning it from a feeling into a visual expression. In evaluating artwork with this in mind, the viewer is looking for and understanding what the artist is expressing emotionally.

WASSILY KANDINSKY'S YELLOW-RED-BLUE

Wassily Kandinsky's *Yellow-Red-Blue* (1925) is an abstract painting filled with shapes and colors. To analyze it using the expression aesthetic theory, one would imagine the artist's process and think about what emotions are being expressed through this artwork. According to the theory, the artist is working out their own emotion while creating the artwork, and this emotion is not fully expressed until the artwork is completed. In this painting, Kandinsky used a combination of bright primary colors, abstract and geometric shapes, and a variety of lines. The eye is led throughout the piece with these lines, and the bright colors catch the eye as well. Primary colors give a sense of simplicity and straightforwardness, and the lines go back and forth from order to a more chaotic feel. The brighter yellow is balanced by the large, darker hues of red and blue, and emotionally the more geometric and brighter left side contrasts with the organic shapes and squiggles on the right, suggesting a contrasting inner turmoil.

Career Opportunities in Art

USING PORTFOLIOS FOR CAREER-RELATED PURPOSES

In addition to using portfolios for assessment and college entrance purposes, they are also used for interviewing for art-related careers. Throughout college, a student will keep their best work. This could be in digital form or a hard copy. Then when interviewing for a position after college, they can assemble their best work either as a digital portfolio or as a physical portfolio. The work should be related to the job field that they applied for, and it should show mastery and proficiency in skills they would use for that position. The work should be clean and organized, and it should be presented so that the presentation itself does not distract from their work. Only the best work should be presented, and the artist should be prepared to speak about how the work was created and how these skills would transfer to a position at the company. In addition to the degree obtained at school, an employer will also want to see evidence that the person is proficient in the skills needed for the job, and a portfolio can demonstrate these skills.

JOB DESCRIPTION, EDUCATION, AND SKILLS NEEDED

GRAPHIC DESIGNER

A graphic designer is responsible for the visual design of print and digital items such as billboards, brochures, signs, corporate communications, logos, website graphics, and more. They will need to be able to communicate with clients to assess their needs, create graphics that will meet the needs, and use a variety of tools to create the graphics. A graphic designer must be creative, technically proficient, and able to keep up with emerging technologies. They will collaborate and communicate with illustrators, photographers, editors, copywriters, web developers, salespeople, and printers. Although skill and creativity are important, it is helpful to have a degree in art or graphic design and to have a portfolio of relevant work to obtain a position. It is also important to have a working knowledge of programs such as Photoshop or Illustrator, depending on the position.

Curator

A curator is responsible for preserving items in a museum, as well as acquiring collections and loans from other museums or institutions. They will organize artifacts or artwork for display and for storage and manage a staff to care for, display, and catalog items. The curator can also be involved in advertising for the institution, as well as giving tours and holding workshops. They can help with fundraising and public relations and work on authenticating the origin and age of pieces obtained by the museum. They need strong skills in management, organization, critical thinking, and working with the public. A curator position generally requires a master's degree in history, art, archaeology, or museum studies. The graduate program will likely include an internship in which the student will get experience working within a museum setting, and a graduate might work as a researcher or assistant to get experience prior to obtaining a curator position.

Animator

An animator is responsible for using a computer or traditional art materials to create animations. Computer animators design 2D and 3D animations for a variety of needs, including television shows, mobile apps, and websites. Many animators are self-employed and work on freelance assignment, although it is possible to be employed with a company, too. A bachelor's degree in computer animation is usually required, as well as a portfolio showing a variety of animation skills. Animators will need to be creative and keep up with emerging technologies. They will need to be able to work with a variety of programs and platforms, and a company will want the prospective animator to be proficient in the programs that the company uses. Internships and freelance positions are valuable for gaining experience because companies will give preference to those with experience and a good portfolio.

Game Developer

A game developer is responsible for the design and creation process for video games. This includes games on video game platforms, computer games, and even games played on phones and tablets. The game developer might be involved in the design of the game, as well as the coding, creation of prototypes, storyline development, and other parts of the development process. The game developer will need to be creative, keep up with changing technology, and work with a team that includes programmers, graphic designers, and software engineers. Generally, a game developer will have a bachelor's degree in software engineering or computer science, but they will also need to be creative and imaginative to come up with and develop new and innovative ideas for games. The game developer will also often have certification in programming languages such as Visual Basic, C++, or Java.

Photographer

A photographer is responsible for capturing and editing images with a digital camera and editing software. A bachelor's degree in photography gives the most in-depth and comprehensive training for a career in photography. It includes aspects of marketing and business, in addition to the technical and artistic skills needed for this field. A photographer can work in many fields, including photojournalism, fine arts, commercial photography, and travel photography. Photographers can also specialize in family or special occasion photography. They need to be proficient with photography equipment and editing software, keep up with new technological advances, and understand how to capture photographs that will suit the needs of their clients or their artistic ambitions. A photographer will need to develop an electronic portfolio, and he or she can work as an assistant to gain experience. A photographer will often display work samples in an online portfolio to gain new clients.

Illustrator

An illustrator produces artwork that is used in books and publications. The artwork can be created with traditional art materials or digitally. An illustrator will need to know how to create illustrations in many different styles, to suit the needs of clients and to suit each project. They will need to be proficient with different artistic media when illustrating by hand, or they should be proficient with computer illustration software when illustrating digitally. Although an illustrator can obtain a degree in art, experience, skill, and creativity are valued more than education in this field. An illustrator is usually a freelance worker, accepting projects from clients. There are many different types of illustration, including medical, botanical, and book illustration, as well as illustration for advertising. An illustrator will need to build up a portfolio with a variety of works showcasing their skills and creativity.

Fine Artist

A fine artist is an artist who creates artwork in their chosen media and style to communicate to their viewers through their artwork. Fine arts include photography and illustration, but in general a fine artist will be self-employed and either create artwork of their choosing or artwork that is commissioned by clients. Although an artist can get formal training in their chosen concentration, such as ceramics, painting, or printmaking, a degree is not necessary to be a fine artist. Instead of a traditional degree, an artist can learn from private classes or an apprenticeship under an artist skilled in their chosen medium. A fine artist needs to be highly proficient in their chosen media, and he or she also needs good communication skills to communicate with clients and galleries. These artists might need to make oral presentations about their work or create a written artist statement to explain their work.

Architect

Architects are responsible for designing residential and commercial buildings that are safe, aesthetically pleasing, and within a budget. They will need an understanding of building materials and architectural styles, as well as creativity and good communication skills. In general, an architect will need a five-year bachelor's degree or a master's degree, as well as a multi-year internship before taking the required state licensing exam. An architect will also consider the impact of the building on the surrounding area or community and can redesign and reuse previously existing spaces. The architect will factor in environmental considerations, work with sustainable design, and decide on building materials to suit a building and site. The architect will also consider the use of interior space in a building, designing the interior to suit the needs of the occupants. An architect needs effective communication skills to speak with clients and to advise people and organizations about the use of space and the design of buildings, working with the clients to find a solution to fit their needs.

Fashion Designer

Fashion designers design clothing and apparel for a variety of needs, and they are responsible for the creative process of designing garments. They are also involved in producing and marketing the clothing. There are associate's, bachelor's, and master's degrees available in this field, and each will provide the student with a different level of understanding and proficiency of the field. The bachelor's and master's degrees will address more advanced skills including marketing, business, and retail issues in fashion. Fashion designers design clothing, shoes, and accessories and will need to understand past fashion trends while keeping up with the current trends. They might design one-of-a-kind pieces or work with a team to design lines of mass-produced fashion that will be sold in retail stores. A fashion designer should be creative and have a solid understanding of technical skills, materials, and proportions when designing clothing.

Art Educator

An art educator is responsible for teaching art processes and art history to students of all ages. To teach in a formal setting, such as K–12 or higher education, a degree in art is needed. For K–12 teaching, the educator must obtain teaching certification in their state, as well as a bachelor's degree in art education. This will include a student-teaching experience in a school setting. For higher education, the educator will generally need one degree higher than what they plan to teach; for example, a master's degree would be needed to teach undergraduate courses. An art educator will need to have an understanding of materials, techniques, and art history, as well as pedagogy, assessment, and classroom management. Strong communication skills and a passion for art are also useful for this field. Art education can be a competitive field, so an educator might need to substitute teach or work in a related position prior to obtaining a position in a school.

Collaboration between Artists

Collaborative Art

There are several ways that artists can collaborate to reinforce **group identity**.

- Artists can use their shared cultural, political, or social identity to share their experiences. Collaborating on projects helps marginalized or underrepresented groups to have a voice. Artists during the Harlem Renaissance, for example, collaborated and promoted Black culture while sharing a sense of pride and identity.
- The use of common colors, symbols, or patterns helps groups to reinforce their sense of identity and unity.
- Artists collaborating on installations or murals that are located in spots significant to a community can create a project that educates others about the artists' histories and values.
- By collaborating on art, artists can document traditions and preserve cultural practices.
- Protest art can involve collaborating to create work that advocates for change or demands rights while reinforcing group identity.

Artist Co-Ops

An **artist co-op**, or **artist cooperative**, is an organization that is owned and operated by a group of artists. The artists within the co-op share resources and collaborate. They use the co-op as a way to showcase and sell their art. Together, the members maintain the space. Many artist co-ops have a gallery where the members can display and sell artwork, and that space will have a lower commission rate than outside galleries.

- Artist co-ops are supportive environments for artists. They allow the artists to stay in control over their own work. They also help build a sense of community among artists. Co-ops play a role in the local community by organizing art events and helping artists engage with the local public while contributing to the local culture.

Chapter Quiz

Ready to see how well you retained what you just read? Scan the QR code to go directly to the chapter quiz interface for this study guide. If you're using a computer, simply visit the online resources page at **mometrix.com/resources719/osatart** and click the Chapter Quizzes link.

Pedagogical Content Knowledge

Curriculum and Instruction for Art

Discipline-Based Art Education

Discipline-based art education (DBAE) involves educating across the following four disciplines: aesthetics, art history, art criticism, and art production. The desires of this approach are to make art education more in line with other disciplines and to standardize the framework for assessment and evaluation within art. With this approach, it is believed that art is for all students, not just for those who have a talent or skill in art creation. It does retain studio art and art creation, but it does not focus solely on the creation of artwork. The goal of this approach is to help students appreciate and understand all types of art and to be able to discuss art using art terms. Curricula created with this approach should give equal weight to the four disciplines and include content from a wide range of visual arts, including other cultures and various styles.

A DBAE Lesson Plan

A lesson plan based on the DBAE model will include aesthetics, art history, art criticism, and art production. The lesson could be involved and may take several class sessions to complete. The lesson would integrate these parts into the study and connect them all together. If students are learning about a specific artist or art style, for example, they would learn about the history and significance of the artist or style, discuss the aesthetics of the style or the artist's artwork, produce an artwork in this style, and talk about art criticism in relation to the style. The lesson could begin with an introduction and guiding questions to get students thinking about the artist or style, and then it could lead into the history of the style. After discussing the history and an explanation of how it is made, students could produce their own work and then talk about how to judge the work aesthetically.

The Backward Design Curriculum Model

The backward design curriculum model begins with the identification of the desired results of a lesson, deciding on acceptable evidence that the lesson was successful and learning occurred, and then planning the instruction based on the desired results and acceptable evidence. In identifying the desired results, the instructor should consider what skills the students should master or what knowledge they should gain from the lesson. They identify big ideas to get across to the learner and what they should remember after the lesson. Next, they should consider assessment methods to think of how to find out if the lesson was successful. The students will need to be able to prove that they have mastered the skills or gained knowledge. After this, the instructor can begin to consider how to deliver the information. He or she will consider teaching methods, materials, and resources to get the information to the students.

Teaching for Artistic Behavior

Teaching for Artistic Behavior is a choice-based approach to teaching art. Students have a choice as to what they will work on, and they learn by practicing problem solving in art. To begin the class, students will observe a short demonstration or participate in a discussion. Some students might try to emulate the technique presented, whereas others use this knowledge for an idea that they have already decided upon. Students will share ideas and collaborate, working as a community of artists. They will learn to persevere through problems and come up with creative solutions. Because students will be working on individual projects, the teacher will work with the students individually or in small groups. They will work at their own pace and assess their progress as they work. They will also learn to speak about and share their work, as well as write an artist statement.

5–6-Year-Old Students

Five-year-olds have limited fine motor ability. They are learning to print and will still often reverse letters and numbers. They have difficulty copying words from a board and will focus on one word at a time because their visual tracking is not developed. At age six, their tracking ability makes reading much easier, but spacing and staying on a line is still difficult. Activities should be chunked into short sessions, with 15–20 minutes being the maximum for quiet sitting. This age group needs carefully planned and consistent guidelines, but at the same time they enjoy active exploration of materials. They can become repetitive for fear of making a mistake when trying something new and will focus more on completing projects quickly than doing it well. These students will need encouragement to continue to finish a work to a satisfactory level of completion and may need to be redirected many times to finish it.

7–8-Year-Old Students

At seven years old, students begin to work more tidily and focus on completing assignments. They tend to enjoy working alone, and they may work slowly, erasing constantly to correct their mistakes. Their ability to reflect on their work is beginning to grow, so introducing self-assessment of artwork could begin now. Printing and drawing go from large to much smaller at this age, and students may have trouble filling up their paper when asked to. Eight-year-olds will be more social and full of energy, working to complete work quickly, and socializing and talking while working. Their pencil grip is maturing, and they can handle more lengthy assignments. They enjoy working in groups and beginning to take on responsibilities. They place importance on peer assessment of their work and may need help with organizational strategies. Eight-year-olds may overestimate their abilities, so shortening assignments or chunking them may be helpful.

9–10-Year-Old Students

Nine-year-olds have increased coordination, which leads to a greater ability to show detail and greater control over a pencil. It is helpful for nine-year-olds to practice with various fine motor skills, including drawing, painting, and fiber arts. This age group is still learning to read and is taking pride in finished works as well as paying attention to detail. Nine-year-olds are competitive and may give up easily when trying to accomplish tasks, so encouragement is helpful. Ten-year-olds enjoy tracing and copying. Their fine motor skills are continuing to increase, and they can begin to use tools such as rulers and templates successfully. They are cooperative and are beginning to be satisfied with their abilities, as well as helping their fellow students. They enjoy being recognized for their efforts and accomplishments and can be productive and conscientious with their schoolwork and homework.

11–12-Year Old Students

Eleven-year-olds are ready to use their fine motor skills to explore more refined skills such as calligraphy, block printing, and new painting techniques. They may enjoy fiber work such as weaving and can use art as a way to channel and express their emotions. They learn well in groups, and they enjoy hands-on learning, as well as puzzles and challenges. They would rather move on to new work than reflect on previous work. Twelve-year-olds are beginning to show skill in specific areas of interest and can set more realistic goals. They have patience and confidence for practicing fine motor skills and are beginning to show interest in more complex skills such as clothing design or architecture. This age group is good at assisting their peers and may begin to show leadership qualities. Their peers' opinions are more important than the teacher's, and their insight and empathy are increasing at this age.

High School Students

High school students tend to have high energy and much more refined fine motor skills than previous grades. They are beginning to have abstract reasoning abilities and are skilled at both self-critique and peer-critique methods. Students in this age group are interested in expressing themselves through art, music, and other creative outlets. They are interested in math and science, as well as geography, current events and world conflicts, the use of natural resources, and basic physics and biology. They are ready to engage more in group discussions, and they are more willing to revise their work and try things multiple times. This age group can learn well in cooperative group situations. They may complain of being bored, but they respond well to variety and challenges in the classroom. At this age, they may enjoy looking at a problem from many sides and considering multiple solutions.

Students with Physical Disabilities

To work with students in the art classroom who are physically disabled, it is helpful to offer choices in media. If a student is not comfortable with or is having difficulty with a particular media, accommodations can be made to use different media (e.g., oil pastels instead of painting). Students with physical disabilities or gross motor issues might find a larger painting or drawing surface easier to work with. Taping the paper to the table can help hold it in place. Tempera paint can be put into a refillable applicator for easier application. Scissors with a double grip can allow the teacher to assist with cutting. Weighted tools can help students hold their materials more steadily and obtain greater control. Some students might find it easier to grip and control larger tools, including thicker pencils, thicker or larger paintbrushes, or thicker pastels or crayons. Glue sticks or larger glue applicators might be easier to control than standard white glue containers.

Students with Mental Disabilities

For students with mental disabilities, chunking projects into small, manageable parts will be beneficial. Presenting one step at a time will make the project easier to work with and giving the student only materials for each step might also help. Flexibility with the project is also helpful because the student might take it in a different direction than originally intended. Large paper can be easier to work with and taping the paper to the table will help the student so that he or she will not need to hold it down. Simpler assignments with a low number of materials that are easy to use and easy to clean up will be beneficial to the student. Frequent praise will encourage the student to continue to work on their project. Some students might be able to create a modified version of the assignment that the main portion of the class is working on, whereas others might need something tailored for their abilities.

Visually or Hearing-Impaired Students

Students with visual impairment can use paint with sand added to it, so that they can feel their design once it has dried. A glue gun can be used to create an outline they can feel for coloring. These students may enjoy working with clay and other materials with a tactile sensation. They will likely find it beneficial to work with larger paper or larger media and will also benefit from being in the front of the room or close to any material demonstration.

Students with hearing impairment may benefit from another student taking notes during a lecture. Making sure the student can see your face when you talk or touching their arm or shoulder to get their attention can be helpful. In some situations, you might wear a speaker with a microphone to make your voice louder so that a student with hearing impairment is able to hear you in the classroom. Again, these students will likely benefit from being in the front of the room or close to any demonstration.

Students with Behavioral Disabilities

When working with a student with behavioral disabilities in the art classroom, it can be helpful to assign tasks or appoint the student as a helper in the classroom. They can count or pass out supplies or help with cleaning up at the end of class. Praise the student often when they are on task and be consistent with rules in the classroom. Find positive things to say about their efforts or products and allow extra time or accommodations with materials if needed. For example, they might find it enjoyable and soothing to work with clay. These students might find it easier to work in a secluded area of the room because this could help with their concentration on the project. The student could benefit from assignments being broken down into smaller parts and frequent check-ins on their progress.

Art Lessons and Activities

Grades K–3

Students in grades K–3 should be strengthening their cutting skills by learning to cut along a line and cutting out shapes. They can practice applying glue with glue sticks and with white glue. These students can practice folding paper, including the accordion fold, and they can begin weaving paper. Drawing shapes and different types of lines and coloring in an area with a solid color are good skills for this age group. They can describe texture, recognize space with regard to overlapping and near or far, and describe personal reasons why they like or dislike an artwork. They can name and recognize the primary colors, as well as warm and cool colors, and they can practice mixing colors. Modeling clay into shapes and experimenting with clay materials can begin at this age. These students can also begin to learn about and recognize significant artworks from major artists and styles.

Grades 4–6

Students in grades 4–6 can begin to recognize and describe the elements of art and principles of design in artwork. They can recognize and use positive and negative space, use one-point perspective, and use correct proportions when drawing faces and bodies. Students in these grades can begin weaving fabric, practice graphic lettering including calligraphy, and practice and improve their brush skills for painting. These students can create and describe a value scale and a 12-hue color wheel and use value in drawing to create realistic shadows. They can use art vocabulary to discuss themes and subjects in artwork and explain how thoughts, experiences, and feelings are expressed in artwork. They can recognize and describe different types of balance and symmetry, as well as the difference between geometric and organic shapes. These students can make connections between art and personal experience and begin to "read" an artwork by identifying what the artist is expressing.

Grades 7–8

Students in grades 7–8 can further practice and strengthen the use of value and shading to create realism. They can practice printmaking skills, use stencils, and continue to strengthen their skills in creating perspective in artwork. These students can begin to layer colors to create new colors and demonstrate the use of the elements of art and principles of design in their artwork in three-dimensional artwork. They can demonstrate and recognize symmetry and asymmetry and use hand building techniques to create ceramic projects. These students can express preferences for different artworks and explain their reasoning. They can describe the feelings and experiences they are expressing in their own artwork and analyze the feelings and experiences expressed in others' artwork. They can describe similarities and differences in artworks and recognize and create foreground, middle ground, and background in artwork to demonstrate space.

High School

Students in high school will continue to use value and shading to portray items realistically. They can draw from life and from photographs and use a grid system to accurately portray a photograph or printed image. These students can focus on longer projects and work with oil paints to achieve blending and glazing in their work. They can work with a pottery wheel and continue to practice hand building techniques. Hand lettering and pen-and-ink work including cross hatching and stippling can be introduced and strengthened at these grade levels. Students can create more realistic and detailed work with graphite and colored pencils and express preferences to work with the media of their choice to achieve their artistic goals. They can present their art and describe the elements and principles, as well as their process for creating their art.

Incorporating Historical Art Concepts

Elementary

Elementary students can begin to invent stories to go along with historical artworks and compare their stories to the actual story behind the artwork. They can compare scenes and people from history with what is common in the present day and describe how clothing or other parts of the artwork are different from today.

This can lead to a discussion about what life was like at that time in history and why the artist was portraying that scene. They can view historical artworks and describe their feelings about the works, as well as whether they like or dislike them. These students can learn about and recognize major artists and artworks, and then they can create a project in the style of that artist to further reinforce the concepts. They could learn to recognize the subject and styles of historical artworks and group artworks by subject and style. Students could create their own portrait or self-portrait after a discussion about why painted portraits were important in history.

High School

In the high school art classroom, students can practice identifying the elements of art and principles of design used in artwork throughout history. They can also begin learning about how the elements of art and principles of design apply to modern and abstract art and discuss the purpose and motivations behind these types of artwork. They can research artists and find artists whose style they enjoy and then find ways to emulate that style through their own artwork. They could analyze the perspective techniques used in Renaissance art and learn about the significance of different art movements. Students could act as a curator, deciding how to put together a collection for a museum to showcase a particular style, movement, or period of time. They could also examine how self-portraits throughout time are similar to and different from modern-day "selfies."

Presenting Student Artwork for Display

There are many possible methods for presenting student artwork for display and increasing the visibility of the school's art program. Art can be hung in the hallways of the school, on bulletin boards, or in display cases. Sculptures and three-dimensional art should be placed in display cases to keep them safe. Two-dimensional work can be attached to black poster board with a 2–3-inch border showing, or it can be matted with matboard. Exhibits can be timed for when parents will be in the school for other purposes, such as enrollment or open house. Artwork could be rotated in other teachers' and administrators' classrooms and offices or the school library. Artwork can be entered in local competitions and displayed in local businesses. Photos of artwork could be submitted to the newspaper, and art shows could be arranged for the local library or mall.

Student Evaluation of Famous Artwork

Students can use various methods to evaluate famous artwork. They can give their initial impression and explain whether they like or do not like the artwork and then explain why. Students can then study the artwork further, looking at the details and the subject, as well as the use of design elements and principles. It might be helpful to give the student a list of elements and principles to look for in the artwork. Students can also read about the artist and the artwork to gain a greater understanding of the context of the artwork and the intentions of the artist. After students evaluate their initial subjective reaction to the artwork and their carefully studied objective evaluation, they can compare the two and think about what changed, if anything, and why. Background and contextual knowledge of the artwork and artist could change students' opinions of the artwork after giving them more insight into why the artwork was created.

Student Self-Evaluation

One method for students to evaluate their own artwork is with the rubric provided for the project. A student can self-evaluate using the rubric to see if they are meeting the criteria for the project, prior to the artwork being evaluated by the instructor. This can help the student understand how their work will be assessed. Older students might take notes, whereas younger students could use a pictorial system such as smiley faces to rate their work on a rubric.

Students can also create their own criteria for evaluating their artwork. A student might need guidance creating their own list of criteria. Younger students could use a simple checklist, whereas older students could use a more complex rating system for this. Students could be asked to choose three or five criteria by which to evaluate their work, including use of materials and cleaning up their workspace.

Necessary Student Knowledge

For a student to appreciate artwork, it is helpful for him or her to have a vocabulary to express what they are seeing. Students need to know what the elements of art and principles of design are and how to discern them in different types of art. They should understand how to describe what they are seeing in subjective and objective ways, to explain the success of an artwork, as well as to explain whether they like or dislike it. It is important to go beyond the basics and be able to explain why the student likes or dislikes the work. Background knowledge of an artist and art movement is helpful, too, to understand where the artwork fits within art history and whether the artist was successful at expressing themselves in this style. Students should also understand how to find and read an artist statement and/or description of the artwork to glean more information for appreciating an artwork.

Fostering Independent Learning about Art

Independent Learning About Art

For students to learn independently about art, they must know how to find valid information and have a desire to seek out that information. To promote a desire to learn more about art independently, it is helpful to expose students to many various artists, artworks, styles, and materials in the classroom. If a student is interested in the current topic and wants to know more, then opportunities for enrichment can be provided. Instructors can show students how to find information online and how to check if a source is valid. They can provide books to find further information as well and arrange a tour of the library so that the librarian can point out a section for additional resources for the art classroom. The instructor can also encourage students to bring in their artwork and ideas from home and incorporate those in the lessons in the classroom, tying in their independent work to the classwork.

Connecting Ideas Between Art and Student's Lives

Elementary Students

Elementary students are interested in their friends, family, and pets, as well as themselves. They also enjoy talking about and expressing their favorites of different categories, including food, animals, or games. This age group is beginning to explore who they are in the context of a larger group. They excel in experimenting with materials, and they might be more interested in the process than in the final product. They are comfortable taking risks with materials and are willing to use new materials. To connect ideas between art and their lives, elementary students could create artwork about themselves, such as a self-portrait, or about their pets, family, and friends. They could create artwork about their activities outside of school, such as sports or trips they have gone on. They could create artwork about some of their favorite items, to express what they like.

Middle School Students

Middle school students, like elementary students, can still be egocentric and focused on themselves. At the same time, they are developing their own interests and hobbies, as well as figuring out what they are skilled at doing. They value their friends' input, while becoming more self-aware and individualistic. Students in this age group are beginning to take more pride in their finished work. They are less apt to experiment and are more likely to be critical of their work. To connect their lives to artwork, middle school students can create autobiographical artwork including themselves and their new interests. They can work collaboratively with their friends and classmates to create artwork about what they want to express or what they deem is important. Their increased coordination and attention to detail can lead to longer and more involved projects in which they can express their feelings or show details about their lives that they wish to share.

High School Students

High school students are beginning to distance themselves from their parents and teachers as sources of information and turning instead to their friends and peers. This age group is interested in fairness and justice, as well as current events. They value their friends and social standing and are beginning to think about how they will fit into the adult world. To connect their lives to their art, students could create an autobiographical painting, sculpture, or collage of what is important to them, which could include their friends, their room, their car, or their home. High school students could also portray issues in their artwork that are important to them, such as environmental or political issues. This age group enjoys expressing themselves creatively and can express their identity through artwork. Their motor skills are refined enough that they can express themselves successfully through many different media. Having a goal that is connected to their lives and that they find significant will yield a higher quality of artwork.

Technology

Creating Artwork

Technology can be used as part of creating traditional artwork. A student can watch videos and read tutorials to learn new art techniques, as well as to perfect or practice techniques that they already use. They can read about different methods and materials and see how other artists use these methods and materials.

Students can also use technology for the creation of artwork itself. Many free or paid programs can be used, including Adobe Photoshop, Adobe Illustrator, or even Microsoft Paint. A student can use these programs to create and then print out digital artwork. A desktop or laptop computer with a trackpad or mouse could be used, or a student could use a tablet with a stylus to draw and edit artwork directly on the screen. Students can use digital cameras to capture images for their artwork and use the photographs as source imagery for traditional artwork or use them in their digital artwork.

Learning About Artwork

With technology and the Internet, a student can virtually tour a museum and see artworks that they might not be able to see in person. Students can use technology to read about artists and artworks. They can see the newest artwork from various artists and view new shows in museums and galleries. A museum will often have their collection available to view online, including the artwork that is not currently on display. In addition to this, museums will often produce extra online content to allow people to zoom into artwork or focus on certain artists or collections, furthering the viewer's understanding. In addition to viewing artwork, students can read about artists and artwork from many different sources, including museums, artists, educational websites, and even online dictionaries. Online courses are available for students to learn more about an artist, a technique, or more about art in general.

Locating the Meaning of Unfamiliar Terms

When a student locates an **unfamiliar term** when learning about art, an educator can supply the student with the appropriate sources to locate the meaning of the term.

Dictionaries provide the definitions of words. A student can find a term in a dictionary and see its meaning, pronunciation, and the word's origin. The dictionary also gives antonyms and variant spellings. If the term is found in a sentence or paragraph, the student might be able to use context clues or familiar words within the text to figure out its meaning. The student might also find that the word is similar to another familiar word. They might already know the root word, suffix, or prefix and be able to determine the meaning from its parts. If they remove the prefix, suffix, or both, they might more readily recognize the root word. If the text that the word is located in has a glossary in the back, the student can use the glossary to find the word's meaning. The glossary works as a dictionary that is specific to that text. It defines words within the text that the reader might not recognize.

For art-specific terms, a guide like the *Bulfinch Pocket Dictionary of Art Terms* is helpful. A regular dictionary will likely include the art term but may also have other definitions of the word. The word *capital*, for example, will be defined in a dictionary as an important city or town in a region. The art dictionary, though, will define it as the head of a column or pillar.

Texts and Technologies Used to Retrieve Content-Related Information

When finding **content-related information**, it is important that **students** use reliable sources. Available texts and online sources may have a wealth of information, but the student will need to discern between reliable and unreliable sources. Sources that anyone can edit, like blogs or Wikipedia, are not considered reliable. The student should look for official publications, scholarly articles, and reputable organizations. The information should include an author's name, and the author should be an authority on the topic they are writing about. Students should avoid sources that present biased information and instead look for sources that give an unbiased point of view. Online videos from reputable sources like professional artists, educational resources, and art material manufacturers can help students learn or hone their techniques.

Other sources of reliable information include:

- Art material manufacturers, like Golden or Winsor & Newton, often create educational material that helps students learn more about how to use the art materials.
- Art-related trade magazines, such as *Artforum* and *ARTnews*, can help students find relevant and emerging information about artists and techniques.
- Museums, including the Museum of Modern Art (MOMA) and the Louvre, offer information on the artists and artwork they exhibit.
- Artcyclopedia, which is a fine art search engine, and the *Art & Architecture Thesaurus* offer further information about art terms, art techniques, and artists.

Museums as a Learning Medium

A museum can incorporate touchscreen technology for visitors to find out more about a particular artist, painting, or art movement. Museums can also use audio technology to create a docent-led tour experience with headphones and a guidebook. These recorded tours can allow a visitor to have an in-depth tour of the museum on their own time and at their own pace. A docent-led tour can include a prearranged phone conference with an artist as part of the experience, and the visitors on the tour can ask the artist questions. Video can also be used as technology in museums. TV screens can show the video art of different artists, played on a loop for viewers to stop and watch. They could also show an artist talking about their work. These videos might be shown in the gallery area, or they may be put into a special viewing room separate from the gallery where the sound will not distract other visitors.

Assessment in Art Classrooms

Formative Assessment

Formative assessments should inform students about their progress continuously through a course. The teacher can monitor students' progress and intervene if there are issues. They help the teacher understand students' learning styles and needs. A formative assessment can help the teacher see where students are in relation to the learning goals, and then the teacher can help students get closer to those goals. These are nongraded assessments in which students can practice their skills and get to know their deficiencies in understanding prior to taking a graded assessment. Formative assessments should be engaging, and art education offers many opportunities for creative work. In an online classroom there is the opportunity to use interactive assessment methods to engage the student. The teacher should model or demonstrate what good work will look like; the student internalizes the goals and process, and he or she is eventually able to see their progress to the goals themselves. Formative assessments can include exit slips, journals, sketchbooks, or even a short ungraded activity.

Summative Assessment

Although art is generally subjective in nature, it is still important to have a summative assessment at the end of a period of instruction to assess student learning. Students can demonstrate their understanding of concepts through performance assessment such as art creation or a demonstration of their use of techniques or materials. Students could also create an oral presentation explaining their artwork, the elements and principles within their art, or their understanding of a concept that was presented in class. Another summative assessment technique is the use of written tests, which could include selected response questions or short answer and essay questions. The summative assessment should provide proof that students have reached the learning goals for that lesson or unit of study before moving on to other topics. Through the results of the summative assessment, the teacher can determine if the students have met the objective for the lesson or unit of study.

Review Video: Formative and Summative Assessments
Visit mometrix.com/academy and enter code: 804991

Performance Assessment

Performance assessment is an assessment method that is often used in visual arts because through a performance assessment, students can demonstrate their art-making skills. A performance assessment is an authentic task in which students show what they are able to do. This could include the creation of an art project from start to finish, their problem-solving methods for creating art, the demonstration of their skills with a particular technique or medium, or even the creation of a portfolio. Performance assessments allow the instructor to assess a student's performance against their prior performance, rather than against a standard benchmark. The instructor will often provide a rubric or checklist for a performance assessment, so the student can gauge their own progress toward their goal. Students are able to demonstrate what they have learned while also seeing their progress as compared with past performances.

Metacognitive Skills

Metacognitive skills are skills that help a student understand and regulate their own learning. It is a process of thinking about your own thinking. These skills include monitoring one's own comprehension, self-assessment, and correcting work based on the self-assessment. A student with strong metacognitive skills can approach and solve a problem effectively, assess their own progress, and adjust their processes based on their own assessment. In an art classroom, it is important for a student to be able to approach an artistic problem, find solutions, reflect on their processes throughout the project, and adjust their approach based on the results. A student can use a rubric for the project to see if their progress is meeting the goals of the project and adjust his or her approach to meet these goals. Modeling self-assessment strategies in the classroom and having students practice assessment to reflect on their own artwork can strengthen these metacognition skills and help them work independently toward a goal.

A Portfolio

A portfolio is a collection that represents a student's body of work. It can show a student's progress, and it allows students to showcase their best work. It gives evidence of a student's learning and growth throughout a project or course. Portfolios can be used as either a summative or a formative assessment technique, or it can include some elements of both. As a formative assessment, a portfolio will show the development of a student's work. Students can chronicle their work as they progress and show the steps taken to create an artwork. A summative portfolio will show a broad range of finished work, and it will display the student's progress and growth throughout a unit or course. The summative portfolio will not include everything they created in class; rather, students will curate their work and decide which works they want to showcase within the portfolio. A portfolio will generally be assessed by a rubric.

Using Rubrics to Assess Art

Rubrics are used to assess student work with set criteria. This is especially useful for art projects, which are generally thought of as being subjectively assessed. Using a rubric to assess artwork will help the instructor grade all work fairly and equally. The teacher sets the expected standards of performance and then assesses the work objectively based on these standards. It is helpful to give the rubric to students while explaining the project, so that the students will understand what the goals of the project are and how their work is being assessed. Then they can work toward reaching the goals on the rubric. The students can assess their own progress throughout the project and adjust their processes to reach these goals. This enhances metacognition skills. Rubrics also help the teacher assess student work efficiently and fairly. All work is graded by the standards set on the rubric, and it is not compared to other students' work or graded subjectively. Rubrics can also expose gaps in student understanding because all students are assessed by the same standards.

STANDARDS-BASED ASSESSMENT

Standards-based assessment in visual arts focuses on a student's work toward and mastery of a standard. This includes establishing levels of proficiency and assessing the student's proficiency level for each standard. This will not include things that are outside of the standard, such as effort or class participation.

The teacher will develop topics for instruction based on standards, and then he or she will decide what skills students will need to master for these standards. They will establish developing, proficiency, and mastery levels for each skill and then assess the students' work based on these levels. The rubric is created in advance with the lessons, and the student is aware of what they will be learning as well as what they will be assessed on. Standards-based assessment can better communicate student achievement and mastery of skills to students and parents. It can also provide teachers with evidence to reflect upon and adjust their teaching.

CROSS-CURRICULAR CONNECTIONS

Many cross-curricular connections can be made between the art classroom and other subjects. Reading, writing, speaking, and listening standards can be met while writing artist statements, writing about the elements and principles found in an artwork, making oral presentations, researching a project, and listening to other students' presentations. Reading can also be connected to art while exploring book illustrations and how they relate to the text of a novel. Connections can be made to history while explaining the historical context of artworks and art movements. The science of color mixing and light as well as how oil- and water-based materials react to each other touch on science subjects. Measuring paper for cutting or measuring to create a grid for artwork relates to math. Math is also used when scaling an image up or down, understanding the size of a famous artwork, or converting units of measurement.

Art Classroom Management

SAFETY

DRAWING AND CUTTING TOOLS

When using drawing and cutting tools in the art classroom, safe practices should first be modeled by the teacher. Safety issues should be covered in the lesson and demonstration. Elementary students should be given age-appropriate scissors, and they should be instructed to walk with the scissors pointing away from their body if they need to move around in the classroom with scissors. High school students can begin to use paper cutters, utility knives, and X-Acto knives, although proper safety procedures should be covered first and their use should be monitored by the instructor. An X-Acto knife should always have the cap put back on it when not in use, and a utility knife should be retracted back into its handle. If a cutter has a guard, it should be kept in place. Drawing materials should be kept out of mouths, and pencils, like scissors, should be carried while walking with the point facing away from the body. Students should be instructed on how to safely use a pencil sharpener, or in younger elementary grades the instructor can sharpen the pencils. All sharp materials should be counted at the end of class.

CLAY AND CERAMICS

When using clay and ceramic materials with elementary grades, it is important for students to understand not to put clay in their mouths and to wash their hands after using clay. If it is an air-dry clay, it should always be stored in an airtight container or bag to keep it from drying out. For older students using clay tools, the instructor should model safe use of clay tools such as a wire cutter or loops. All tools should be washed with water and dried before storing. The tables and tools should be wiped down with a wet paper towel or rag to remove dust because clay dust is hazardous to breathe. Firing student pieces in a kiln should occur while students are away, if possible. If this is not possible, students should be instructed to stay away from the kiln because of the heat and potential for burns.

Painting

When working with painting materials, students should understand that no paint or brushes should be put in the mouth. Some paints, such as cadmiums and cobalts, should not make contact with skin. It is generally not good practice to paint with fingers unless it is a designated finger painting medium. When working with any paint, it is important to clean the brushes with appropriate solvent or water so that the paint does not dry on the brushes. Although acrylics, watercolor, and tempera can be cleaned up with water, oil paint requires solvent such as turpentine to clean brushes and surfaces. Turpentine should be handled carefully and not poured down the sink. It should be stored in a cabinet with proper MSDS sheets and a lock so that the teacher and other necessary staff have the only access. Oil painting also requires proper ventilation due to the fumes.

Material Safety Data Sheets

An MSDS sheet, or material safety data sheet, contains the information for the potential hazards associated with a material, as well as how to properly use the material. It describes the health, fire, reactivity, and environmental hazards for the material. These documents are created by the manufacturer of the material and should be read and understood before using the material in the classroom. Students should be instructed on how to properly use each material, what to avoid doing, and how materials should be cleaned up and stored. A fire extinguisher should be in the classroom in case of any flammable materials. All materials should be stored properly, and safety gear should be worn if necessary, including gloves, aprons, and goggles. Hazardous materials should be stored in a fire-resistant, locked cabinet, and all materials should be cleaned up at the end of each class. A designation of AP (approved product) or CP (certified product) should appear on materials for younger students. More hazardous art materials can be used in high school with proper supervision.

Proper Care and Storage of Materials

At the end of each art class, all materials should be cleaned up and stored in their proper place. Procedures should be explained by the teacher at the beginning of the year, and there should be a designated place for each material. Proper care should be explained and modeled at the beginning of each lesson. All surfaces should be wiped down at the end of each class to minimize dust and particles. Brushes should be washed thoroughly and stored in a jar with the handle end down, to protect the bristles. Caps should be put on markers and paints, and glues should be closed so they do not dry out. Drawers and bins should be labeled so students know where to put their materials when they are done. Solvents should be stored separately in a fire-resistant cabinet, and solvent-soaked rags should be stored in an airtight Occupational Safety and Health Administration-approved container to prevent spontaneous combustion. Clay should be stored in an airtight container to prevent drying, and wet cloths should be used to wipe up clay dust.

Chapter Quiz

Ready to see how well you retained what you just read? Scan the QR code to go directly to the chapter quiz interface for this study guide. If you're using a computer, simply visit the online resources page at **mometrix.com/resources719/osatart** and click the Chapter Quizzes link.

OSAT Practice Test

Color Images

Some of the questions and explanations printed in this book refer to colors or techniques that are difficult to represent in grayscale. Many of the images included in your practice test are available in color in our free interactive version of this test. For a better testing experience, please use our interactive practice tests found on your online resources link.

Want to take this practice test in an online interactive format?
Check out the online resources page, which includes interactive practice questions and much more: **mometrix.com/resources719/osatart**

1. Which of the following architectural styles is known for the use of pointed arches, gargoyles, and a sense of upward visual movement?

a. Classical
b. Art Nouveau
c. Gothic
d. Baroque

2. Vincent van Gogh, Paul Cézanne, and Paul Gauguin are artists associated with which style of art?

a. Post-Impressionism
b. Surrealism
c. Fauvism
d. Cubism

3. Which of these terms refers to a performance or event created in the context of fine art?

a. Happening
b. Installation
c. Sculpture
d. Plein air

4. When a piece of clay is partially dry but not completely dry, it is ________.

a. bisque
b. greenware
c. leather hard
d. bone dry

5. Which of these painting techniques involves the application of thick layers of paint with visible brushstrokes?

a. Sfumato
b. Sgraffito
c. Wash
d. Impasto

6. In Leonardo da Vinci's *Mona Lisa,* he used a painting technique to give a smoky, cloudy appearance and soften the appearance of any hard lines. Which of the following techniques does this describe?

a. Sgraffito
b. Sfumato
c. Velatura
d. Imprimatura

7. Which of the following is an example of an accommodation in the classroom for a student with behavioral disabilities?

a. Using large paper and taping it to the table
b. Outlining a design with glue
c. Using larger tools and offering choices of media
d. Working on the art project in a quiet area of the room

8. Claes Oldenburg was an American sculptor in the 1960s known for creating large-scale Pop art sculptures, often of food items. How did his work challenge the traditional means of sculpture?

a. He challenged the traditional media of metal and marble by sculpting with wire.
b. He painted his sculptures, which was not traditionally done.
c. He challenged the traditions of sculpture by using assistants to create his works.
d. He changed the traditional hard medium of sculpture to a soft, changeable format.

9. Which type of assessment in the art classroom best reflects a student's ability to apply art-making skills?

a. Performance
b. Traditional
c. Formative
d. Summative

10. Which statement best describes the purpose of sculptures in the Classical period in ancient Greece?

a. Sculptures sought to capture the true likeness of a person.
b. Sculptures were made to honor gods and goddesses.
c. Sculptures were used in fertility rituals.
d. Sculptures were created to provide a resting place for a soul after death.

11. Which of the following best describes this sculpture as analyzed with the formalism aesthetic theory?

a. This sculpture evokes feelings of warmth and closeness due to its color and form.
b. This monochromatic sculpture is red, and it is asymmetrically balanced, leading the eye in arcs toward the ground.
c. This sculpture would be more successful if it represented a recognizable object.
d. This large sculpture is intimidating; the red color adds to the menacing appearance.

12. Which of the following was NOT a goal of the artists of the Impressionist movement?

a. To capture fleeting moments of time
b. To portray the momentary effect of light on a scene or object
c. To depart from depicting a scene in a realistic manner
d. To portray exaggerated scenes and heightened emotions

13. Hierarchical proportion was used in many cultures to denote relative importance of figures, including Mayan, Renaissance, and Ancient Egyptian artwork. Which of the following describes the hierarchical proportion with which figures would be portrayed in Ancient Egyptian artwork?

a. People of higher status are portrayed on a larger scale than those of lower status.
b. People of higher status are portrayed on a diagonal higher than those of lower status.
c. People of higher status are portrayed more realistically than those of lower status.
d. People of higher status are portrayed with larger features than those of lower status.

14. An artist wants to try using both a wax- or an oil-based medium and a water-based medium, but does not want any resistive effects. Which method of layering these multimedia materials would best achieve this purpose?

a. Layering acrylic paint over oil paint
b. Layering watercolor paint over encaustic paint
c. Layering tempera paint over oil pastels
d. Layering crayon over watercolor paint

15. A tertiary color can be created by mixing which of the following?

a. Red and yellow
b. Yellow and orange
c. Blue and yellow
d. Orange and green

16. Which of the following was NOT an architectural need or advancement that led to the construction of skyscrapers?

a. The invention of the first safe passenger elevator
b. The development of load-bearing walls for construction
c. The refinement of the steel process which led to steel skeletons in buildings
d. The need for more vertical buildings to create more space in cities

17. Which of the following art related careers will be least likely to depend on the use of computer graphics and image editing programs?

a. Illustrator
b. Photographer
c. Curator
d. Graphic designer

18. Which of the following would reinforce the goals of the Feminist art movement?

a. Portraying women in a more abstract manner
b. Creating artwork that supports stereotypes about traditional female roles
c. Excluding modern art from the canon of artwork made by women
d. Embracing materials traditionally tied to their gender in artwork made by women

19. Which photographic technique will result in a clear and focused subject with a background out of focus, as in the following image?

a. Using a larger aperture
b. Using a higher ISO
c. Using a slower shutter speed
d. Using a greater distance from the camera to the subject

20. This painting shows religious subject matter with elongated figures, unnatural poses, and dramatic lighting. During which art period or movement would this have most likely been painted?

a. Medieval
b. Renaissance
c. Mannerism
d. Romanticism

21. How was the Postmodernist art movement similar to the Dada art movement?

a. They both sought to portray dream-like scenes with accuracy.
b. They both sought to depart from the traditions and authority of previous art movements.
c. They both sought to bring attention to the contributions of previously unrecognized artists.
d. They both sought to explore the emotional response of the artist.

Refer to the following for question 22:

An EC teacher gives children an art activity of illustrating and labeling plants or animals by name that they learned about in a science unit. However, one student in the classroom has difficulty focusing on her project and is often found wandering away from her desk, distracting other students.

22. Which of the following would be the LEAST helpful accommodation for this student?

a. The student's project should be broken down into smaller chunks.
b. The student should be given larger materials and larger paper to work with.
c. The student should be given a secluded area in the room to work and concentrate.
d. The student should be given frequent praise during the project.

23. A teacher writes their curriculum focusing first on setting the goals of instruction, then the assessment methods and the lesson plans. Which curriculum design method is this teacher using?

a. Teaching for Artistic Behavior
b. Discipline Based Art Education
c. The TABA method
d. Backward design

24. Which of the following describes a student's use of metacognitive skills in the art classroom?

a. A student uses a rubric to assess their progress toward reaching their goals.
b. A student answers an essay question about an artist's life.
c. A student creates a sketch in their sketchbook drawn from real life.
d. A student uses different media than they are used to for creating artwork.

25. An artist paints thin, transparent layers of oil paint on top of another layer of oil paint that has already dried. What is this technique called?

a. Alla prima
b. Impasto
c. Glazing
d. Plein air

26. Which of the following paint supports would be most ideal for an egg tempera painting?

a. Canvas
b. Paper
c. Masonite
d. Linen

27. Which of the following art skills would be most appropriate to students in Kindergarten through 3rd grade?

a. Drawing with two-point perspective
b. Mixing secondary colors
c. Calligraphy
d. Working with oil paints

28. Which of the following safety practices would NOT be done in the art classroom as a result of the SDS sheets?

a. A fire extinguisher is kept in the classroom due to flammable materials.
b. An apron, gloves, and goggles are used with certain corrosive printmaking materials.
c. Solvents are kept in a fireproof cabinet.
d. The blade of a utility knife is retracted when not in use.

29. Which of the following art movements did NOT aim to portray their subjects in an exaggerated or idealized way?

a. The Ashcan School
b. The Hudson River School
c. Romanticism
d. Neoclassical

30. What surface would have been used for this painting from the Byzantine era?

a. Wood panel
b. Linen
c. Canvas
d. Paper

31. Which of the following describes how the artist used the elements to create contrast and emphasis in this artwork?

a. The artist used primary colors to contrast against the neutral colors throughout.
b. The artist used the contrast of warm and cool colors to help the orange buildings stand out against the green.
c. The artist used a wide variety of textures to create emphasis in the artwork.
d. The artist used different values and shapes throughout the artwork to create emphasis in the artwork.

32. How did the Impressionism art movement react against the advent of photography in the art world?

a. Impressionist artists sought to paint as quickly as possible to capture fleeting moments in time with a sense of realism.
b. Impressionist artists wanted to use minimal colors to capture a scene.
c. Impressionist artists wanted to work indoors rather than out in the field.
d. Impressionist artists sought to capture an impression of a scene rather than a faithful reproduction.

33. An art museum wishes to incorporate technology into their new exhibition showcasing Pop art. Which of the following would NOT be an effective way to incorporate this?

a. Touchscreen technology could give the viewer more information about the artists.
b. Multiple video screens showing the artists explaining their process could be set up together in the gallery.
c. A docent-led tour could include a pre-arranged video call with an artist to discuss their work.
d. Visitors could be provided headphones and a guide book for a self-led tour experience.

34. Which of the following statements accurately describes an ethical standard relating to artwork?

a. Permission should be obtained if using source materials that are not public domain or out of copyright.
b. Copyright for an artwork begins once the artist files for copyright.
c. Copyright laws are primarily determined on the state level.
d. It is permissible to draw or paint a copy of a famous artwork and sell copies of it.

35. Which of the following architectural elements is featured in this photograph?

a. Triangulated pediment
b. Flying buttress
c. Ornamental parapet
d. Transept

36. Which of the following painting techniques would NOT be used to create texture in an artwork?

a. Sgraffito
b. Dry brush
c. Wash
d. Impasto

37. Which of the following principles of design helps to create the focal point in this painting?

a. Contrast
b. Movement
c. Balance
d. Rhythm

38. Which of the following is NOT a tool commonly used for printmaking?

a. Burnisher
b. Brayer
c. Gouge
d. Mandrel

39. Which of the following was a significant contribution of artists during the Renaissance art period?

a. Lost wax casting
b. Linear perspective
c. Paint in tubes
d. Acrylic paint

40. A wooden sculpture of a youthful human figure shows symmetry and is visually abstracted. It is used for religious purposes. In which culture was this sculpture most likely created?

a. Ancient Roman
b. Mycenaean
c. African
d. Egyptian

41. Fresco was a technique often used in the Renaissance art period. Which of the following best describes this process?

a. Oil paint was applied to wet plaster.
b. Pigments mixed with plaster were applied to a surface.
c. Tempera paint was applied to dry plaster.
d. Pigments mixed with water were applied to wet plaster.

42. Which of the following is a technique used to create a more interesting composition in an artwork or a painting?

a. Intaglio
b. Rule of thirds
c. Trompe l'oiel
d. Middle ground

43. Which of the following best describes some of the characteristics of Baroque architecture?

a. Pear-shaped domes, marble or faux finishing, and bronze gilding
b. Hemispherical domes, columns, and decorative pilasters
c. Semicircular arches, barrel or groin vaults, and thick walls
d. Circular domes, pendentives, and mosaics

44. Which of the following is NOT an example of relating context to an artwork?

a. Finding more information about the cultural values of African artists
b. Reading about the social movements at the time of Harlem Renaissance artwork
c. Practicing similar techniques of a Pointillist artist
d. Researching a Dada artist's values and personal views

45. Which of the following color schemes did Vincent van Gogh use to create contrast in this painting?

a. Analogous
b. Complementary
c. Triadic
d. Tetradic

46. Which of the following is NOT a way to improve the composition of a still life?

a. Arranging the items in a symmetrical grouping
b. Overlapping items rather than having the edges touch
c. Using realistic perspective
d. Including a focal point in the arrangement

47. Which of the following describes a similarity between Minimalist art and Color Field painting?

a. The use of mainly primary colors
b. Paint extending onto the edges of the canvas
c. A focus on consumer items as the subject
d. Large, flat areas of color with minimal brush strokes

48. Which of the following color schemes was used to create this painting?

a. Split complementary
b. Triadic
c. Complementary
d. Tetradic

49. Which of the following will most likely benefit a person seeking a career in graphic design?

a. Certification in programming languages such as Visual Basic, C++, or Java
b. An apprenticeship under an artist skilled in their chosen medium
c. A working knowledge of programs such as Photoshop, Illustrator, and InDesign
d. Experience with pedagogy, assessment, and classroom management

50. Which of the following is NOT a common file format for images?

a. JPEG
b. GIF
c. AVI
d. PNG

51. Which of the following is an example of a triadic color scheme?

a. Orange, green, and purple
b. Blue, green, and purple
c. Red, yellow, and orange
d. Orange, blue, and green

52. This photograph, one of the first works of Modernism during a time of many immigrants coming to America, was captured by which photographer?

a. Alfred Stieglitz
b. Edward Weston
c. Dorothea Lange
d. Louis Daguerre

53. Which of the following color schemes is evident in this artwork?

a. Triadic
b. Tetradic
c. Analogous
d. Complementary

54. Which of the following is NOT an accurate difference between acrylic paint and oil paint?

a. Acrylic paint dries much more quickly than oil paint.
b. Oil paint is more flexible than acrylic paint when dry.
c. Acrylic paint can be cleaned with water, while oil paint requires solvents.
d. Oil paint has no visible color shift when it dries, while acrylic paint becomes darker when it dries.

55. The concept of infinity is often used in patterns in Middle Eastern art. What is one common symbolic interpretation of why these patterns are used in Middle Eastern art?

a. They contrast the infinity with man's finite existence on earth.
b. They are useful for covering large areas of walls.
c. They allow different artists to easily copy the same pattern.
d. They represent the magnitude of the soul.

56. Which of the following is NOT a characteristic of traditional Japanese woodblock printing?

a. They often depicted landscapes, history, geishas, and scenes from everyday life.
b. They used large, flat areas of color in the composition.
c. They used primarily black for the prints.
d. They began by drawing in ink then gluing it to the wood block for carving.

57. A comic book hero wears a costume that evenly features red, blue, and yellow. Which of the following best describes the character's color scheme?

a. Dichromatic
b. Monochromatic
c. Analogous
d. Triadic

58. An artist wants to create a pen and ink drawing with a lot of detailed work. Which surface would work best for this endeavor?

a. Watercolor paper
b. Canvas
c. Illustration board
d. Charcoal paper

59. Which of the following is NOT a common oil painting medium?

a. Poppy oil
b. Linseed oil
c. Grapeseed oil
d. Stand oil

60. Which of the following best describes the daguerreotype process?

a. An image is created on paper coated with silver iodide.
b. An image is created on a silvered copper plate.
c. An image is created on a glass plate.
d. An image is created on a tin plate.

61. This metalworking technique involves forming metal threads into a lace pattern. Which of the following is the name of this technique?

a. Filigree
b. Enameling
c. Fusion
d. Soldering

62. Which of the following forms of printmaking was applied in this image?

a. Relief
b. Serigraphy
c. Lithography
d. Intaglio

63. Which of the following watercolor techniques would this artist have used to create the hazy sky and clouds in this painting?

a. Dry brush
b. Wash
c. Crayon resist
d. Wet on wet

64. If an artwork is analyzed by the formalism aesthetic theory, which of the following would NOT be included in the analysis?

a. The artist used primarily warm and neutral colors in the painting.
b. The trompe l'oeil technique creates an optical illusion in this painting.
c. The lighter objects contrast against the dark background.
d. The ribbons and the feather have a smooth implied texture.

65. An artist's oil painting has dried and the paint has begun to crack. Which of the following is a possible cause of this issue?

a. The artist varnished the oil painting after it dried.
b. The artist mixed linseed oil with their paint.
c. The artist did not prime the canvas before painting.
d. The artist worked in layers and used a glazing technique.

66. Which of the following color schemes is primarily used in this artwork?

a. Complementary
b. Triadic
c. Analogous
d. Tetradic

67. This painting by Vincent van Gogh uses which of the following color schemes?

a. Complementary
b. Triadic
c. Warm
d. Analogous

68. Which of the following was a reason that Baroque architecture spread throughout South America in the 1600s and 1700s?

a. South American architects read about this style and began to use it.
b. Spain colonized Central and South America.
c. Architects from France emigrated to South America.
d. Baroque architecture was a reaction against the previous Neoclassical architecture.

69. Which of the following video file formats would be the most ideal for saving and sharing a high-definition video?

a. MP4
b. WMV
c. MPEG
d. MOV

70. Which of the elements of art would best direct the viewer's eye when representing this road in an artwork?

a. Color
b. Line
c. Texture
d. Value

71. Which of the following is NOT an aim of video sculpture?

a. To integrate video aspects into an object, location or performance.
b. To diverge from the standard narrative video configuration.
c. To present videos in new and innovative ways.
d. To show a video in a linear format with a beginning and end.

72. Which of the following best describes how the artist used color in this artwork?

a. The monochromatic color scheme simplifies the artwork and helps the viewer focus on the subject.
b. The warmth of the greens and blues creates an inviting and happy scene.
c. The analogous colors help the viewer's eye flow through the scene.
d. The warm colors advance and draw the viewer's eye, whereas the cool colors recede.

73. How does the traditional creation of porcelain challenge the perception of the "Made in China" slogan, which calls to mind mass-produced products made inexpensively in China?

a. Porcelain is no longer made in China.
b. The creation of porcelain is labor intensive.
c. The materials used for porcelain are very expensive.
d. Porcelain parts can only be made by artisans.

74. This painting is an example of which of the following painting techniques?

a. Alla prima
b. Plein air
c. Trompe l'oeil
d. Sgraffito

75. During which of the following artistic movements would this painting have been created?

a. Neoclassical
b. Mannerism
c. Medieval
d. Post-Impressionism

76. Which of the following best describes a way that visual art has influenced popular culture?

a. Artists appropriated images from comic books to use in their artwork.
b. The bright colors and repetition of Pop art were subsequently used in fashion and advertising.
c. Mass-produced objects were a subject in the artworks.
d. Artists used commercial methods such as screen-printing.

77. Which of the following best describes why watercolor paper should be stretched before it is painted on?

a. So the paint will adhere to the surface
b. So the colors will mix properly
c. To make the paper into a larger surface
d. So that it will not warp

78. Which of the following principles of design is most evident in this painting?

a. Balance
b. Contrast
c. Emphasis
d. Rhythm

79. If an artist wanted to create a drawing with a great amount of detail, which of the following drawing instruments would be best suited for this?

a. Vine charcoal
b. Red conte crayon
c. 2H pencil
d. Black chalk

80. Which of the following is an instrument used to support and steady the artist's hand while painting or drawing?

a. Mahlstick
b. Tortillon
c. Frisket
d. T-square

81. If an artist wanted to use pen and ink to emulate the visual color blending of the Pointillism art movement, which of the following would be the most appropriate technique?

a. Stippling
b. Cross hatching
c. Hatching
d. Wash

82. Which of the following painting surfaces does NOT need to be primed with a primer before it is painted on?

a. Wood panel, when using oil paints
b. Canvas, when using acrylic paints
c. Wood panel, when using egg tempera paints
d. Watercolor paper, when using watercolor paints

83. Which of the following best describes the artist's use of elements to convey space in this painting?

a. The shapes of the buildings make them appear farther in the distance.
b. The lines of the trees make them appear closer in space.
c. The texture of the trees and bushes makes them appear closer in space.
d. The lighter colors and values recede, whereas the darker colors and values advance in space.

84. Which of the following describes the main issues that were expressed through the Muralism art movement of Latin America?

a. The rights of women and children
b. Freedom of speech and artistic expression
c. The desire for better schools and education
d. Political and social justice

85. An artist creates a sculpture from a block of marble, carefully removing pieces by use of a chisel. Which of the following sculptural techniques is this artist using?

a. Casting
b. Modeling
c. Subtractive sculpture
d. Assemblage

86. Which of the following terms describes the method with which this fiber art was created?

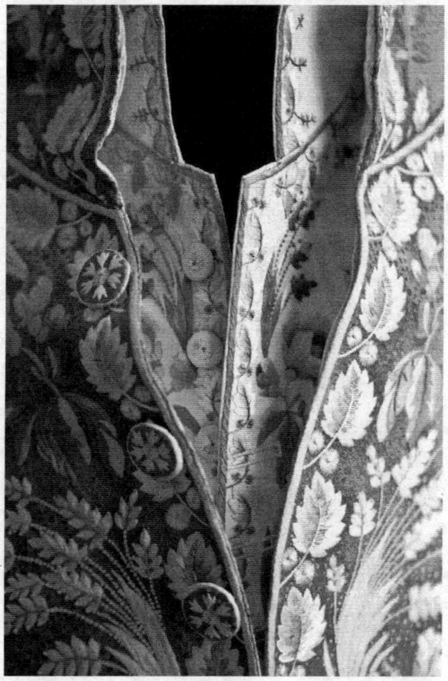

a. Embroidery
b. Weaving
c. Knitting
d. Crochet

87. Which of the following terms refers to hanging artworks in groupings on the wall at, above, and below eye level?

a. Exhibition-style
b. Gallery-style
c. Salon-style
d. Museum-style

88. Which of the following best describes why Ansel Adams created black and white environmental photographs instead of color?

a. Color photography had not yet been invented.
b. If the photographs were in color, they would be mainly green.
c. He did not have experience with producing color photographs.
d. He could control the outcome of the prints better with black and white.

89. Which of the following cultures would have produced this dot style painting?

a. Aboriginal
b. African
c. Chinese
d. Brazilian

90. Which of the following media was first accepted as a fine art in the early to mid-1900s?

a. Oil painting
b. Photography
c. Performance art
d. Gouache

91. Which of the following describes an analysis of this artwork using the formalism aesthetic theory?

a. The artist loosely represented a horse as the subject of this artwork.
b. The artist expressed his feelings through the varied use of lines.
c. The artist used both primary and secondary colors in this artwork.
d. The artist used the subject to express his experience with equestrianism.

92. What is the most commonly recommended minimum dpi for printing an image?

a. 300 dpi
b. 720 dpi
c. 100 dpi
d. 500 dpi

93. An art critic analyzes this artwork's repetition of color, shapes, and lines, as well as the unity created throughout the piece by these elements. The critic is using which of the following aesthetic theories of art criticism?

a. Emotionalism
b. Formalism
c. Functionalism
d. Imitationalism

94. Which of the following is NOT one of the names for this method of composition for art and architecture?

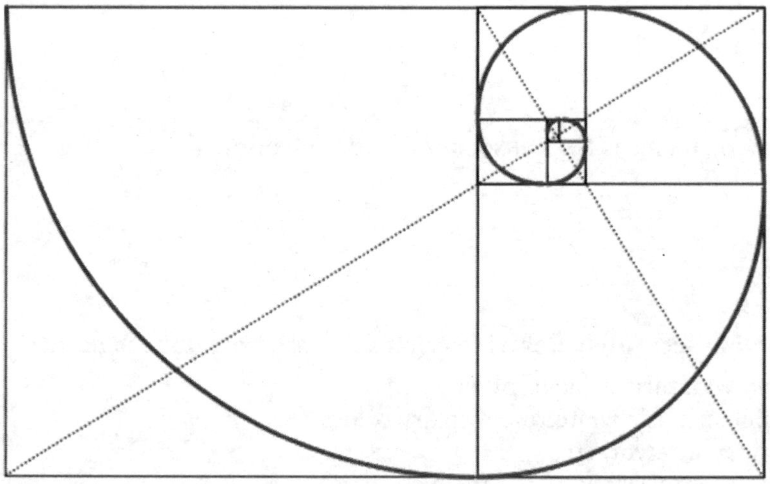

a. Golden Mean
b. Pi
c. Golden Ratio
d. Fibonacci spiral

95. In this painting, the larger area of red on the left is repeated in small amounts in different areas on the right. This is an example of which principle of design?

a. Movement
b. Contrast
c. Symmetry
d. Unity

96. Which of the following metals used for jewelry making is an alloy of antimony, tin, and copper?

a. Pewter
b. Silver
c. Aluminum
d. Titanium

97. Which of the following terms is NOT associated with knitting?

a. Chain stitch
b. Purl
c. Casting on
d. Stockinette

98. Which of the following accurately describes characteristics of gouache paint?

a. It can be thinned with turpentine or other solvents.
b. It is only available in black, white, and primary colors.
c. It cannot be re-wet or reworked.
d. It is opaque and dries to a smooth, matte finish.

99. Which of the following types of clays is an earthenware that is generally a reddish-brown color and is more porous and less durable than other types of clay?

a. Stoneware
b. Terra cotta
c. Porcelain
d. Raku

100. Which of the following artworks was instrumental in the acceptance of fiber arts as an artistic medium?

a. Kara Walker's "Gone"
b. Yayoi Kusama's "Dots Obsession"
c. Judy Chicago's "The Dinner Party"
d. Miriam Schapiro's "Big Ox No. 1"

Answer Key and Explanations

1. C: Gothic architecture, which was a style used in Europe from the mid-12th to the 16th century, is known for its tall designs with a sense of upward movement. This was a departure from the previously dark, damp buildings of the Romanesque style. Gargoyles were used as drainage spouts, and pointed arches were a commonly used visual element in this style.

2. A: Van Gogh, Cézanne, Seurat and Gauguin are all associated with the Post-Impressionism movement. This movement sought to explore the emotional response of the artist and was a departure from the naturalism of Impressionism. These artists used bold colors and while they portrayed real-life subjects, they also began to use distorted, geometric forms in their artwork. They sometimes used exaggerated colors and bold outlines as well.

3. A: A happening is a performance or event created in the context of fine art. These began in the 1950s, and they include audience participation as a main component. Happenings can be planned or improvised, and are meant to be a changing, unique work of art that cannot be preserved in a museum. Happenings might include music, dance, poetry, or performance, and can have a large or small audience depending on the artist's intentions.

4. C: When clay is partially but not completely dry, it is leather hard. At this stage, the piece can still be carved or trimmed. When the piece is completely dry, it is considered bone dry. A bone-dry piece is fragile and cannot be carved or trimmed. An unfired ceramic piece is called greenware, and after the piece is fired once in a kiln, it is considered bisque. A bisque ware piece can be glazed and fired again.

5. D: The impasto technique is the application of thick layers of paint, usually with oil or acrylics. The visible brushstrokes can become a visual element that leads the viewer's eye around the painting, and the paint can be applied by a brush or a palette knife. With this technique, the artist can create texture a control how the light reflects off of the layers of paint. Vincent van Gogh was known for working with this technique.

6. B: Sfumato is a technique in which the painter creates a hazy, smoky atmosphere, reducing the appearance of harsh lines in the artwork. *Mona Lisa* is an example of this, with soft transitions throughout the painting. Da Vinci masterfully built up layer upon layer of paint to create this soft appearance. This can also be used to represent objects in the distance to create the appearance of atmospheric perspective and haziness.

7. D: An accommodation is a change to instructional materials, assessments, or settings that enable a student to engage in the curriculum without changing the goals or rigor. Students with behavioral disabilities may need help minimizing distractions and triggers that upset them. Instead of changing the project by replacing the media or changing the way the project works, a teacher can accommodate these students' needs by minimizing distractions. One way of doing this is by allowing the student to work in a quieter side of the room or by providing them with noise-cancelling headphones. Students with disabilities should not receive modifications (changes to the content or rigor) or be removed from the general education classroom unless they absolutely need it. Their right to the least restrictive environment must be respected.

8. D: Claes Oldenburg was an American sculptor known for creating large-scale Pop art sculptures. He created soft sculptures, often of food items, beginning in 1962. In doing this, he changed the traditional hard medium of sculpture to a soft, changeable format that challenged the idea of sculpture. Oldenburg was later known for his large-scale outdoor sculptures of ordinary objects, including a clothespin and a rubber stamp.

9. A: A performance assessment is an authentic task that focuses on the student's ability to demonstrate their art skills or their use of methods and materials. Traditional assessment consists of standard tests, such as multiple choice and essay tests. A formative assessment tests a student's understanding and progress throughout a course, while a summative assessment checks a student's knowledge at the end of a unit or lesson.

10. B: Sculptures in the Classical period in ancient Greece were made to honor their gods and goddesses. The technical skill of Greek sculptors allowed them to depict human anatomy with great accuracy, and at the same time they idealized the human figure. They often depicted figures and scenes from mythology and used sculptures to adorn temples. The statue of Zeus at Olympia was created during this period in ancient Greece.

11. B: The formalism aesthetic theory is based on analyzing the artwork's success of using the elements and principles; it does not analyze the feelings or intentions behind it or even the abstraction or representational nature of the art. The emotionalism aesthetic theories investigate the expressive qualities of the artwork. Imitationalism looks at whether an artwork successfully represents what it sets out to represent.

12. D: Artists of the Impressionist movement sought to capture fleeting moments in time and the momentary effects of light. They were departing from the realistic depiction of previous art movements, such as Realism, and using the newly invented paint in tubes to paint outside to portray these moments in a new way. Artists of the Romanticism movement portrayed exaggerated scenes and heightened emotions.

13. A: In the hierarchical proportion used in artwork in ancient Egypt, scale was used to show the importance of people in relation to each other. People of higher status would often be sculpted or drawn as larger than those of lower status. This proportional organization would not necessarily be used in battle scenes or more chaotic portrayals of groups of people.

14. D: To prevent a water-based medium from being resisted by an oil or wax-based medium, it is recommended to layer the water-based medium underneath the oil or wax-based medium. Acrylic, watercolor, and tempera are all water-based, while oil paint, encaustic, and crayons are oil and wax based, which will all resist the water-based medium. Layering a water-based medium on an oil or wax-based medium can cause the top layer to not stick to the bottom layer.

15. B: A tertiary color is created by combining a primary color with a secondary color. The tertiary color will be named by combining the names of the two colors used. In this instance, the name of the tertiary color would be yellow-orange. The primary colors are red, yellow, and blue, while the secondary colors are orange, green, and purple or violet.

16. B: The refinement of the steel process, which led to steel skeletons for buildings, allowed buildings to be constructed at greater heights. The steel skeletons allowed builders to depart from load-bearing walls, which did not allow for tall buildings such as these. The invention of the first safe passenger elevator, as well as the need for more vertical spaces to save room, also led to the construction of skyscrapers.

17. C: An illustrator will most likely need to be proficient at using computer graphics programs such as Adobe Photoshop and Illustrator for their work, although some work can be completed by hand as well. A photographer will use digital photo editing software to refine their photographs before printing or publishing them online. A graphic designer will use a range of computer graphics programs to create their designs. A curator would be the least likely to need proficiency in these programs.

18. D: In the Feminist art movement, female artists began to embrace and use materials that were traditionally tied to their gender, including embroidery and textiles. They sought to challenge stereotypes and cultural attitudes and bring attention to the contributions of female artists throughout history, including all art movements. They used new media that was not yet male-dominated to communicate with their viewers and used self-portraits, appropriated images, collage, and other methods to get their messages across.

19. A: A larger aperture will result in a clear and focused subject with the background out of focus, otherwise known as a shallow depth of field, creating a clearer focal point in the photograph. To create a shallow depth of field, you would use a larger aperture and decrease the distance from the camera to the subject. A higher ISO changes the sensitivity to light but does not affect depth of field, and shutter speed can be slowed to blur motion, but will not affect the depth of field.

20. C: The Mannerism style, beginning at the end of the Renaissance in the 1520s, focused on mainly religious subject matter and included techniques such as elongated limbs, dramatic lighting, and unnatural, artificial poses. These artists departed from the compositional techniques of the Renaissance period and created compositions on a more flattened plane. They also experimented with portraying emotions in their artwork and using bright colors.

21. B: Both Postmodernism and Dada art sought to depart from the authority and traditions of previous art movements. Dada was considered "anti-art," challenging the previous ideas of art. Postmodernism was anti-authoritarian and refused to recognize the authority of any previous art movement, questioning authorship, originality, and subjectivity. They both wanted to move forward in their own way without relying on previous ideas and traditions.

22. B: In this situation, larger paper and larger materials would be the least likely accommodation to help this student. This accommodation is more often given to students with physical disabilities or vision impairment. A student with behavioral disabilities should be given a secluded area to work in, have their assignment broken down into smaller chunks with frequent check ins, and should be given frequent praise to help them stay on task during the class.

23. D: Backward design entails starting with the end point, or the goals of instruction, and then basing the assessments and the lessons around meeting those goals. The backward design method entails identifying what skills or knowledge the students should master by the end of the lesson or unit, then designing the instruction and assessments for the students to master the skills and information.

24. A: A student uses their metacognitive skills to assess their own learning, and this can include self-assessment and correcting their own work based on their self-assessment. When a student uses a rubric to check their progress toward reaching their goals, they are using their metacognitive skills. These skills help a student understand and regulate their own learning, and, when the student uses them, they can get themselves closer to their learning goals.

25. C: When an artist paints layers of transparent oil paint on top of one another after each layer underneath has dried, this is called glazing. Glazing is a technique used to build up colors that will blend visually, without blending them on the palette. Glazing is often used to create complex colors such as skin tones. The artist needs to understand the transparency of different pigments to use this technique.

26. C: Egg tempera requires a rigid support so that the paint will not crack or flake off the support. Masonite or a wood panel would be the most ideal support for this paint. On paper or a fabric such as canvas or linen, the paint will crack and flake. To use these flexible supports, the paint also needs to be able to flex to some degree.

27. B: Mixing secondary colors is an appropriate skill to be introduced in these early grades. Students should be learning to name and recognize the primary and secondary colors and begin to mix the secondary colors as well. Using two-point perspective, hand-lettering, and using oil paints are all skills appropriate to introduce in later grades, such as middle or high school.

28. D: The safety while using a utility knife is not dictated by the SDS sheets. The Safety Data Sheets explain the hazards associated with certain materials, and what precautions should be taken because of these hazards. This includes flammable or corrosive materials that are used in the art classroom. Students should understand how to properly use, clean up, and store each material that they are using.

29. A: The Ashcan School sought to portray life and people in a realistic, unidealized manner and thought the working class was a worthy subject. Artists of the Romanticism movement portrayed scenes with exaggerated and heightened emotions, while artists of the Neoclassical movement portrayed people with themes of heroism and classical mythology. The Hudson River School depicted idealized landscapes of the views surrounding the Hudson River Valley.

30. A: A painting from the Byzantine era would have been made on a wood panel for several reasons. In Byzantine panel painting, canvas and paper were not used yet for paintings. Canvas became popular during the Renaissance times since canvases were able to support larger works and make them lighter. This painting would have been done with tempera, which will crack if flexed, so using a non-flexible surface like a wood panel would be ideal for the medium.

31. B: In this painting by Gustav Klimt, a limited color palette of oranges, greens, and neutrals was used to create contrasts and emphasis throughout the artwork. There is repetition of shapes and values throughout, as well as a repetition of textures in the buildings and trees. The majority of green helps the white and orange to stand out further, and this arrangement leads the viewer's eye around the painting in a circle.

32. D: While the artists of the Impressionism movement tried to capture fleeting moments in time, like photography, they also reacted against photography by capturing an impression instead of a faithful reproduction. Impressionist artists often worked outdoors to capture the play of light on the scene and used a wide range of colors to imitate the light they saw. Their loose brushstrokes and vivid colors captured the impression of a scene rather than a realistic reproduction of it.

33. B: While video screens showing the artists discussing their artwork or showing video artwork are effective ways of incorporating technology in an exhibit, having multiple screens playing in one gallery can be distracting. One video screen per gallery, or video screens in separate viewing rooms, would be preferable so that they do not distract the visitors from each other or from another artwork.

34. A: If not using your own source material, and the source material is not out of copyright or in the public domain, you should obtain permission from the source. Copyright for an artwork begins once the artwork is completed. Copyright laws are primarily federal. It is not permitted to sell a copy of a famous artwork as your own.

35. B: This photograph features a pair of flying buttresses, which are masonry supports that transmit the thrust of a roof or vault into the outer support. The flying buttress is an inclined bar that flies out from the wall to carry the weight of the vault or roof. This type of support was developed in Gothic architecture, departing from the previously hidden supports. The flying buttress was instrumental in supporting the high ceilings characteristic of Gothic churches.

36. C: A wash is a large, flat area of color. Sgraffito involves scratching through paint to reveal the layer or surface underneath, and this can add texture to a painting. With dry brush, the artist loads paint onto the brush with minimal water or oil medium, and this can create a scratchy texture in the painting where the brushstrokes are visible. Impasto painting involves layers of thick paint, which can create a texture.

37. A: This artist used contrast to create the focal point of the painting. The light value of the bar, coupled with the bright red of the clothing, draw the viewer's eye. These both contrast heavily with the dark background and the muted colors throughout the rest of the artwork. Together, the light line and red clothing catch the viewer's attention and emphasize the tightrope walker in the painting.

38. D: A mandrel is a tool used to size and shape a ring for jewelry making. It is a tapered piece of metal on which rings fit. A burnisher is a smooth metal tool used to smooth the surface of the plate for intaglio printmaking. A brayer is a rubber roller used to roll ink onto a surface for printmaking. A gouge is a tool used for relief printmaking, used to cut away parts of the surface before applying ink.

39. B: Renaissance artists were the first to use linear perspective in their artwork, giving it greater realism and more accurate depth. Prior to this, artists were aware of the relation of sizes for objects close up or far away, but Filippo Brunelleschi is credited with discovering geometric perspective in 1413, and artists began using vanishing points and horizon lines following this discovery.

40. C: African sculptors often used wood to create masks and sculptures of human figures. They emphasized symmetry and pattern, and would stylize, or visually abstract, the figure rather than depicting the figure in a naturalistic way. These sculptures were often used for religious purposes including display on altars or use in rituals. They would emphasize youthful characteristics as well as health and physical strength.

41. D: The fresco technique involved mixing pigments with water and applying the mixture to wet plaster. Once the plaster dried, the pigments would be visible. This made the pigments and the painting into a permanent part of the wall. The painting technique is time sensitive since the paint must be applied while the plaster is still wet. This technique was used by Michelangelo on the Sistine Chapel ceiling.

42. B: The rule of thirds is a compositional technique used in painting, photography and other two-dimensional artwork to add visual interest to the composition by not putting the subject in the center. The scene is divided into three parts both horizontally and vertically, the subject is centered on a point where those dividing lines intersect. In a landscape, the horizon line will often fall on the lower line.

43. A: Baroque architecture is characterized by pear shaped domes, marble or faux finishing, and bronze gilding, among other things. It originated in Italy in the late 16th century. Hemispherical domes, columns and decorative pilasters are characteristics of Renaissance architecture. Semicircular arches, barrel or groin vaults, and thick walls are characteristics of Romanesque architecture. Circular domes, pendentives, and mosaics are characteristics of Byzantine architecture.

44. C: Context describes the related conditions or circumstances around which something occurs. Understanding the context can help a person understand the artwork better, by looking at the circumstances in which the artist was working in at the time. This can include their environment, the historical events and traditions happening, their cultural values, the social movements at the time, and even the artist's personal values and commitments.

45. B: In this painting, *Café Terrace at Night* (1888), van Gogh used complementary colors to create contrast and make the colors stand out from each other. The bright orange and various blues used throughout this artwork are complementary, lying directly across from each other on a color wheel. Complementary colors create contrast and work to make each other stand out further, adding more visual depth to the artwork. They also make each other appear to glow.

46. A: A still life arrangement will have a better and more interesting composition when it is asymmetrical. It can be centered but should still have elements of asymmetry. Using incorrect perspective can be distracting to the viewer. Having edges of objects touch rather than overlap causes spatial ambiguity rather than showing which object is closer. A focal point should be included in the arrangement to draw the viewer's eye.

47. D: Color Field painters and Minimalist artists both used large, flat areas of paint in their artwork with minimal brush strokes. Color Field painting is also characterized by the extension of the paint to the edges of the canvas, suggesting the colors go on for infinity. Neither group focused on using primary colors, although the De Stijl art movement did. Pop art used popular and consumer items as their subjects.

48. C: This painting by Agnolo Bronzino uses a complementary color scheme, meaning that the main colors in the painting are directly across from each other on the color wheel. The woman's dress is green, whereas the background is red. Red and green are complementary colors, and they help each other stand out and appear vibrant in an artwork. Other complementary combinations are blue and orange or yellow and violet.

49. C: A graphic designer will be responsible for the design of print and digital items. They would not need certification in programming languages, or an apprenticeship under an artist or designer. They also would not need experience with pedagogy, assessment and classroom management. A graphic designer will benefit from a working knowledge of the programs they will likely use for their job, including Adobe Photoshop, Adobe Illustrator and Adobe InDesign, among others.

50. C: AVI is one of the oldest video formats and is not an image format. JPEG, GIF, and PNG are all common image file formats. JPEG stands for Joint Photographic Experts Group. GIF and PNG files both use lossless compression, while JPEG is highly compressed and lossy. They can each be used for specific purposes while saving image files, depending on the desired final product.

51. A: A triadic color scheme is composed of three colors that are evenly spaced around the color wheel. This could be comprised of the three primary colors, or the three secondary colors, as in this example. This would not include analogous colors, which are next to each other, or complementary colors, which are directly across from each other on the color wheel.

52. A: This photograph, titled *The Steerage*, is Alfred Stieglitz's most famous work. Taken in 1907, this photograph depicts families on the lower deck of a boat leaving America and traveling to Germany. This has often been interpreted as an "immigration to America" photograph, although it is not. Stieglitz was on the upper deck of the ship, and he had a view of the lower deck, known as the steerage. From here, he was able to get this view and take this photograph.

53. D: This image, *Paul Gachet* by Vincent van Gogh uses a complementary color pattern by using colors on opposing sides of the color wheel. By using cold blues as the predominant color in this work with oranges as a warm contrast, it brings balance and contrast to the image, which serves to reduce tension, while adding to the intensity of the artwork.

54. B: When acrylic paint dries, it becomes a sort of plastic that is flexible and will not crack when bent. This makes acrylic ideal for painting on multiple surfaces. Oil paint is less flexible and is prone to crack when flexed. Acrylic does dry much more quickly than oil, and it can be cleaned up with water. It does dry slightly darker when the white binder in the paint turns clear, but oil paint also changes color as it dries.

55. A: Artists in the Middle East often repeat a pattern in a way that could go to infinity. This is often used to contrast man's finite existence on earth. These patterns were also used on surfaces to represent the dissolution of matter, which is another important concept for these artists. These patterns could be highly intricate and ornate.

56. C: While strong black outlines were often used, Japanese woodblock prints used a rich palette of colors. The water-based inks used by these artists provide a large range of colors that could be vivid and transparent. When multiple layers were used, they had to be placed with precision as subsequent areas were carved out of the wood and more ink was applied to the prints.

57. D: The description of this hero reflects a triadic color scheme with the main colors being red, blue, and yellow. A triadic color scheme is evenly spaced around the color wheel. Analogous colors are next to each other on the color wheel. A tetradic color scheme includes two complementary pairs, for example red and green plus blue and orange or yellow and purple plus red and green. Monochromatic would consist of shades and tints of one color.

58. C: Watercolor paper and charcoal paper will both have a rough surface that is not suitable for detailed pen and ink work. Canvas is not suitable to draw on unless primed, and even then, it will have a rough surface. Illustration board is a firm, smooth surface that is made for detailed illustration work. It would be the most suitable choice out of these.

59. C: Poppy oil, linseed oil, and stand oil are all used in oil painting. Linseed oil is the most commonly used, and it offers a quick drying time. Poppy oil is good for lighter colors, as it is less likely to yellow than linseed oil. Stand oil is a thicker version of linseed oil, enhancing the glossy effect but increasing the drying time.